MANAGEMENT PRACTICES AND STRATEGIES IN AN UNCERTAIN ERA

The Indian Experience

MANAGEMENT PRACTICES and STRATEGIES in an Uncertain Era

The Indian Experience

Edited by

V. Sita

Professor, School of Management Studies,
University of Hyderabad, Hyderabad

and

V. Venkata Ramana

Dean, School of Management Studies,
University of Hyderabad, Hyderabad

New Century Publications
New Delhi

NEW CENTURY PUBLICATIONS
4800/24, Bharat Ram Road,
Ansari Road, Daryaganj,
New Delhi – 110 002 (India)

Tel.: 011-2324 7798, 6539 6605
Fax: 011-4101 7798
E-mail: indiatax@vsnl.com • info@newcenturypublications.com
www.newcenturypublications.com

Editorial office:
LG–7, Aakarshan Bhawan,
4754-57/23, Ansari Road, Daryaganj,
New Delhi – 110 022
Tel.: 011-4358 7398

First Published: **July 2012**

ISBN: **978-81-7708-327-9**

Published by New Century Publications and printed at Salasar Imaging Systems, New Delhi.

Designs: Patch Creative Unit, New Delhi.

PRINTED IN INDIA

About the Book

Of late, world economy has been passing through uncertain times. Indian economy is no exception to the general slowdown being experienced by several countries worldwide. The increasingly uncertain economic outlook requires a strategy shift on the part of companies to successfully face the impending downturn. Years of economic growth have made some companies complacent, and now is the time for them to prepare for worst-case scenarios. Winners and losers will emerge during any economic change, and mistakes can be all the more costly during uncertainty. To avoid getting sunk, the first thing to know is that uncertainty is not a time to pull back and hope to come out unscathed.

A downturn can actually be good for a well-managed company. For example, saving costs is one alternative to stay profitable in a period of uncertainty. Acquisitions are also one means to consolidate in times of uncertainty. Ideally, managers should know all of this before a slowdown hits, and should work with the human resources department to develop a strategy for reassessment of employees and other factors of production.

Against this background, this book aims at providing a compendium of articles and literature to the professionals, scholars and researchers on issues relating to managing a company in an uncertain economic era. The 21 papers included in the volume address various issues of managing in an uncertain era in a lucid way. The book provides an excellent opportunity for all those interested to update their knowledge on the concepts, processes and methodology in the Indian context. Curricular issues on the topic should also be an added attraction to the management teachers and researchers.

About the Editors

Dr. V. Sita is currently Professor at the School of Management Studies, University of Hyderabad, Hyderabad. She has 3 books to her credit and several papers published in professional journals of repute including *Asian Economic Review*; *South Asian Journal of Management* and *Academy of Management Journal*. She has travelled to USA, Singapore, Hong Kong, Malaysia, Dubai, and Canada on academic assignments. She is the recipient of several awards including the Indo-French Exchange Scholar Award (2008) by the Government of India, Best Case Study Award (2005) by UNDP, and the IIM-A Alumni Research Award (2006).

Dr. V. Venkata Ramana is Dean, School of Management Studies, University of Hyderabad, Hyderabad. Widely travelled, he has visited USA, UK, Europe, and Middle-East on academic assignments. He is the recipient of following awards: Vemuri Seshayya Sastry Gold Medal (Ph.D.); Rotary International Award in 1998; AICTE Career Award for Young Teachers in 1999, and Navatarangalu Award. He has published 4 books. He specializes in marketing management, and corporate environmental management.

Contents

Contributors

V. Sita Professor, School of Management Studies, University of Hyderabad, Hyderabad.

A. Suryanarayana Professor, Department of Business Management, Osmania University, Hyderabad.

Sukesh Koka Director HR, Hackett Group (India) Limited.

A. Jagan Mohan Reddy Associate Professor, Institute of Public Enterprise, Hyderabad.

S. Suman Babu Senior Research Fellow, SMS, JNT University, Hyderabad.

A.R. Aryasri Director, School of Management Studies, Jawaharlal Nehru Technological University, Hyderabad.

K.V.S. Raju Department of Management Studies, GRIET, Hyderabad.

K. Mamatha Associate Professor, Vishwa Vishwani Institute of Systems and Management, Hyderabad.

G. Srinivas Rao Faculty, Secunderabad Post-graduate College, Secunderabad.

Radha Iyer Faculty, Human Resource Development, K.J. Somaiya Institute of Management Studies and Research, Vidyavihar, Mumbai.

Swagatika Panda Faculty, Human Resource Development, K.J. Somaiya Institute of Management Studies and Research, Vidyavihar, Mumbai.

D. Anil Kumar MBA Student, Osmania University, Hyderabad.

M. Vinay Chandra Sai MBA Student, Osmania University, Hyderabad.

Aditya Sriram Student, Indian Institute of Technology, Kharagpur.

Aniket Student, Indian Institute of Technology, Kharagpur.

Harish S. Vangala Research Associate, Centre for Organization Development, Hyderabad.

B. Savitha Faculty, St. Francis Degree College and Research Scholar, SMS, University of Hyderabad.

Mohd. Moiz Research Scholar, Centre for Knowledge, Culture and Innovation Studies, University of Hyderabad, Hyderabad.

S.C. Vetrivel Assistant Professor, School of Management Studies, Kongu Engineering College, Perundurai, Erode.

B.K. Swain Professor, National Institute of Rural Development, Hyderabad.

R. Sreenivasa Rao Assistant Professor, Department of Management Studies, MBA Programme, Sir C.R. Reddy College, Eluru, Andhra Pradesh.

G.V.S. Ravindra Babu	Assistant Professor, Department of Management Studies, MBA Programme, Sir C.R. Reddy College, Eluru, Andhra Pradesh.
Ch. Jayasankara Prasad	Department of Business Management, Krishna University, Machilipatnam.
Y. Ramakrishna Prasad	Department of M.B.A., Gokaraju Rangaraju Institute of Engineering and Technology (GRIET), Hyderabad.
M.K. Padmalatha	Soft Skills Trainer, Eluru, Andhra Pradesh.
Sunitha Ratnakaram	Associate Professor, Vishwa Vishmani Institute of Systems and Management, Hyderabad.
Venkama Raju Chakravaram	Associate Professor, Narsimha Reddy Post-graduate College, Hyderabad.
I. Anand Pawar	Assistant Professor, Department of Commerce, Dr. B.R. Ambedkar Open University, Hyderabad.
K. Chandra Sekhar	Vice-President, (Project Sales), Robo Silicon Pvt. Ltd., Hyderabad.
G.P. Sudhakar	Faculty, ICFAI, School of Information Technology (ISIT), Hyderabad.

Editors' Note on the Book

The increasingly uncertain economic outlook means a strategy shift is in order, or at least illustrates the urgency of planning for a downturn. Years of economic growth have made some corporations complacent, and now is the time for them to prepare for worst-case scenarios. Winners and losers will emerge during any economic change, and mistakes can be all the more costly during uncertainty. To avoid getting sunk, the first thing to know is that uncertainty is not a time to pull back and hope to come out unscathed.

A downturn can actually be good for a well-managed company, as organizational experience worldwide evidences different ways and means to get over uncertainty. For example, saving costs is one alternative to stay profitable in a period of uncertainty. Saving costs is one thing, but a firm also has to reinvest in other areas. Intel Corp. provides an example of how spending more during a period of uncertainty can be beneficial.

Acquisitions are also one means to consolidate in times of uncertainty. Though a firm has to have enough cash—asset values fall during a recession making potential targets a cheap deal. Management at DuPont anticipated as far back as 1999 that a slowdown was on the horizon due to weakening demand in its primary customer markets. As a result, the chemical giant slashed capital expenditure to buy up seven companies.

Advertising is another area where companies can boost spending. Typically, advertising drops in a slowdown, creating an opportunity to take advantage of the reduced clutter in the marketplace. It was during the 1991 recession that Intel launched its successful "Intel Inside" campaign. Similarly, computer maker Dell Inc. increased its marketing budget, which helped to boost its market share. Recessions also inevitably result in job cuts, and managers have to be prepared to cut staff. That requires taking a hard look at employees to identify those, whom the company cannot afford to lose.

Performance is just one factor; employees with skills are important, and keeping workers in positions with steep learning curves may also be crucial.

Ideally, managers should know all of this before a slowdown hits, and should work with the human resources department to develop a system for ongoing reassessment of employees. But hanging on to talented employees will be difficult in a downturn. In the previous era of recession, workers typically waited for the rebound before reassessing their options. Given the changing work arena and the increasingly mobile nature of work, many people feel there are plenty of other opportunities around the world. Thus, all these issues drive the organizations towards new processes, and changed mindset in a majorly *service economy* across the globe.

If this being the scenario in one country or continent, *What if* a global uncertainty hits as the globe is experiencing as on now? The variance of GDP growth rates across countries is at its lowest point in thirty years; never in recent history have economies been so closely in step with each other. This increases the odds of a synchronized global economic downturn, which means that companies will have nowhere to turn to shift supply. In such an extreme scenario, companies should keep answers ready for some questions. Do you have the cash reserves to help consolidate your industry and save jobs? Have you evaluated which competitors you should acquire based on your core businesses? Or, if you have a weaker financial position, have you identified where you can cut costs without cutting out the heart of your business? Where are you making your profits and generating the best R&D to renew product lines? Where do you hold the most competitive cost position? What about good governance and managerial practices? What alternate models—Public private partnerships for example—enhance strategic choices? What is the role of corporate Governance and what ethical standards govern companies in tiding over/managing the situation? What are the implications of all these for managers and management educators? What are the lessons for developing countries like India?

Against this background, the book primarily aims at providing a compendium of articles and literature to the professionals, scholars and researchers on issues relating to managing in an uncertain economic era. More specifically, the book seeks to include views of the experts on the issues and experience of Indian organizations from a multi-stakeholder perspective—policy makers, managers, academics and beneficiaries in the organizational process in India. The theme is contemporary and includes emerging patterns/changes relating to managing in an uncertain economic era.

The book addresses various issues of managing in an uncertain era in a lucid way. The book provides an excellent opportunity for all those interested to update their knowledge on the concept, processes and methodology in the Indian context. Curricular issues on the topic should also be an added attraction to the management teachers and researchers.

We place on record a deep sense of gratitude to a number of people who have directly or indirectly helped us in the completion of this book. The Vice Chancellor and the administration of the University of Hyderabad merits mention for their support and encouragement in our academic endeavours. We are also thankful to the authors of the scholarly papers included in this volume.

We particularly appreciate the efforts of Ms. M.P. Aparna, Research Scholar, School of Management Studies, University of Hyderabad, for her support in the finalization of this volume. The enduring support of our family has always energized us in turning our dreams into reality. Special mention is also due to many well wishers, whose names have not been included, but their support is whole-heartedly acknowledged.

Thanks are, of course, due to Mr. Sandeep Sury, Chief Executive, New Century Publications, New Delhi and his team of professional editors for their co-operation, excellent editing and formatting of the work.

Hyderabad
June 2012

V. Sita
V. Venkata Ramana

[illegible] B. (1988), "Management training needs [illegible]", *Industrial and Commercial Training*, Vol. 20, [illegible] pp. [illegible]

Hackett, M.[illegible] and Smallwood, [illegible] (1987), "Now for a [illegible] different look at needs analysis", *Training and [illegible] Journal*, Vol. 41, No. [illegible], pp. 75-79

[illegible] (199[illegible]), "[illegible] in Trends in Training and Development", *International Journal of Human Resource Management*, [illegible]

McClelland, S.B. (1993), "Training needs assessment", *Journal of European Industrial Training*, Vol. 17, No. 1, pp. 1[illegible]

McClelland, S.B. (1994a), "Training needs assessment data-gathering methods: Part 1 survey questionnaires", *Journal of European Industrial Training*, Vol. 18, No. 1, pp. [illegible]

McClelland, S.B. (1994b), "Training needs assessment data-gathering methods: Part 2 individual interviews", *Journal of European Industrial Training*, Vol. 18, No. 2, pp. [illegible]

McClelland, S.B. (1994c), "Training needs assessment data-gathering methods, Part 3 focus groups", *Journal of European Industrial Training*, Vol. 18, No. 3, pp. [illegible]

McClelland, S.B. (1994d), "Training needs assessment data-gathering methods: Part 4 on-site observations", *Journal of European Industrial Training*, Vol. 18, No. 5, pp. [illegible]

Moore, R. J., "A case study approach to training needs analysis", Journal of European Industrial Training, [illegible] 1/3, pp. 23-28

Moore, M. L., Dutton, P., "Training Needs Analysis: Review and Critique", *Academy of Management Review*, July 1978, [illegible] 545.

Moreno, R. (1973), "Determining Organizational Training Needs", *Personnel Psychology*, Vol. 26, pp. 479-[illegible]

O'Driscoll M.P., Taylor, P. J., "Congruence between theory and practice in management training needs analysis", *International Journal of Human Resource Management*, [illegible] 3, Issue 3, pp. 593-603.

Salas, E. and Cannon-Bowers, J. A., "The Science of Training: A Decade of Progress", Annual Review of Psychology, [illegible] 471-499.

Schneier, C.E., Guthrie, J.P. and Olian, J.D. [illegible] approach to conducting and using [illegible] assessment", *Public Personnel Management*, [illegible]

1

Human Resources Strategy During Uncertainty

V. Sita

Managers analyze many situations and take a number of decisions in a day. Each decision is the outcome of the process which usually involves two kinds of things–*first* going back to understand the past and the *second* looking forward to predict the future. Looking backward is suggestive and evolves diagnosis and individual judgment. It also involves making links between unconnected events, understanding the cause and effect scenario and looking at the theory to take it forward. On the other hand predicting future involves thinking forward and depends on mathematical models.

A manager needs to account a number of variables and factors and besides based on certain rules, regulations, guidelines and practices in the organization. Managers use both these types of thinking most of the time but are unaware of the differences between the two. This makes them lead to decisions which put them into trouble at times. Managerial awareness on this leads to improved decision making capability.

It is also true that the traditional approach to strategy is based on the assumption that managers can predict the future by applying a set of analytical tools. The approach worked initially for the organizations but the later part of the 20th century was marked by uncertainty and turbulence, thus making the tools of analysis redundant. Managers looked for a strategy to predict the future in uncertain business environments.

Levels of Uncertainty

Organizational experience reveals that there are four levels of uncertainty that the managers have to confront (Courtney, Kirkland, and Viguerie, 1999). They are as follows:

Level 1: At level 1 manager can develop a forecast of the future that gives a *clear enough future* for strategy development. It may not exactly forecast in an uncertain situation but it sufficiently provides strategic direction towards a decision. For e.g., when the Indian aviation industry was opened up, the major domestic airline- Indian Airlines – had to develop a strategic response to the entry of a low cost competitor–Air Deccan into its airport hubs. Should the airline major respond with a low cost service or should it surrender the low cost segments to Air Deccan or should it compete aggressively on price, service, promotions, deals to drive the new entrant out of the market.

The airlines managers need to analyze the different issues to decide through research and other analytical tools. In such cases originations can chart out a clear enough future in uncertain times and predict the future.

Level 2: At level 2, managers can describe the future as one of the *alternate outcomes*. The most probable outcome could be predicted but not the exact one. Managers and businesses which depend on regulatory and legislation confront the level 2 uncertainty. The major telecom players had to strategize when the sector was opened up in the 1990s to take care of the new entrants into the telecom market in India. Although the telecom regulation was pending, the broad guidelines were clear to the players and the industry observers as well. There was uncertainty on the passing of the bill in the houses of parliament but no amount of analysis can predict how long it will take to pass the bill and implement it. This makes the managers difficult to decide as a whole lot of network infrastructure and other processes needs to be put in place before entering into the market.

Level 3: At level 3, future can be predicted on continual companies in emerging markets or entering new geographical areas face this level of uncertainty. An American or a Japanese company deciding on entering into the Indian or Chinese market is a classic example of this level of uncertainty. Companies cannot decide on potential customer penetration anywhere between 10-40 percent as it is difficult to plan in that range. Moreover, companies need to strategize differently for different products and services. Research only provides a broad range and it makes managers difficult to decide on a new technology, product, cost or profitability.

Level 4: At level 4, there is *true ambiguity*, which makes it virtually impossible to predict. Research cannot identify scenarios or a range and even the identification of the variables defining the future becomes difficult. This kind of uncertainty is rare as it often migrates to the other level most of the time but companies do experience such uncertainty. For e.g., companies in the Indian context which were doing well in certain sectors did experience this kind of uncertainty when their where diversifying their products and services in view of the opportunities that where available after globalizing the Indian economy. The Tatas, Reliance Industries are successful companies in the Indian economy today but they faced this level of uncertainty concerning their entry into IT and other opportunities in 1990s.

Uncertainty and dealing with uncertainty thus demands a more flexible approach than situational analysis. As time progresses, companies in most sectors will be required to tackle strategy problems because of the varying level of uncertainty. It is very important that strategy formulation and strategy analysis needs to be tailored to the level of uncertainty that the company faces. Decisions made during such levels of uncertainty, surely impacts the organizational survival. Among the most important decisions that the company engages in relates to the organizational work force.

According to the Bureau of Labour Statistics (BLS), the US economy has lost more than a million jobs from June 2008 till today. The housing and credit crises have wiped out approximately 3 trillion dollars in market cap. Many people have seen their savings and retirement funds lose more than 25 percent of their value in just the last two-three months. The lack of available credit threatens to push thousands of businesses—large and small—into bankruptcy or out of business. All these evidence recessionary trends and it is difficult to predict how long the situation continues and how bad the impact would be. Such situation forces the company to be focused and planned and careful in dealing with people management issues. These are important because organisations spend more that 50 percent of their budget for work force related expenses. Moreover, talent management and competency management drives efficiency and productivity. The HR decision during uncertain times relate to retaining or reducing staff levels, eliminating jobs, laying off people, VRS packages, cost cutting by outsourcing , off showing, reducing benefits, compensation, training budget, hiring freeze etc. organizations need to predict the future and take pragmatic HR decisions to eliminate waste and improve profitability in the organisations.

Role of Analytics

Managers make decisions using the data and the information at their disposable. Organisational experience evidences that most decisions especially relating to HR or people management could not use the right type of data needed for making critical decisions. Organisations could survive and grow struggling with the data they had with their disposal, but in uncertain situations there is no room for poor decision making. Managerial decision making function in contemporary organisations has acquired a strategic significance and the implication of a wrong decision can be disaster for the organisation. HR decision making is all the more complex with the lack the appropriate matrix that can measure human capital, the worth and value of human effort etc. Evidence also suggests the use of work force analytics as the key decision support tool. Experience also suggests that it provides the needed certainty to uncertain situations. The role of analytics can be seen in the following ways.

1. **Link to Strategy:** Organisations use work force measures to connect business strategy and human capital management. Managers will be able to understand possible risks in strategy execution by monitoring the measures. In an uncertain situation, the core strategy takes a back seat, as the operational challenges are immediately focussed. It is not advisable to push back the core strategy which often contributes to strategic decision making. For example, competency management prepossess the awareness, usage and application of competencies in HR functions. The process requires the identification and application in various HR functions which takes time from an organisational perspective. But organisation growth presupposes the sourcing of talent and bringing the employees on board immediately which negates the whole idea of managing the competencies. The HR strategy should be linked to the overall business strategy and critical measures to hire new employees based on competencies has to be done in the given competency framework. Any change in the strategy to suit the uncertainty would lead to revisiting the measures to have a re-look at the alignment. Thus, at any given point of time strong alignment to overall strategy has to be ensured. Analytics do have a role to play in providing the measures for improved HR decisions.
2. **Identifying Value Drivers:** Organisations do have certain key drivers which add value to the outcomes of HR decisions. These assume much more significance in uncertain times. For example, managers should analyse which HR practices or programs lead to meaningful outcomes, how can the organisation cut cost in acquiring talent , developing talent and all the same retaining talent, how am organisation can differentiate between the core

and non-core HR activities, what strategic direction an organisation can provide for the learning capabilities of employees while cutting cost etc. Work force analytics provide the key decision support tools in identifying these values drivers in HR decision.

3. **Talent Management:** Talent management presupposes talent acquisition, talent development and talent retention. HR decision on talent management relate to talent groups critical to strategic and operational execution and groups that cost more to acquire, develop and retain. Any HR decision which refers which talent pool should be carefully taken because of its implications to strategy. The leaders, successors, the star performer etc. fall into this category. HR decisions on talent management thus assume significance in such context. The role of analytic should reduce the negative impact on organisation.

4. **Work Force Information:** A strategic shift or even a minor change in strategy will automatically affect the organisational structure. Any restructuring has to have the right description of the workforce information to address the change in the situation. Organisations confront such situation in uncertain times. Since, the change in the situations is so fast, organisations are unable to have readymade information to fall back during uncertainty. Examples like the total number of employees on the roles of the company, the distribution between permanent and contract employees, the location in which they work, their service matter, their performance rating, the compensation package, their job role, skills sets, productivity, cost per employee, etc. becomes an important data base for taking right decisions. Analytics can integrate the data and provide them in charts/figures so that the organisation can use whenever they need it for easy analysis.

5. **Workforce Performance and Productivity:** Uncertainty entails not only restructuring in terms of jobs, positions and people but also rethinking on products and service that

an organisation offers. Decision on businesses, products lines, location of operations, business strategy impacts the productivity and performance of the employees and the organisation. At the organisational level the financial parameters occupy the centre stage thus, losing site of the workforce productivity and performance. While the customer, market and financial decisions are important, HR decisions also assume significance as they impact the work force performance. At a time when estimates cannot be relied upon, exact information leading to better decision on people related matters become crucial in uncertain situations. Global experience in different sectors has led to proven results in terms of outcomes, profitability and growth of the companies in the long run. The *Intel Inside* campaign during recession of the 1990s is a classic in the US is a classic example of such decision making. Thus, every organisation has to leverage and invest in analytics and related tools not only to evaluate but also to lay a solid foundation for improved HR decision making to leverage the data base especially in uncertain times.

References

Courtney. H, Kirkland. J and Viguerie P. (1999), "Strategy under Uncertainty", Boston: HBR Press, pp. 1- 32.

Einhorn, Hillel and Hogarth, Robin (1999), "Decision-making: Going Forward in Reverse" included in *Managing Uncertainty*, Boston: HBR Press, pp. 131-146.

J. Blintiff Richie and Erin Hillman (2011) "Making High Certainty HR Decision in Uncertain Times", www.HRwiki.com.

2

Human Resources Management (HRM) in Uncertain Times

A. Suryanarayana

There is a fast-growing and high-quality body of empirical research to demonstrate that HRM policies have an impact on organizational performance. Traditionally, the HR function has not, been thought of as a repository of strategic insight or advantage. However, innovative ideas can be proposed and considered to remedy this situation. It would be imperative to suggest some intermediate-term indicators or proxies to assess whether HRM in a given organization is moving in the direction and for being "strategic" in its orientation. Strategic HR in such firms is more closely involved in the design of activity-based costing systems, information systems, and quality programs. It is also involved sooner and more centrally in long-run strategic decisions, such as mergers and acquisitions, changes in technology, and decisions regarding sourcing and location of facilities. Thus, managing changes assumes significance in contemporary context. Management of change presupposes an agent of change who takes care of the change management issues leading from the front.

Change Agent

A change agent is the person who initiates, stimulates, or facilitates a change program, and may be an internal or external to the organization. Change begins with the intervention of the change agent in the system to be changed. The internal change agent is already a member of the organization—typically someone from the HR or OD Department. An external change agent is not previously associated with the client system. Internal and external change agents have their own advantages and disadvantages. An approach that attempts to maximize the advantages while minimizing the disadvantages is to use both internal and external agents. Intervention refers to the change agent's entry into the client system and includes several different roles and activities.

They have a variety of styles or approaches. One way to view the styles is based on the degree of emphasis that is placed upon two inter-related goals or dimensions of the change process. One of the goals is *effectiveness*, the degree of emphasis upon goal accomplishment. The other goal is *morale,* the degree of emphasis upon relationships and participant satisfaction. The styles are not mutually exclusive and all of them can be effective, and they are interrelated. A change agent may transition from one style to another to meet changing client system needs and deal with diverse situations. Frequently, some combination of the styles may be applied. The change agent must decide exactly when, how, and with whom to intervene. The receptivity of the system to change must not be overlooked or taken for granted but ought to be carefully probed and realistically determined prior to further intervention. Globalization along with economic and political turbulences and information technology revolution tended to bring in radiant transitions in business with concomitant changes in management structures and systems, particularly after the year 2000.

These transitions brought paradigm shifts in business practices like functional business practice to process reengineering and standard products to customization and in management practices such as division of labour and specialization to generalization and multi-skills. However, the recent global economic slowdown has the potential to reverse the process. These transitions are aimed at change leaders besides centring on building competencies for businesses to become and remain vibrant and competitive in the ever-changing economies.

The premise An attempt is made in this conceptual Paper to impart a "Change Agent's perspective" to Human Resource Management innovations while managing employees by enlisting the disciplines of economics, psychology, and sociology, and drawing on careful disciplinary scholarship that exists on the theme. This paper is based on the following four premises. They are as follow:

First, human resources are vital for organizational success or failure. It is perhaps going too far to say that excellent HR policies are sufficient for success. But, success with poor HR policies is probably impossible, and the effects of improved and innovative HR policies on organizational success are potentially enormous. Moreover, competitive advantage built and achieved through superior HRM is more sustainable and harder for competitors to emulate than some other bases of achieving competitive advantage. HR policies and practices must be tied to overall organizational strategy. Until recently, something of a leap of faith was required to believe the management of human resources has big effects on the bottom line. But no longer: There is a fast-growing and high-quality body of empirical research demonstrating that HRM policies have an impact on organizational performance, to quote Alan Blinder, "it appears that changing the way workers are treated may boost productivity more than changing the way they are paid, although profit sharing or employee stock ownership combined with worker participation may be the system of all".

Second, HRM is too important to be left to HR specialists. For, HRM to be successful, Change Agents, external or internal, must be involved. From the overall strategy of the organization to day-to-day logistical operations, management must understand and be sensitive to the role played by the organization's human resources.

Third, just because successful HRM is a key element to success of the organization, it need not be necessarily be concluded that the concern and involvement of change agents is crucial. Human resources constrain the strategies that the organization can and should carry out, so that insofar as change agents are concerned with setting and implementing overall change strategy, directly or indirectly, they would be foolish to ignore the organization's HR policies. Employee expectations and attitudes are crucial to HRM, and change agents have a pre-eminent role to play in setting the "tone" of the employment relationship. The implementation of the firm's HR policies is best done with the participation of line managers in the field, rather than being left to HR specialists. *The primary responsibility of change agents is to influence the hearts and minds of people, consistent with the culture of the organization, so that they care more about the firm's business than competitors care about theirs.*

Finally, the fourth premise that, nostrums are just. HRM is too complex to be turned into slogans. To understand HRM, change agents must reach back to the basic economic, social, psychological, and legal forces that impinge on employment, which means that we must reach back to economics, psychology, sociology, and the law. And they must reach back to all of these complementary ways of thought. Any approach that stresses one to the exclusion of others will be incomplete and potentially misleading. "One-size-fits-all" nostrums and prescriptions built from one and only disciplinary lens may contain wisdom, but they may miss as much as they hit. Even while invoking the social sciences, one should be able to minimize the jargon and maximize plain English. Concrete examples should replace abstract principles. Any attempt to integrate the basic social sciences that have a tradition of mutual indifference, if not hostility, has its own pay-offs.

Objectives: Based on these four premises, the objective of this paper are to construct frameworks by which anyone—as a Change Agent or a student of Change Management—can better analyze and craft innovative HR policies in his organization. HR policies are part of a system—they should not be considered piecemeal. Human resources are capital investment and not cost. Human resources are difficult to shift or modify and hence, the HR strategy needs to be right at the start, or the companies would probably pay the price later. This paper primarily examines those frameworks that shed light on some crucial HR issues confronting management today, such as management of a diverse workforce, Total Quality Management (TQM), the outsourcing of labour, and downsizing an oversized organization.

Strategic and Innovative HRM

The HR function has not, traditionally, been thought of as a repository of strategic insight or advantage.

- Many—perhaps even most—firms play lip service to the strategic importance of HR, and increasingly many firms regard their human resources as key strategic variables. But this rarely extends to the HR function itself.
- This reflects a tendency for HR specialists to focus on mundane day-to-day bookkeeping and service provision; a perception of HR specialists as turf protectors; and an HR subculture that emphasizes and hence attracts "warm and fuzzies," rather than strategic hard-edge types.

Innovations are needed in HR for strategic advantage. Innovative ideas can be proposed and considered to remedy this situation. Some of the ideas are listed below:

1. Spin off from HR the mundane service and record-keeping tasks, or at least, separate these "service centre" tasks from strategic HR.
2. Have line managers directly involved both in formulating HR strategy and policy and in making nontrivial judgment calls in HR administration.
3. Use HR professionals as advisors to general managers and as evaluators of general management performance in HR.
4. Staff "Strategic HR" with people who are at least nearly general managers, with specialized HR training, but also with the training and attitude of general managers.
5. Have unit-level HR report directly to unit-level line

management, with only an indirect report to Corporate HR.

6. Push the formulation of HR policy out to units and subunits, unless you have a very substantial reason for centralizing. Decentralization should be the null hypothesis.

Moreover, serious attention is also highly recommended to the following activities of HR:

1. Creating metrics for measuring HRM performance.
2. Designing experiments in HR administration.
3. Most importantly, creating a management culture that stresses the importance of HR as a task of general management.
4. Avoid creating a culture of dependency of line management on HR specialists. As it is generally difficult to find accurate explicit measures of how general managers do in managing their human resources, particularly over shorter time frames, more intrinsic and intangible motivators—in other words, "culture"—must be enlisted.

It would be in fitness of things to suggest some intermediate-term indicators or proxies to assess whether HRM in a given organization is moving in the directions that are generally recommended to become and for being "strategic" in its orientation. The firm should be able to witness an increasing diversity over time in the "origin" and "destination" points for individuals posted in the central HR function, with line and general management positions being more and more frequent as routes into and out of postings in HR.

The organization should have been in a position to develop, maintain, and attend to metrics that assess the performance of line managers and individual organizational units in recruiting, managing, and developing employees. These metrics, perhaps experimental at first, are the ones that are increasingly embedded in the organization's performance management routines and are attended to at all levels of management. These metrics may, out of necessity, vary from context to context, even within a single organizational unit. In one setting, the appropriate measure might be one of senior management 'bench strength": how many talented and qualified candidates exist within the organization to fill vacancies in a set of high-leverage positions.

In another setting, it might be a measure of human capital renewal, reflecting the amount of ongoing education employees have obtained through company programs, professional development activities, conferences and workshops, and the like.

But what should have been common to all such measures is that they are connected tightly to the overall strategy or mission of the company and unit.

Beyond formal filings and reports, the company should be providing informative reports on its human and intellectual capital, so that investors, customers, potential employees, and others can see how the organization defines, measures, and manages its human capabilities.

The company's website should have a link on its home page leading to human resources that provides more information than just job postings and contact information. Strategic HR in such firms is more closely involved in the design of activity-based costing systems, information systems, and quality programs, and is involved sooner and more centrally in long-run strategic decisions, such as mergers and acquisitions, changes in technology, and decisions regarding sourcing and location of facilities.

They conduct assessment of alignment and internal consistency of HR policies on a regular and formal basis, not only at headquarters, but also by each line manager. Where the line manager has oversight over a business unit with distinct HR policies and practices, the focus is on consistency with overall corporate HR strategy. Where HR is centrally located, they keep the focus on how well policies and procedures match local conditions. In that organization, this process would be comparable in regularity and importance to the routine strategy, budget, and planning exercises and, ideally, would be closely integrated with them.

To assist this effort, they may be making use of tools such as benchmarking studies, enabling a manager to make comparisons against other organizations operating within similar contexts, surveys of current and prospective employees, which allow managers to gauge whether the organization's HR practices have transmitted and reinforced a set of values that are internally coherent and consistent with what management intends, and other research conducted either internally or in conjunction with external partners to evaluate the key HR drivers of profitability.

In such companies, perhaps most importantly, all else being equal, we can observe a reduction over time in the prevalence of HR staff specialists within organizations, as HRM comes to be seen as part and parcel of "management pure and simple" and therefore a key determinant of how managers are hired, developed, and rewarded. Change Agents, external and/or internal, should be able to take advantage of these concepts and frameworks to move the organizations in the strategic direction.

Diversity in Staffing and Recruitment

Diversity is one of the important process considerations relating to staffing and recruitment and deserves a special mention. There are compelling social reasons, and in some jurisdictions, legal requirements for maintaining a workforce that is as demographically and socially diverse as the general population. At the same time, organizations may face external economic pressures to increase or decrease diversity. Customers and clients may resist dealing with certain types of individuals, or they may insist on it. And for internal reasons, organizations may find that diversity is helpful or problematic.

One case for diversity is that it broadens the perspectives

the firm can bring to bear in specific decisions. Insofar as the firm is able to choose among alternatives with some discernment, then having more diverse viewpoints represented will widen the set of alternatives considered, leading on average to better decisions. Diversity can also help the firm to reach out to and then serve a broad clientele. An Indian firm, for example, that wishes to extend operations or sales to virtually anywhere in world, may find invaluable resources in the ethnically and racially diverse population of India. That precisely gives it a competitive advantage over firms that recruit from more homogeneous populations. Particularly in transactions involving trust, ambiguity, and intensive communication, some similarity between an employee and the external constituencies with whom he or she interacts can be an asset.

On the other hand, that same argument can cut the other way. Whereas diversity may be an asset externally in relating to heterogeneous constituents, it may be a liability internally in some instances. Spontaneous trust will usually be stronger between socially similar individuals and in cases where the individuals share a social environment beyond the workplace—most dramatically, in family businesses—the ability to punish bad behaviour with social sanctions is increased, which in turn increases trust. In particular, an organization with a more interdependent technology may find itself favouring a relatively more socially homogeneous workforce.

Thus, private organizations benefit in some ways from a diverse workforce, but diversity can also have private countervailing disadvantages. Society, on the other hand, generally has a strong preference in hiring and staffing that is non-discriminatory. Consequently, a private organization may face societal pressure to be come more diverse than it finds privately optimal.

Organizations that wish to realize the benefits of diversity, both for themselves and for society, can blunt some of the costs by screening for alternative forms of homogeneity or, alternatively, by creating them "artificially." For instance, recruiting students who attended similar educational institutions or majored in the same subject or served in the military or have the same off-work hobbies may produce some of the same benefits of homogeneity, while still permitting a labour pool that is heterogeneous on racial, ethnic, gender, and other lines. And exposing new recruits to similar formative experiences and socialization can often create the same types of bonds that usually exist *a priori* among individuals who are homogeneous along racial, ethnic, or other dimensions.

Total Quality Management

Total Quality Management (TQM) consists of an overriding philosophy or super-ordinate goal of improved quality (zero defects), a distinctive set of production techniques, and a cluster of HR practices aimed at broadening and empowering production workers. Recent research in various industries suggests that productivity and especially quality is improved by adopting production techniques or the cluster of HR practices characteristic of TQM, but adopting the combination of the two is especially powerful. Total quality efforts must extend to suppliers, as quality problems presented by suppliers cannot be tolerated. Suppliers unwilling to accept TQM ex-suppliers; suppliers who accept TQM are rewarded with long-term, stable relationships.

Turning to the human resources dimension of TQM, line workers are best situated to monitor and improve the production process because they are closest to problems that arise and as they possess unrivalled knowledge about the production process. They must be carefully selected and then given the training and tools necessary to carry out their special functions, including on-the-job training, frequent job rotation, job enlargement and enrichment, and free sharing of information. They must be given the authority and autonomy to make changes in the production process. When they are organized in self-managing teams, channels of communication between line workers and all levels of the hierarchy must be kept open. They must also be motivated to act as responsible partners by being given employment guarantees and premium compensation, being treated with respect by their nominal superiors, etc. Thus, TQM requires selection and adoption of a very particular context-specific high-commitment HRM practices.

The plants that combine both the operations and HR facets of TQM are likely to be ahead of the pack of firms that implement TQM. Similarly, adopting a manufacturing strategy based on quality and adhering to a "human-capital-enhancing" approach to HRM (e.g., selective staffing, intensive and broad training, group incentives, pay-for-skill, all-salaried workforce), reflect favourably in several metrics for assessing organizational performance. We have to consider training investment made by firms initiating a TQM program. Often a first step in such programs is to train line employees in both communications and tem-participation skills and in process-control techniques. These are valuable skills for any employee. But it is the extent to which they complement other human capital the employees have and will come to have—as their jobs are enlarged and enriched, and as they learn more about the firm's entire production process—that really gives these skills value.

Downsizing

Firms downsize for a variety of reasons, including cost cutting, increased flexibility and adaptability, enhanced focus, enhanced productivity, as part of organizational policies, to broaden skill bases by using outsourced staff, and in hopes of improving shareholder equity. Recent upsurges in downsizing are often attributed to intensified competition, decreased product life cycles, escalating costs and legal liabilities associated with employees, falling costs of substitutes including outsourced employees, and increased discipline from capital markets, which seem to endorse downsizing.

Existing evidence about the effects of downsizing suggests the following conclusions:

1. The impact on the firm's bottom line in terms of both operating profits and financial market performance is mixed and largely transitory.
2. Employee morale and attitudes suffer, which can be especially costly in environments that emphasize creativity.
3. It may not be the least able employees who leave. Instead, some downsizing programs unwillingly encourage the more able and valuable employees to depart.
4. Downsizing can have a substantial negative effect on the local community, although some commentators argue that these effects are temporary and, if avoided, lead to far worse consequences down the road.
5. The overall moral from the available empirical data is that downsizing works best when tied to sensible restructuring of the organization's work practices, because:

- Organizations that restructure are more likely to be addressing the real problems and opportunities they face.
- Morale among those left behind is likely to be higher if management projects a clear vision of what the problem has been and how things will get better, than if they merely downsize reactively to "cut fat."

Organizations that contemplate downsizing should first contemplate alternatives. If companies must downsize, process considerations become very important. There are no easy answers in how to downsize, but the following should be kept in mind:

1. Communication with employees is critical.
2. Employees should be co-opted into the process as much as possible, and it should be made clear that alternatives were considered.
3. Distributive and procedural justice should be carefully attended to.

4. Both the leavers and the survivors should be supported, the former with "services" and the latter with training and a sense of where the downsized organization is headed.
5. On balance, targeted layoffs seem a better bet than uniform, across-the-board layoffs.
6. Layoffs that target for that favour more senior workers have advantages and disadvantages on both legal and organizational grounds.
7. Consider thoroughly the interests of the communities involved, what you can do to mitigate the impact of the layoffs, and whether it isn't in your organization's interest to be a "good citizen" of the affected locales to protect your reputation as such.
8. Legal considerations should be attended to carefully, though they cannot and should not be determinative. Careful planning, rationalization, and documentation may be an important "cover" in the face of lawsuits.

Outsourcing

Organizations nowadays are increasingly relying on outsourcing to meet their employee force requirements, by hiring "temps" from labour contractors, purchasing specific services from independent contractors, and employing a host of strategies intermediate between these two. The bottom line is that outsourcing is generally a bad idea for activities that:

1. Are part of the organization's "core".
2. Are closely linked spatially, technologically, or socially to core activities.
3. Depend on workers internalizing the organization's welfare.
4. Require high levels of firm-specific human capital.
5. Involve workers who are socially similar to regular employees.

Outsourcing is usually a better idea for jobs that require workers who don't fit within the culture of the organization or whose skills and other attributes make them atypical for the firm, and for tasks the oversight of which would divert management attention from core activities.

1. In outsourcing tasks that are highly interdependent with core activities, maintaining trust and cooperation with regular employees carrying out those core activities is paramount. Consequently, it is often advantageous in such cases to make use of contingent workers (part-timers or temps) who resemble or are compatible with the client's workforce, or to retain contractor firms whose cultures and HR practices are similar to those of the client.
2. In outsourcing tasks that are strategically important, quality and the ability to monitor results are paramount. It is often beneficial in such cases to spin off a separate organizational unit to handle such tasks; or to develop long-term relations with the labour suppliers or independent contractors involved, so that they have incentives to develop firm-specific knowledge and to maintain quality.

Some organizations have chosen outsourcing in an attempt to avoid or minimize legal liabilities. If outsourcing is thought of for these reasons, take good legal advice; it isn't as simple or straightforward as is thought. "Assigning" former employees to an independent labour contractor or serviced provider and then "hiring" them back as outsourced labour can be contentious, particularly when the former employees remain closely tied to regular employees, which will make it less legitimate to treat the two groups differently. An alternative to the downsizing/outsourcing combination, especially for employees who are "under- worked" in the organization, is to enable those employees to provide services to external clients, as well as internally.

Conclusion

The creed (or philosophy) of a company when clearly expressed and enthusiastically used creates the foundation of a corporation's internal and external personality. For a corporation to quickly establish itself and maintain a high product standard while growing rapidly it will be important to develop an ethical, aggressive, responsive, and stable impression on customers, distributors, employees, and vendors as soon as possible. Perhaps most importantly, the ultimate quality of a company is largely determined by the character of its employees who are attracted into employment and develop because of the company's environment. Firms that invest heavily in building a strong system of employee commitment and organizational attachment from the outset generally require significantly fewer administrative overseers some years later.

Until quite recently, the management of human resources was regarded as a low-level technical specialty, involving people who specialize in filling out government-mandated forms, conducting wage and morale surveys, handling initial recruitment interviews, and the like. HR Department has been one of the places to send good, solid managers who fell off the fast track at some stage or another. Accordingly, most general managers had few and limited tools with which to think intelligently and analytically about HRM in particular organizations.

The contrast is most vivid with traditional Japanese firms, where managing human resources is the single most important duty of middle-level general managers, and success in these tasks is a prerequisite for advancement into top management. Senior HR managers in large Japanese corporations are, if anything treated as the elite. There is an increasing awareness of the importance of managing the human resources. HR departments are outsourcing some of their lower value-added activities, such as payroll and benefits processing, to remake themselves into leaner, more "high-end" business partners.

Change Agents have to become increasingly aware that their innovative skills in thinking about HRM need polishing at least and, in many cases, a complete makeover. However, the need of the hour is to come up with innovatively crafted frameworks on some of the crucial HR issues confronting organizations/managements today, such as outsourcing, diversity, TQM, and downsizing. If they persevere, the conceptual frameworks so created will illuminate some of the important HR issues of current concern.

References

American Management Association (1997) Corporate Job Creation, Job Elimination, and Downsizing: Summary of Key Findings, New York: American Management Association, Viewable online at http://www.amanet.org/survey/97survey.htm.

Bennet Harrison and Maryellen R. Kelley (1993) "Outsourcing and the Search for 'Flexibility,'" *Work Employment and Society* Volume 7, June, pp. 213-35.

Brian Becker and Barry Gerhart, (1996) "The Impact of Human Resource Management on Organizational Performance," *Academy of Management Journal,* Vol. 39, August, pp. 779-801.

Bruce Caldwell and Marianne Kolbasuk McGee (1997), "Outsourcing Backlash—Many Companies Aren't Getting What They Wanted from Their Outsourcing Deals," Information Week 650, September 29, p. 14.

Jane Auman and Brian Draheim (1997), "The Downside to Downsizing Benefits Canada, http://www.benefitscananda.com/Content/managed/mc13_feature.html.

Kathy Williams and Charles O'Reilly (1998), "Demography and Diversity: A Review of 40 years of Research," included in Barry M. Staw and L. L. Cummings (eds.), Research in Organizational Behaviour, Vol. 20 Greenwich, CT: JAI Press, pp. 70-140.

Mark A. Youndt, Scott A. Snell, James W. Dean Jr., and David P. Lepak (1996), "Human Resource Management, Manufacturing Strategy, and Firm Performance," *Academy of Management Journal,* Vol. 39, August, pp. 836-66.

Martin N. Baily, Eric J. Bartelsman, and John C. Haltiwanger (1994), "Downsizing and Productivity Growth: Myth or Reality? CES Discussion Paper 94-4, Washington: U.S. Bureau of the Census.

Rebecca D. Eisen, "Dealing with Downsizing: What to Do Now to Prepare for a Possible Layoff", viewable online at the Web site of Brobeck, Phleger and Harrison LLP: http://www.brobeck.com/sslitle/88.htm.

Richard Peish (1995), "When Outsourcing Goes Awry," *Harvard Business Review*, Vol. 73, May-June, p. 24.

3

Resource Engagement in Uncertain Situations

Sukesh Koka

"The greatest tragedy in America is not the destruction of our natural resources, though that tragedy is great. The truly great tragedy is the destruction of our human resources by our failure to fully utilize our abilities, which means that most men and women go to their graves with their music still in them." Oliver Wendell Holmes has said the above words in the context of America but globally this is the phenomenon that has plagued the business systems time and again. Everyone knows about the story of the ant and the grasshopper and everyone admires the foresight of the ant but everyone wants to be the grasshopper.

This symptom is mutually interpolated between individuals and organizations alike. This paper is aimed at how human resource systems and organizations should adopt and implement a foresight that can not only help them evade the imminent slowdown but also create a star image among employer and employee communities alike. It provides steps for organizational preparedness to face the situation and march towards organizational renewal and growth.

Recession Leading to Uncertainty

Deploying the right resource at the right time and at a right place is considered to be one of the key factors for any successful business. This practice becomes much more important when the business is not doing good or when we are facing an economic slowdown. Economic slowdown is what is defined as Recession; a situation where the buyers do not have money to spend; the manufacturers do not have enough cash flow to produce goods. This is a cycle and owing to this the employees lose their jobs, as the organizations get into losses, which in-turn increases the un-employment rate in a country.

A similar situation to a recession was prevalent in the IT industry 10 years back when the dot-com bubble burst. Several organizations closed their operations, many individuals and organizations lost money in the share market and few people could never come out of the financial loses they made till date. And here we are, again, with a much bigger economic crisis situation termed as a "Global Recession", the worst the world has ever seen since the Great Depression which occurred in the year 1929. The global markets have tumbled, share markets crashed, many industries are making recurring loses quarter by quarter Unanswered questions bothered the practitioners and the researchers alike. Some of them are—so how is that we have not known this Tsunami coming our way?

How is it that all the management gurus in the world could not predict a way out? What can be worse than a bank which has the deposits of individuals is not able to pay back as there is no cash with them? How come all the liquidity has vanished in the sub-prime crises? In this great economic melt-down we saw every country has lost money and so did the organizations and individuals. Could the answer be that we were not prepared? Or did we not observe the warning signals? Now who is going to bail out the SMEs which are the worst hit? Would the SMEs come back to normalcy at all? Whatever may be the cause, the fact that organizations have to address these issues to survive and grow.

Uncertainty: Impact on Human Resources

In a slowdown, it is the personnel who lose their jobs first as the organizations are not able to pay salaries to them. Organizations slice the manpower to shred the pay load as the first step and then take up drastic cost cutting measures to decelerate the cash flowing out of the company. The support staff is reduced and in this process HR, Recruitment, Training, marketing, corporate communications etc departments either stop working or operate with lean staff. But this could be perceived as only a stop gap arrangement, then how would the business improve now?

Several organizations witnessed additional responsibility to the middle management so that the business could still function normally and some resources are moved completely into a new role terming the process as Job Rotation. Even by doing this, many organizations have failed to bail themselves out from this economic depression as most of the employees might just look at this as an stop-gap arrangement so that they could search for other opportunities and some might just accept the new work as there are not many options available in the market. On the other hand, the organization spends lot of money towards the notice period of the employees and they again spend money in training the new deployed manager externally.

Though the cash is flowing out, organizations might feel that this is a better situation as the future is very uncertain. Now what could be a possible solution for this kind of challenging situation? How does the company increase the efficiency of the deployed resources and increase business to move up the profit ladder? Does the organization have the right resource if so; have they been engaged in the right job?

In many organizations particularly in the SMEs the recruitment teams generally validate the job seekers against the role and hire them. The real attributes, strengths and weaknesses of the job seeker are not completely explored. Few very important traits of individuals like adaptability, perseverance skills etc are not checked at all. Partially, because the recruiters are under pressure to close the position or they do not know how to select the right candidate.

At the tough times of recession this creates a very big issue which is mostly invisible. Individuals who are not willing to embrace the change would have a tough time in accepting the new role or accepting additional responsibility. The stress levels might increase and they might also get mentally harassed as the contribution of every resource comes out very clearly and so does the efficiency and performance. This is mostly because the teams are understaffed and working is under constant pressure to perform so that they could retain their jobs. So what could be the possible solution for a catastrophic situation like this? Which are these "Right Resources" who could be given additional charge/work or new role?

Employees learn from their mistakes and experience. If this is so, leadership is also about being pro-active to situations. Keeping in mind the past experience in the IT industry, organizations have to be very careful while hiring the resources at all the times. A soldier's mettle is seen in the war field and not at the training camp and same might be the case with the organizations. Below are few methods/ ways of taking up proactive steps at the time of hiring resources in order to be prepared for tough times. The crux here is to hire the right resource and engage the resource in a job which suits their skills best.

1. **Select the Right Resource at all the Times:** Immaterial of what ever is the situation, it is essential for the HR department selects the right resource for a particular position. It's important that they thoroughly screen the candidate and select the candidate without compromising on any of the skills. Selecting a wrong candidate succumbing to pressure lays a week foundation and it might not act in building a strong team.
2. **Look for Resources which are High on Perseverance Quotient:** At tough times all the resources are need to run an extra mile for the organization to perform and at juncture the perseverance skills of a candidate play a vital role. The resource should be able to try and perform beyond his normal capacity to achieve the goals. It essential for them to move out of their comfort zone and

stay focused on their goals firmly.

3. **Look for Resources which are High on Adaptability Quotient:** This is one of the most important attribute of an individual which the HR folks gauge from the company perspective at the time of interview however it is very essential that the resource is gauged on the adaptability quotient from the personality angle. Individual who are high on the adaptability quotient are very easily embrace the change and team. They create minimal or no friction when it come to team dynamics. They are the ones who embrace the change looking for achieve their targets.
4. **Look for Resources that Have the Zeal to Take My New Challenges at All Times:** Select candidates who are open for new challenges, who are willing to take risk, who are enthusiastic to achieve new heights against candidates who are just looking for a routine job which just fills their time. These resources are the one who are ready to run a new race every day morning, their passion to achieve the goals is what they always look for.
5. **Look for Resources that Have a High Appetite for Career Growth:** Candidates who have a high appetite for growth in their career always look for new avenues to add to their skill set. They look forward to learn every skill which they may like. And at time of recession they always look forward for opportunities where in they could add additional responsibility to their portfolio.
6. **Select Resources Who Accept Job Rotation as a Healthy Practice:** Hire resources who believe that job rotation is a healthy process. Individual contributors refrain themselves from getting into a new job after working in a particular role for a long time. They prefer becoming a specialist in the field and remain the same throughout their life rather than trying new avenues. These people would become non-performers if they get into a role which they do not like.

7. **And of Course Look for Leadership Skills:** This is one of the most important factors while hiring resources in to the company for leaders stand stall at the time of crisis. They take the onus of the situation and act tactfully to get the organization into profits. People with no leadership skills generally give up in tough time before working towards a task.

One of the biggest challenges for any organization at the tough times of business or at time of economic recession is to engage the right resource for a job and for this planning has to be done from the day the resource joins the organization; just to stay put and be prepared for tough times in business. Merely drawing a plan when we are in deep sea would not help. The below described methods can be a few of them and these are purely based on my experience. These may be termed as few pro-active steps an organization can take up in order to prepare their manpower for rough business weather. These steps would help an organization in a big way to train an engage manpower in the right direction to achieve the desired results.

1. **Identify the Primary and Secondary Interests of the Resource at the Time of Joining:** Apart from the skills which the candidate would possess for the applied job, we always need to identify the secondary interests. Many recruiters may feel that having secondary interest might not be good as the performance on the primary interest is diluted. But this might not be the case. It is just that job seekers do not reveal their secondary interest at the time joining. Most of us always have secondary interest and plans we always make for our future.
2. **Have a Selected Group of Resources Exposed to Functioning of the Other Departments:** As a regular practice we need to have the resources of one team work on the job of other teams which are closely related. Like recruitments team can work on the sales calling, the Presales team can take up project management; the Delivery team can be involved in recruitments and so on...

This practice will ensure that the departments are inter linked, the resources would have a practical experience on how the other team works and eventually the respect for the other teams also increases when they face the delivery challenges.

3. **Have a Systematic Job Rotation Plan as Part of an Appraisal:** Have a job Rotation plan as a compulsory option for all the resources in a systematic manner. Job Rotation should be used only for promotions, transfer or when resource utilization is less. The objective of job rotation has to be only for taking to the employee to the next level of management and should not be given as a promotion for good work.
4. **Fire the Secondary Skills of the Resources at all Times:** As a practice always keep fuelling the secondary skills of the resources. Have them as part of the annual appraisal plan. Have the resources work on these as fulfil the ambitions and also achieve something for the company. A word of caution should be that the secondary skills should be inline or something related to the business. This cannot be a practice of arts and music for self-interest.
5. **Keep the Teams Trained for Handling Change Management:** Always have the team trained to believe that adapting to new environments is important. Change Management for the organization is as important as Change Management for an individual. Conduct regular training programmes to emphasize on this point always.
6. **Create Intra-departmental Training Avenues:** As a practice have inter department training programmes happening regularly. These would help in large way in bridging the gaps between and team and also help the team members upgrade their skills and knowledge. This practice is visible in few captive centres.
7. **Do not Hire Manpower in Excess at all Times:** Organizations should have minimum bench strength at all times. Not realistic sales forecast should be carefully

studied before investing in hiring manpower. The funds might as well be used in building a brand image and strengthen the skills of the recruitment team so that they could turn around quickly with the resources when the organizations are in need.

8. **Hire Contractual Staff for Seasonal Positions:** When there are flow of work on a particular project or when a short team SPV is created then it is highly advisable to hire resources on contract from vendors for this particular work. Because when the project is completed the cost would automatically go down. If FTEs are always taken the resource management would become a challenge for the company when the project comes to an end or gets cancelled for various reasons.

By following the above steps, the organizations would be able to create a healthy atmosphere at office. The personnel feel at all times that the organization is always investing on the current and the future needs of the resources. On the other hand, the organization is preparing their resources for a situation where there is a turbulence or recession and when this hits the market their resource would take up the changing business scenario more like an opportunity to learn and go to the next level in the career rather than an option which has been given to retain them. The urge to perform and grow in the new role would be higher for the individual and thus there would be a flow of adrenaline into the system. The new job on which the individual is engaged might also see better results than expected and would surely bail out the company from financial crunch. This might be the right formula to prepare for uncertain business scenarios and to achieve this it is essential for the top management to look at this plan very seriously.

Hence, to summarize, identification of the right resource for the company is the one of the most important factors for the success of any business. Nurturing the talent at all times and preparing the personnel for tougher times is always advisable. Having discussed the methods and approaches in screening a capable incumbent and also the procedures through which the individuals can be utilized on multiple roles, the focus is mainly on giving a transparent picture with in the organization in order to elicit a positive environment that can accept change and work towards it. By taking up these steps an organization can be prepared to engage a right resource for a right job and achieve the desired results in this uncertain economic era. Having prepared the resources with a transparent outlook towards uncertainty, the change would be embraced by the resources as a challenge for growing rather than looking at it as a stop gap arrangement.

The human resource department plays a very vital role in making this happen and to reiterate this has to be taken as one of the strategic objective rather than a tick mark operational activity by the management. At the time of recession leading towards uncertainty, engaging the right resource who is trained, skilled and packed with motivation to achieve the new challenging tasks might work as an elixir for the organization.

4

Recession Blues for Human Resources

A. Jagan Mohan Reddy

The commencement of the millennium brought with it a real breakaway from the past. The future belongs only to those managers who can manage people well. Besides being a necessary criterion to stay and succeed in business, there is also a more harmonious and plus point to managing people well. Managers derive a sense of satisfaction and experience a feeling of fulfilment, when they collaborate with the employees in a wholesome manner. Four issues are assumes significant during the first decade of the 21st century. They are as follows:

1. Recruitment of talented employees.
2. Retention of talented employees.
3. Building better and more improved skills in such employees.
4. Achieving higher levels of performance from such employees.

Hence, people management matters most in the current context. There is yet another and altogether different demand placed on the corporate management. Quick innovation and fast response time are required to meet the ever-expending customer needs and tastes. Against this background, the paper highlights the reflections of the author on the issues that the HR faces in uncertain organizational context.

Challenges

The global melt down/recession has thrown up several challenges for the HR professionals such as cutting staff with out loosing talented workforce, keeping employees in position with steep learning curves etc. In fact no one needs an introduction to the word recession in these times. Though Indian economy is still growing, organizations are taking all possible steps to ensure that they survive through these uncertain times of global recession. One such change has taken place in the recruitment and training departments of most organizations.

According to a recent survey conducted by the Boston consulting Group, when organizations were asked about the steps they are taking to respond to this crisis, the following responses were received.

1. Cutting back on recruitment (69 percent).
2. Cutting back on company events (54 percent).
3. Cutting back on bonuses linked to company performance (45 percent).
4. Laying off temp employees (43 percent).
5. Laying off regular employees (34 percent).
6. Cutting back on individual training (33 percent).
7. Cutting back on technical training (31 percent).

This data evidences that out of the seven measures taken to control costs, five are related to the area of recruitment and training. The cost cutting strategies of organizations relating to recruitment and training departments the change their outlook when the times change from a high growth environment to an uncertain environment of recession is shown in Table 4.1.

During the times of recession, the demand-supply gap tilts in favour of the employer. So, there are more people available than what the market demands. Secondly, the overall risk appetite of the organization reduces dramatically, thereby making the organization resort to the safer options. Thus, organizations tend to look for people who are a perfect fit for a role instead of looking at resources who are 'generally smart' but need a time of 3 to 4 months before they can start producing results.

The recruitment strategy and training strategy go hand in hand. Similarly, training strategy during the boom and recession era also differs (Table 4.2). It is quite evident that organizations will cut down on training budgets to save costs in times of recession.

Table: 4.1 Cost-cutting Strategies of Organizations

Dimensions	During Boom	During Recession
Cost of hires	Get the people on board at any cost	Low cost services for hiring
Hiring	Longer interval planning hire First, get customer's later	Temping Just-in-time strategy
Quality of hiring	Ready to employ hiring lower Expectations of right fit (Question-is the candidates trainable) Easy on productivity	Ready to deploy hiring perfect fit Redeployment/multi-skilling do more with less.
Quality of hiring	Over hire (growth + attrition hiring)	Organizational cleaning –Correcting the pyramid
Risk appetite	High	Very low

However, business still needs competent people who can deliver services to the customers. Part of this responsibility is shifted to the recruitment team where they are mandated to find the 'right-fit' candidates who do not need long training cycles. Business teams, who provide 'project- specific' training to new members of the team, so that the overall training costs could be minimized, share part of the responsibility.

Uncertainty: Response from the Organizations

The consensus of economists surveyed by the National Association of Business Economists (NABE) is that the recession of 2007-09 is over. More positive economic prospects should be a reason for rejoicing. But the financial haemorrhaging of the recent downturn resulted in companies scrambling with short-term fixes and painful cuts. Now, as a result of such increased short-term thinking, executives feel they are not in a position to ride the next economic upswing. In fact even when times were flush, there was concern that too much short-term thinking had dominated business thinking.

Table 5.2: Training Strategy during Booms and Recessions

Dimensions	During Boom	During Recession
Type of Training	Personal Development, Education for freshers- Functional/technical skills	Project based training (Specific to a gap in project)
Training out look	Train at will across board Employer sponsored employee development	Self initiated skill up gradation
Trainers	Heavy reliance on third party trainers	Mostly in-house
Training budgets	High	Minimum

Forbes in a study of 200 large companies revealed that leading executives are concerned about the cutting that took place over the past years has hobbled their future growth prospects. Talent recruitment efforts are one area where companies have cut too far and wide. Strategically, organizations need to be aggressively courting the best talent available, and planning and developing the next workforce. However, operationally, organizations are still in bare-bones cut mode. More than one in five executives surveyed (22 percent) said their company's recruiting and retention efforts did not accurately reflect current or updated strategic goals. Further more, a quarter (25 percent) indicated that their organizations' training and development programs didn't align with strategic goals. This may not be surprising, but executives interviewed say that short-term operational thinking will not help long-term growth.

Workforce reductions and hiring freezes have been key elements of the cost-cutting measures companies have had to take through the current recession. With staffing taking a backseat to other measures, executives are not necessarily focused on talent issues. For example, recruiting, retaining, and training employees ranked 12th on the list of current operational priorities and only moved to 9th on the list for priorities in 12 months.

Yet with economic recovery, companies can expect additional pressure to retain their most valued employees and they will face a more competitive market for recruiting new talent. So aligning human capital management to strategic and operational goals may be more important than ever for future success. In the light of above, a question arises as to what the companies should dos and don'ts.

Dos and Don'ts for Companies

First, the companies need to fight fear of recession—because fear causes confusion amongst the employees as well as employers.

Secondly, they should not react in a way that can cause distress and confusion. For instance cutting quickly the frills–such as the late leavers drop facility, team-parties, outings and sometimes even the birthday cake, etc., seem very common but may not help. Lean practices or good but they should not be seen as resorting to knee-jerk reactions. If you have an overall Lean-Drive' and do it with employee involvement, they themselves will suggest very good ideas. But one-sided reactive actions can lead to losing employee confidence and add to cynicism.

Thirdly, this is the right time to invest to find out what brings value or what employees value. Is it the brand identity, job challenge, leadership or a sense of belonging? Discover and invest in the positives. During recession or bad times, attrition drops and it is time to use it to your advantage. So, whatever positive investments you make will create an amplified effect on the workforce which is more stable.

Fourthly, good communication, good communication matters all the time and more so during bad times. Keep your communication channels open (to suggestions) and responsive (to queries).

Fifthly, this could be the time for HR to get very innovative. For instance this could be the opportunity to educate employees to focus on customer value if it has not already been done. Successful companies are already doing such things. A Medium-sized IT company's CEO told me recently: "We have asked employees to spend 20 percent of their time in any of the corporate development activities. To come forward in teams to suggest projects which will help develop the organization." He added, "The response has been very good–an employee team came forward to refurbish the company web site and has been doing a good job." This is applicable to bigger organizations as well but smaller companies can achieve far more easily due to the size. Economic recession does offer opportunities of a different magnitude to the HR professionals but there are challenges that confront the HR fraternity.

Managing HR Risk

Risk in relation to human capital has now gone significantly beyond the traditional remit of the human resources (HR) department. With current economic challenges and in an increasingly complex regulatory environment, managing HR risk has become an increasingly important issue for global executives. According to Ernst & young's recent global HR risk survey of Fortune 500 CFOs and HR executives, talent management and succession planning were viewed as strategic issues having a high presence in terms of their impact and likelihood of occurrence with in an organization.

Closely following in the surgery results were professional ethics/tone at the top, pay and performance alignment, regulatory compliance and employee training and development. Managing all stages of the talent cycle-recruitment, training and development, performance management, retention and separation–has become a key performance indicator for the best-run companies. As business is contemplating transformation programme within their HR management strategies, managing these risks successfully can deliver significant financial (and non-financial) benefit. Equally, if not managed effectively, the issues surrounding human capital can leave skills gaps in the business and seriously damage its performance and reputation.

Work Force Composition

Unlike the other countries, which are going to be saddled with aging work force (e.g., 42 percent of the Japanese population is credited to be aged 60 or over by 2050, India is going to have a much younger work force. And a major chunk of this work force will be from the Y generation (born 81 onwards). The HR practices of the past helped attract, retain and engage the "baby boomer" generation and generation X (Gen X) that largely constituted the workforce for the last 25 years or so. But it is unlikely that these people practices will equip and empower HR leaders to get, keep and motivate Gen Y which is dramatically different in its aspirations, capabilities and outlook. Some of the key attributes of Gen Y are given below:

1. Value learning; acutely afraid of obsolescence.
2. Value instant gratification; want goals set on Monday, review done on Wednesday and rewards declared on Friday!
3. Enjoy action over pep talk.
4. Work hard but value work-life balance.
5. Willing to listen, but have a mind of their own.
6. More entrepreneurial; higher risk appetite.
7. Willing to be led, refuse to be managed!
8. Outspoken, often blunt; speak their mind without fear.

9. Question authority; respect expertise.
10. Do not like a job just because the pay-cheque is good.
11. Value learning and advancement opportunities more.

Even more important is that the millennial do no fit into any single mould. Each of them may have much in common, but they are also individualistic in their aspirations and motivations. An understanding of the millennial workforce and designing the appropriate people programme and processes are key to building significant competitive advantage in the coming years.

By definition, best practices are best only in an organizational context. It is a misnomer to assume that what is a best practice for one organization will deliver similar value to every other organization. In other words, "best practices" represent the efficiency dimension of HR practice while "best-fit" practices add to the effectiveness. Next practices in HR must be designed to satisfy two important and distinct criteria: (a) suited to the millennial workforce; and (b) tailored to the context of an organization.

Building a Culture of Employee Appreciation

Making employees feel appreciated so that they work harder and be more loyal seems like a simple concept. But there is often a disconnect between the type of appreciation employees want and what their managers think they want, according to a recent study by the International Association of Administrative Professionals and Office team, a staffing company in Menlo park, California. Managers responding to the survey ranked promotions and cash bonuses as the two most effective ways of recognizing employee accomplishments, but workers said they preferred an in-person thank-you or having a job well done reported to senior management. In other words, though a decent bonus will always be a highly coveted form of recognition, employers often underestimate the degree to which workers value kind words delivered face to face.

That may sound like good news for companies looking for inexpensive ways to show appreciation to employees. In many ways, though, it's easier to hand over a bonus than to create a culture in which saying thank you is a regular occurrence. "Especially during tough economic periods, it's important to give people face time and basic human appreciation on a regular basis," says Debra Condemn, a business psychologist and founder of Manhattan Business coaching in New York City. "A plaque may be nice for 15 minutes, but once it goes on the wall, people tend to forget about it."

Doing More with Less

In the last six months, a significant number of HR professional have lost their jobs. The resultant pressure on HR to service employees with a smaller team is very evident. The reduction in budgets also means that HR professionals have to deliver on the same agenda with less access to external resources. Can HR respond to this challenge and, if so, how?

We have seen above how the recruitment and training departments change their outlook even the times the change from a high growth environment to an uncertain environment of recession.

Employee Engagement

Over the years, we have transitioned from employee opinion to satisfaction and now to engagement. In more recent times, corporate India has often relied on Gallup's Q 12 (there are, of course, other methodologies that are also available to understand and measure employee engagement. And, if one were to closely look at the drivers of this engagement, it comes back to clarity of expectations, regular and meaningful feedback on performance, recognition and reward, help with performance improvement and, finally, support to foster growth. Currently, organizations accept engagement as equal to profit.

What then is the business case for this increased attention?

It's simple: engagement = profit! Research shows that engaged employees are more productive employees. They are more profitable, more customer-focused, safer, and more likely to withstand temptations to leave the organization. In the best organizations, engagement is more than an HR initiative–it is a strategic foundation for the way they do business. Organizations that have optimized engagement have 2.6 times the earnings per share (EPS) growth rate compared to organizations with lower engagement in the same industry.

Opportunities for HR

It is true that HR professionals face challenges but economic recession also provides opportunity for HR. Dave Gartenberg, Director HR of Microsoft UK, reportedly said recently: "In turbulent times more than any other, there is not only the opportunity but the need for HR to provide leadership to the business. The ability to attract and retain workers when times are really tough requires leaders to be at their best." Many feel that issuing pink-slips and managing layoffs are the biggest challenges that HR faces today; but there is far less wisdom in this belief because the real challenge that confronts corporate HR today is to utilize this period of recession as an opportunity.

Some of these opportunities are as follows:

1. **Consolidate Workers:** Workforce consolidation is a huge opportunity that any organization has nowadays. This is not only in terms of having a leaner workforce, but also in redeployment of the workforce to improve utilization and efficiency.
2. **Streamline Salaries:** For the past few years most industries have seen above-normal salary hikes due to the pressure of retention. In fact, India Inc recorded the steepest salary hikes in Asia for seven years running till 2008, according to Hewitt Associates. But the recession has changed things dramatically. Salary freezes and pay cuts have suddenly become the order of the day. This

period can be viewed as an opportunity to streamline salaries and cut costs.

3. **Make Organizations more Performance-centric:** The recession has forced organizations to take a close look at the workforce and identify the real performers. The non-performers have either found their way out of the organizations or have been put on a short notice to 'deliver or perish'.
4. **Identify Real Talent:** The renewed strict focus on performance alone for survival in organizations has not only exposed low- and non-performers, but has also brought to the fore 'real talent' in the organization.
5. **Develop Talent as Leaders:** A recession gives us the right time to wisely invest in the development of talent, both in terms of skill sets and in the form of future leaders. The focus has to be on how much they are investing in their employees and what skill sets they will need to grow to improve their businesses in the future.
6. **Review and Restructure Policies:** The mad pace of hiring, training and appraising seems to have come to a screeching halt. And if not to a complete full stop, the rate is low and slow. This also gives HR the time to revisit its policies, compare them with best-in-class practices and restructure them for maximum effectiveness in the present and the future.
7. **Build Employer Brand:** Despite the fact that many companies have put a freeze on hiring, both hiring talented people and retaining them will continue to be a challenge for HR. Hence, keeping the employer brand intact and re-building the same could have a cascading impact later.
8. **And Lastly, Communicate and Build Trust and Morale:** Communicating with employees not only remains one of the greatest needs of HR, but is also an opportunity to build the trust and morale of people during tough times. It is vital for HR to see that the morale of employees does not sag while the organization is sailing through rough

waters. So, we have looked at some of the challenges that HR professionals have to cop with and also discussed the opportunities that the recent economic depression has thrown up.

Now let's look at some of the ways and means through which HR professional can successfully overcome the challenges and in the process not only create and communicate but also deliver value to the organization.

What needs to be done?

1. **Building Competitive Advantage:** The many personal and corporate tragedies of low tide have blurred our memory of what high tide as like but India's long term trajectory means that our ability to find skilled people at the right time will again, at some time in the not so distant future, become the binding constraint for company growth and expansion. The skill crisis has not gone away; it has just been deferred and it is coming to bite us with compound interest.

   The question for the HR fraternity to introspect about is do we pass the two tests of Noah? The first on is that predicting rain is not worth anything but building the ark is all that counts. The second is that the best time to build the ark is when it is not raining. In other words, have we taken any specific actions to build our supply chain? Have we used low tide to prepare for the next high tide? Timing is everything in life and things that are possible in low tide seem impossible in high tide.

2. **Adopting Development Programme:** Human Resources development has been defined as essentially consisting of three C's competencies, commitment and culture. As we know all three are needed to make the company operations efficient. Without competencies many tasks of the company may not be completed in line with company's vision of exceeding customer's expectations. Competencies are not merely related to single individuals. They can be related to team members in the departmental teams.

3. **Cost Optimization as Against Cost Cutting:** The most significant effect of downturn on organizations across the globe is their unified need to cut costs. With limited scope to expand their top lines, companies innovate with seemingly bright ideas to improve their margins through cost reduction-but the more important question is: At what cost to customer value? The short-term focus of cost-cutting is primarily on bolstering margins. This strategy, though a working model, is often detrimental to the organization in the long run. Some of the immediate effects are on the organizational environment, such as blaming cost-cutting measures for lapses in delivery and quality. Customers are often very sensitive to these changes and rightly so, as they become unintentional recipients of the cost-cutting exercise. Cold air-line food is a good example. Cost optimization, which focuses on customer value rather than just on cost reduction, has emerged as a viable alternative. Organizations understand that cost optimization is not a one-time initiative but a focused effort that also brings about sustainable cost benefits.
4. **Opportunity to Innovate:** A lot of 'knee-jerk' and over-reactions are seen in the past months. It seems that there is a 40 year cycle for the occurrence of recession, historically. Just as plants renew themselves in a frosty winter, the economy often odes a renewal during a prolonged contraction-some times, as proven in the past, it is an opportunity to innovate and try out new things. That's the school of thought I belong to. During the 1930s, new industries such as consumer electronics and plastics were created. In the turbulent mid-1970s, the personal computer industry was born, as companies such as Microsoft and Apple founded. The economy didn't look much good then either, with soaring oil prices, rampant inflation, and tumbling stock markets. That didn't stop a young Bill Gates or Steve Jobs from setting up new

businesses. Just as we came out with flying colours in 1930s or 1970s, I am confident that we would also come out of 2009-10 blues. Some of the innovative improvements that could be thought of are as follows:

- **Customer Oriented Innovation:** Areas where your firm had a lead over the competition but was never effectively marketed.
- **Product Innovation:** Possibly ignored new products or incremental innovation-the small improvements in your products that are not only easier to come by but are also easier to sell.
- **Process Innovation:** The bread and butter of corporate innovation-identify the places for improving the processes that allow your organization or the client companies to run smoothly, legally, and more profitably.
- **Strategic Innovation:** Creating fundamental changes in how your company operates an area that requires vision and determination.

Doing a Lot More with a Lot Less: Here are four possible ways in which HR can attempt to do a lot more with a lot less.

Become Self-reliant: In the days of plenty, HR attracted a number of professionals some of whom did not have the time and the inclination to acquire specialized knowledge and skills to perform their roles. With money not being a constraint, many had access to external service providers who gave them ready-to-use 'branded' solutions to meet their needs. As a result, many of these professionals ended up merely orchestrating these engagements rather than ideating, conceptualizing and designing them. So, while the high quality work was being done outside organizations at significant cost, these expensive HR professionals continued to grapple with a huge pile of transactional issues. Today, with access to these specialist services either diminished or cut off; HR professionals are bound to feel helpless.

For HR to do more with less, the first thing that they need

is more competence. In many ways, the slowdown is a golden opportunity for HR professionals to learn the art and science of real HR Management. There are a few illustrative avenues to acquire these HR competencies at virtually no cost: Learn the science of survey feedback: "Survey feedback', which in many ways is the science behind all the modern employee engagement surveys, is a good place to start. HR professionals can learn to design and conduct these surveys themselves. This will take them closer to their employees; teach them what engagement really means on the ground, empower them with a new competence and save lots of money. Compensation surveys: For many years, organizations have had informal clubs through which compensation data was shared among comparable organizations. This gave HR leaders and compensation and benefits (C&B) specialists a first-hand feel for market competitiveness. Today, most of the C&B competence lies solely with C&B consultants. With all the modern-day advantages of professional networking and online information, would it not be possible for HR professionals to do a C&B survey in-house and in the bargain save money and learn a valuable competence?

Recruitment and Selection: The best talent is always head hunted and the best reference checks are always undertaken personally through informal networks. Can HR professionals not use their informal networks to bring on board some high-cost talent and save money in the bargain?

Renegotiate the HR Agenda: In recent years, many HR professionals have taken on a lot more than they can chew and their organizations can digest. In order to make an impact, many have caused an 'initiative overload'. Now is the time to re-order functional priorities and focus on a few vital initiatives. It is, however, important that HR professionals do this re-prioritization in consultation with their business leaders. While most business leaders are likely to welcome this focus, in some cases the negotiation process might not be easy. Business leaders might have conflicting demands or might push hard and the HR team may say "yes" without having the resources to deliver. Business sense and influencing skills are key here.

Organize ourselves differently for many years, rudimentary HR operations including processing of employee requests and resolution of queries were handled by a breed of well-trained clerical staff who not only found great value in doing the job, but also had the 'tolerance to routine 'to do it well. It is my suspicion that many of these jobs are currently handled y so-called qualified HR professionals who not only cost a lot more, but also do it grudgingly. This might be the right time to cerate a new cadre of employee welfare professionals who are a lot more emotionally attuned to the needs of employees and might also be better suited for this role. These employees are likely to give tenure and predictability along with speed and efficiency. Most importantly, they will cost us a lot less.

Become Psychological Green: According to Hendrie Weisinger, author of the Genius of Instinct, being psychologically green means tuning in to your instincts, getting back to basics and back to our human nature. Whereas 'physical green' is analogous to protecting our planet, 'psychological green' is about protecting and honouring our human nature. When HR has to do more with less, more and more HR professionals need to turn psychologically green. Becoming psychologically green will mean that we preserve and promote a healthy organizational work environment. Among all the professions in the world of business, it is the HR professionals who are most psychologically attuned and best equipped to understand the emotions, intentions, dreams and concerns of employees. In these trying times, HR professionals will do well to disconnect from their virtual way of connecting with employees and make a real connection with the human being at work. By listening to them, accepting their vulnerabilities and contributing to their development, we would have gone green and would have truly done more with less!

Getting Your Team Back on Track: Laying people off is difficult and picking up the pieces after a lay-off is even harder. The survivors, who are "the lucky ones" are forced to take on more of the work, put in additional hours and in some cases take a pay cut. All the managers (especially line managers) have a responsibility to get the people back on track after a lay off. The managers undertake the following steps.

1. **Give People Time to Grieve:** Operating as if business is as usual is a mistake. Business is anything but usual. Give your employees a few days to process what has just occurred. Provide them with an opportunity to voice their concerns. Let them talk, while you listen.
2. **Be Empathetic:** Acknowledge the losses that have just occurred. Keep in mind many people may have watched their friends, and possibly family members lose their jobs.
3. **Communicate the New Vision and Direction:** Employees need to know where the company is now heading. Be sure you provide them with as much information as you can regard any changes in the mission and vision of the organization.
4. **Clarify New Roles and Responsibilities:** No matter how senior your employees are, they will need direction. Re-allocate the workload and communicate the changes. Be prepared to provide training, where necessary.
5. **Acknowledge all Success:** It's easy to be so focused on long-term objectives that you miss the small wins that are occurring all around you. Celebrate all successes, not matter how big or small.

Conclusion

One of the most important challenges of the global recession is maintaining the right amount of talent in right quantities at all levels of the organization. Each and every organization needs to focus on human resources from a holistic perspective such that all HR activities are synchronized well. The focus need not be just on axing the people but ensuring that the process of axing is smooth and the human resources should not be left in the midway.

Apart from that, the role of HR is to build a brand among the job seekers in such a way that it engages the axed employees by engaging them constantly. Such an engagement can enhance the brand image of the organization among the job seekers in the days to come else may adversely affect the process of talent acquisition. Since the world is coming out of the blues of recession, this is the right time for the HR professionals of the organizations to take a stock of the physical and psychological status of the existing employees as well as axed employees and re-brand the HR philosophies and policies in such a way that the organizations credibility is catapulted among the eyes of the employees and the new entrants of the organization.

References

Chella, Ganesh, "Doing More With Less" The Hindu-Business Line August 10, 2009.

Ganesh, Sridhar, "Employee Engagement is Key", The Hindu-Business Line, August 17.

Heintz, Nadine, "Building a Culture of Employee Appreciation", B-net September 1, 2009,
http://www. Fast company.com.

Mckendrick, Joe 'Study: "Why Executives are Nervous about the Next Economic Upswing", Smart Planet, October 12, 2009.

Murali, D "Fight Fear of Recession first, The Hindu-Business Line, December 22, 2008.

Raman, K.K., "What Price-Cost Cutting" The Hindu-Business Line September 24, 2009 June 12, 2009.

Srinath, T.T., "What Leaders Need to Do", The Hindu-Business Line, July 20, 2009.

5

Flexi-time as a Strategy of Employee Retention in Uncertainty

S. Suman Babu, A.R. Aryasri and K.V.S. Raju

Companies have responded to the evolving set of issues related to work-life balance by introducing a wide variety of work-life balance practices. While practices vary across companies, most organizational initiatives include several major types of programmes. Most notably, many companies introduce flexible work arrangements—programmes that allow employees to either work during shorter or different hours and/or to work from an alternate location (e.g., flextime, or telecommuting). The dependents' assistance programs (e.g., childcare and eldercare) serve to help employees better meet their responsibilities towards their dependents.

The most cited work-family policies in work-family literature are on-site day care; help with day care costs, elder care assistance, information on community day care, paid parental leave, unpaid parental leave, maternity or paternity leave with reemployment, and flexible scheduling (Perry-Smith et al., 2000). Workplace flexibility is the ability of workers to make choices influencing when, where, and for how long they engage in work-related tasks" (Hill, et al., 2008).

This paper examines the relationship between flexi-time on employee retention as part of a work-life balance practice based on empirical evidence drawn from IT Sector in Hyderabad, India. A total of 300 samples with 30 samples (assistant managers, managers, and senior managers) from each company had been included from the Ten IT companies based on simple random sampling. Managerial personnel from

HR, marketing, finance, operations and technical functions are included in the study.

Literature Review

Both theory and empirical research have suggested a direct relationship between WLB programs and retention (Roehling et al., 2001). What research has not answered conclusively, however, is whether work-life balance itself has a role in this relationship. Rather than helping employees achieve a meaningful balance between work and personal life, these programs may only hold benefits for the employers rather than employees. In light of such arguments and in the context of recent research about the complexities of balancing work and personal life and the importance of balance for individuals' well-being (Friedman and Greenhaus, 2000), it is necessary to investigate whether participation in organizational WLB programs is related to retention through the positive impact of these programs on individual's perceptions of balance.

A related issue that is need of clarification refers to the nature and broad applicability of the work-life balance construct. The majority of past research implicitly assumes that work-life balance is only relevant to women and/or members of families with children (Fredriksen-Goldsen and Scharlach, 2001). Indeed, most researchers have used the term family-friendly HR practices rather than work-life balance practices (Perry-Smith and Blum, 2000). Although recently the topic of shifting focus from work-family to work-life balance has been receiving attention in the popular press (Hayashi, 2001) and at practitioners' forums (Conference Board, 2001, May), academic research has not yet adequately incorporated the salient proposition that work-life balance issues are meaningful for all employees, regardless of gender, marital status, or family responsibilities.

Relationship between Flexi-time and Retention

Flexitime is a work-family practice that allows employees

to have flexible start and finish times, without changing the total number of hours worked, such as a standard 40-hour week in the organisation at the centre of this study (Jarrod M. Haar, 2007).

Employee retention has been linked to flexitime (Gordon and Whelan, 1998; Sailors and Sylvestre, 1994) Compensation, flexible work schedules and training are important tools for retaining employees, employers should not underestimate the power of benefits package (Terry Mullen, 2007). Social exchange theory has been utilised recently to provide an understanding of why work-family practices like flexitime can lead to positive job outcomes (Haar and Spell, 2004). Flexible working may alternatively be referred to as work life balance or work life integration (Smithson and Stokoe, 2005).

According to the National Study of the Changing Workforce, in 2002, 73 percent of employees with high availability of flexible work arrangements reported that there was a high likelihood that they would stay with their current employer for the next year (Bond, Thompson, Galinsky, and Prottas, 2002, p. 34). "Women are somewhat more likely (79 percent) than men (68 percent) to use flextime when it is available" (Galinsky, Bond, and Hill, 2004). "Roughly equal proportion of young women and men in this age group (Generation X) work flexible schedules. In addition, 25 to 34 year old women were more likely than women of other ages to have this kind of flexibility in their jobs" (DiNatale and Boraas, 2002).

Organizations with Flexi-time as a Retention Tool

Many organizations in IT sector like IBM, Intel, Accenture, Cummins and Hinduja TMT and companies like TATA have tried to adopt many retention tools including helping employees achieve healthy work-life balance by providing flexible work practices and many other initiatives (Rupashree Baral and Shivganesh Bhargava 2006). The work-life initiatives most highly sought by employees today are those that allow for work/life balance. A study at IBM, for example, found that the ability to balance work and life was a key driver for the top performers the company was most eager to retain (Chief Executive, 1999).

IBM India: IBM offers its employee's options like flexible workweek schedules, working from home, part time employment, dependant child care, family counselling, and leave of absence programs etc. which can be labelled as family friendly programs. "IBM is committed in providing employees with an attractive and comfortable working environment to maintain a healthy and productive lifestyle. This initiative will help employees deal with the demands of home and family better in these times of hectic schedules and work pressure. Work/life balance is a strategic initiative that helps IBM attracts, motivate and retain the very best talent in the technology industry."

Intel India: Intel claims to provide work-life benefits (synonymously used with family-friendly policies) to help its employees manage work and personal life commitments realizing the fact that managing a job and personal responsibilities is not easy. The range of options includes flexible work schedules, compressed workweeks and alternate work schedules, telecommuting, home office, part-time employment, childcare assistance, resource and referral services and health and wellness benefits etc.

Need for the Study

The major factors that contribute to the interest in work-life balance practices in India are as follows:

1. Higher rates of labour market participation by women.
2. The long hours culture.
3. Work intensification.
4. Working at odd hours.
5. New technology.
6. Global competition.

7. Renewed interest in personal lives/family values.
8. A young workforce.

Scope of the Study

The study is restricted to ten organizations in IT sector. All the ten organizations are situated in the same geographical region of Hyderabad, Andhra Pradesh, India. Due to constraint of time it was decided to evaluate flexitime practice and its retention outcome on the dimensions common to all the organizations in the IT sector. The aspects of looking into flexi-time practice and retention outcomes from different sectors are beyond the scope of the study. The literature review reveals that there are very few studies in India which explore the impact of flexi-time on employee retention. After having extensive discussions with the academicians, key HRD people in IT industry, and colleagues, the research problem has been formulated.

Contemporary organizations, more so in the IT sector, have been discussing on questions like—whether flexitime as a work-life balance practice is being adopted by IT organizations in India and what are its possible outcomes? How flexitime help organization to increase employee retention? Against this background the study seeks to examine the impact of flexitime on employee retention as a work life balance practice in the IT sector.

Objectives of the Study

1. To study existing work-life balance practices in select IT organizations in Hyderabad.
2. To study and analyze the influence of flexitime on employee retention.

Methodology

The primary data was collected from May 2008 to October 2008. The study is based on both the primary data and secondary data. Secondary data was collected from various research journals, books, magazines, websites related to the field of the study. Primary data was collected by administering a structured questionnaire to the junior level and middle level managers of the sampled companies. A 1-5 point Likert Scale strongly disagrees to strongly agree has been used to measure the statements in the questionnaire.

The sample consisted of ten IT companies selected on the basis of non-probability sampling which is non-random in nature. A total of 300 samples with 30 samples (assistant managers, managers, and senior managers) from each company had been included from the 10 companies based on simple random sampling. The size of each of the junior level and middle level management depends on the population of respective cadre of managers. Managerial personnel from HR, Marketing, Finance, Operations and Technical functions are included in the study. Care was taken to see that all the organizations were homogeneous in terms of number of employees (more than 500 each), size (Medium and large scale) and standing of the company (10-15). Descriptive statistics—means, standard deviation have been used as statistical tools. Correlation, regression and ANOVA have also been used appropriately. SPSS 17.0 version was used for data analysis.

Statistical Analysis and Results

The demographic data reveals that 72.7 percent respondent and 27.3 percent respondents Female. The age range was between 25-45 yrs. A majority of them were married (93.3 percent), Tenure of working was in the range of 1-5 yrs. A majority of them were working couples (81.3 percent) and the sector evidenced that single parents working to the tune of 12 percent.

The opinions of the managers on the importance of flexi-time revealed interesting observations.

25.3 percent-34.7 percent felt that flexi-time is extremely important to important, 11.7 percent respondents felt neutral and 14.3 percent-14.0 percent felt somewhat important to not at all important. Moreover, 25.7 percent-35.3 percent respondents felt *strongly agree to agree* on their opinion on quitting a job that did not allow flexi-time, 12.7 percent respondents felt *neutral* and 12.7 percent-13.7 percent respondents felt *disagree to strongly disagree.*

Table 5.1 gives the mean and standard deviation scores for the overall sample of 300 managerial personnel (which includes assistant managers, managers and senior managers). It is interesting to observe that the averages of these domains are almost the same with lesser variation on Employee Stress Reduction. For Flexitime, the corresponding range is 1 to 5.

Table 5.1: Mean and Standard Deviation Scores of 'Overall Sample'

	Mean	Std. Deviation	N
Employee Retention	3.12	1.453	300
Flexitime	3.47	1.357	300

In order to measure the extent of linear relationship between the average Flexitime scores and the average employee retention scores, Karl Pearson coefficient of correlation is computed; and is tested for significance. Table 5.2 reveals that there is a positive correlation between employee retention and flexitime (r=0.648, p=0.000), and is found to be statistically highly significant. For future research, it may be suggested that flexitime can be used to estimate employee retention. Since managerial personnel from all cadres for the purpose of work-life balance practices study are included, it reflects the importance of flexitime to measure employee retention.

The coefficient of determination $R^2 = 0.419$, p=0.000 highlights that Flexitime contributes on Employee Retention to a large extent (Table 5.3). Hence, employee retention can be estimated from flexitime scores.

Table 5.2: Correlation between Employee Retention and Flexitime

		Employee Retention	Flexitime
Employee Retention	Pearson Correlation	1	.648**
	Sig. (2-tailed)		.000
	N	300	300
Flexitime	Pearson Correlation	.648**	1
	Sig. (2-tailed)	.000	
	N	300	300

**. Correlation is significant at the 0.01 level (2-tailed).

Table 5.3: Coefficient of Determination between Employee Retention and Flexitime of 'Overall Sample'

Model Summary				
Model	R	R Square	Adjusted R Square	Std. Error of the Estimate
1	.648[a]	.419	.417	1.109

a. Predictors: (Constant), Flexitime

Model Summary					
Model	Change Statistics				
	R Square Change	F Change	df1	df2	Sig. F Change
1	.419	215.159	1	298	.000

The analysis of variance table (ANOVA) given in Table 5.4 reveals that the regression model fits well for the data (F=215.159, p=0.000).

The regression coefficient and its associated test of significance are given in Table 5.5. The fitted regression model is as follows.

Employee Retention = 0.693 Flexitime + 0.714

From the above regression line, we can estimate the

average score on employee retention for a given average score on flexitime. Further, the population regression coefficient is different from zero as t=14.668, p=0.000. It signifies that when the average flexitime score increases, the average employee retention score also increases proportionately. Hence, the alternate hypothesis "There is significant impact of flexitime on employee retention "is accepted.

Table 5.4: ANOVA for 'Overall Sample'

ANOVA[b]						
Model		Sum of Squares	Df	Mean Square	F	Sig.
1	Regression	264.533	1	264.533	215.159	.000[a]
	Residual	366.384	298	1.229		
	Total	630.917	299			

a. Predictors: (Constant), Flexitime
b. Dependent Variable: Employee Retention

Table 5.5: Regression Coefficient and its Associated Test of Significance for 'Overall Sample'

Coefficients[a]						
Model		Unstandardized Coefficients		Standardized Coefficients		
		B	Std. Error	Beta	t	Sig.
1	Constant	.714	.176		4.059	.000
	Flexitime	.693	.047	.648	14.668	.000

a. Dependent Variable: Employee Retention

Findings

The findings have key implications to IT sector. The study reveals that provision of work-life balance practices like flexitime may benefit organizations by increasing retention rate where employees can perform to the best of their potential and also helps policy makers to frame welfare measures to employees. Organizations should integrate flexitime as a work-life balance practice in core business objectives and also should use as a strategic tool for recruitment and retention of employees. For effective implementation of flexitime as a work-life balance practice there should be both management and co-worker support. Organizations should also consider other practices which will increase retention of employees especially during uncertainty.

Conclusion

During economic downturn or global recession, organizations should adopt flexitime as a retention tool because it does not add any cost to the organizations and moreover it adds many organizational benefits to the bottom line like increased satisfaction and productivity, reduced stress and decreased absenteeism apart from retention of valuable employees.

References

Bond, J. T., Thompson, C., Galinsky, E., and Prottas, D. (2002), Highlights of the National Study of the Changing Workforce.

DiNatale, M., and Boraas, S. (2002), The labour force experience of women from "Generation X". Monthly Labour Review, 125 (3), 3-15.

Formula for retention, Chief Executive (U.S.), (1999), (Chief Executive Guide: The War for Talent), Vol. 46, p. 20.

Fredriksen-Goldsen, K. I. and Scharlach, A. W. 2001, Families and work: New directions in the twenty first century, New York: Oxford University Press.

Friedman, S. D. and Greenhaus, J. H., 2000, Work and family-allies or enemies?, What happens when business professionals confront life choices. Oxford; New York: Oxford University Press.

Galinsky, E., Bond, J. T. and Hill, E. J. (2004), When work works: A status report on workplace flexibility: Who has it? Who wants it? What difference does it make?

Gordon and Whelan, 1998, Gordon, J.R., Whelan, K.S. (1998), "Successful professional women in midlife: how organisations can more effectively understand and respond to the challenges",

Academy of Management Executive, Vol. 12 No. 1, pp. 8-27.

Haar, J., Spell, C. (2001), "Examining work-family conflict within a New Zealand local government organization", The New Zealand Journal of Human Resources Management, Vol. 1, pp. 1-21.

Hayashi, A. M. 2001, Mommy-track backlash. Harvard Business Review, 79(2): 33-42, Conference Board, 2001, May, Work Life Issues. New York, Conference Board.

Hill, E.J., Grzywacz, J.G., Allen, S., Blanchard, V.L., Matz-Costa, C., Shulkin, S., and Pitt-Catsouphes, M. (2008), Defining and conceptualizing workplace flexibility. Community, Work, and Family, 11, 149-163.

Jarrod M. Haar (2007), Exploring the benefits and use of flexitime: similarities and differences, Qualitative Research in Accounting and Management, Vol. 4, No. 1, pp. 69-82.

Perry-Smith, J. E. and Blum, T. C., 2000, Research Notes-Work-Family Human Resource Bundles and Perceived Organizational Performance. Academy of Management Journal, 43(6): 11.

Perry-Smith, J.E., and Blum, T.C. (2000), Work-family human resource bundles and perceived organizational performance. Academy of Management Journal, Vol. 43, pp. 1107-1117.

Roehling, P. V., Roehling, M. V., and Moen, P. 2001, The relationship between work-life policies and practices and employee loyalty: A life course perspective. Journal of Family and Economic Issues, 22 (2): 141-170.

Rupashree Baral and Shivganesh Bhargava (2006), Family-Friendly Policies: Prospects For Indian Organizations, 14th International Employment Relations Association Conference on "Family-Friendly Employment Policies and Practices: An East-West Perspective on Work-Life Balance", 19-23 June 2006, Hong Kong.

Smithson, J., Stokoe, E. (2005), "Discourses of work-life balance: negotiating 'genderblind' terms in organisations", Gender Work and Organisation, Vol. 12, No. 2, pp. 147-68.

Terry Mullen.2007, Achieving an 'A-Player' workforce, Life and Health, 111, 32, p. 20.

6

Role of Employability during Uncertainty

K. Mamatha and G. Srinivas Rao

This paper examines the basic premise that India's vast, skilled labour force will attract a large portion of the global knowledge services industry. In doing so, the analysis not only covers the numbers added to the workforce every year, but also closely examines their employability in a global work environment. It determines that supply-side restrictions are likely to limit the market size to a level far below the figures often suggested by the media and industry players. It proves that the current notions of the enormous potential of this outsourcing industry are based on an overestimated labour supply. It also contradicts the popular notion that as Indian intellectual labour costs rise the cost-differential with developed economies will narrow, causing business to shift to other low-wage countries in the region. It reveals that the cost gap will remain strongly attractive to global companies.

The assumptions underlying the analysis are fairly conservative. Alternate scenarios have also been explored by altering the assumptions to cover a spectrum of possibilities. The demand for labour, which hasn't been estimated, is assumed to come from developed countries and global companies based in India.

Given the flexible concept of knowledge itself, the analysis acknowledges the difficulty in defining the knowledge services industry and, therefore, confines itself to identifying areas in which global companies can expect Indian professionals to provide value to their core businesses. The study does not view this industry merely as a movement up the value chain of the existing business process outsourcing (BPO) industry. Hence, the knowledge services industry goes beyond the traditional cost and time arbitrage advantages that have defined the BPO sector. Hence, the term knowledge services industry is more appropriate to this business rather than the more popular knowledge process outsourcing (KPO).

Knowledge Services Market (KSM)

KSM appears to be like the next big promising step in India's globalization experience. Flush with the success in the low-end off shoring business, India is now looking forward to a slice of high-value jobs, as global companies increasingly scout for capabilities they can't find at home. This is encouraging the growth of the knowledge services outsourcing industry where companies offer their clients value-added inputs for decision making. Competition from other low wage countries in the outsourcing business is also driving Indian companies to move up the value chain. These companies are looking at providing long-term value propositions that cannot be replicated easily as in the case of standardized work in business process outsourcing (BPO). With India's low labour costs, a multitude of skilled professionals proficient in English and enviable software capabilities, the possibility of India getting a large chunk of the estimated US$ 17-billion knowledge outsourcing services industry is strong.

The knowledge services outsourcing industry involves not only companies offering outsourcing services for high-end knowledge work, but also services that deliver enhanced customer value. This includes research and technical work on intellectual property, equity and finance, analytics, market research, clinical research, data management, among others. The knowledge services industry therefore, is about offering value beyond the cost and time arbitrage that defined the success of the BPO business. Hence, we feel the term knowledge services outsourcing industry is more appropriate to this business rather than the popular KPO-knowledge process outsourcing.

Knowledge service companies offer solutions or services that could be, in some cases, intrinsic to the core competency or core business strategy of the client. For instance, private equity firms are increasingly outsourcing work such as the due diligence involved in M&A deals. Farming out highly confidential due diligence functions helps private equity companies to make more deals they would otherwise have passed on because of lack of time and resources for data-intensive work. Further, these companies leverage the outsourced research work to make faster investment decisions. The demand for labour in the KPO sector is assumed to come from developed countries and from global companies based in India. The demand was not estimated and the labour market was viewed entirely from the supply side. Thus, there appears to be an expected shortage of professionals in the advanced economies will drive a general shift of high value white-collar work to India.

Knowledge Services Industry

The knowledge services industry is difficult to define as one needs to consider issues such as the absence of structured processes in knowledge-oriented work. The work profile in this industry isn't simply limited to executing standardized processes but also adding high value through advanced analytical and technical skills. Knowledge services involve outsourcing for largely high-end work to essentially support product development and business processes. This includes research and work on intellectual property, equity and finance, analytics, market research, clinical research and data management among others. The legal off-shoring services business is also part of this domain.

These services could include the entire spectrum of work related to intellectual property from preparing patent applications to IP commercialization. Outsourcing engineering and design work would involve plant design, chip design, and animation. Similarly, we have included judgment-based work in education and publishing businesses, medical content and services as part of the knowledge services domain. The scarce availability of professionals across a range of educational qualifications: doctors, engineers, lawyers, MBAs, chartered accountants, graduates, computer science graduates and PhDs who are likely to fit the skills set required in the knowledge business.

It is found, the availability of people with the right skills set will be seriously constrained by various factors. It is believed that the growth of the knowledge services market in India will be determined more by the size of available labour force than by the dynamics of business demand. These findings have implications for all stakeholders in the knowledge services arena, and especially for companies looking at India as a large potential source of low-wage, but professionally-skilled labour.

Large Talent Pool: The Paradox of Paucity amidst Plenty?

Given the sheer number of qualified professionals India produces, the possibility of finding people with the right skill sets should have been a lot stronger than it is in reality. But companies are finding it increasingly difficult to get the right talent, especially at the middle-management level. The crunch remains despite the annual addition of over 3 million graduates and professional degree and diploma holders to the existing talent reservoir of over 100 million. Every year around 950 business schools in India churn out nearly 90,000 graduates with MBA degrees compared to a mere 13,500 in the UK.

Over 400,000 engineering graduates and 1,500 PhDs are added to the Indian labour force every year. Close to 55,000 passouts of institutes providing masters in computer applications and around 25,000 pharmacists graduated from various institutes in the country. Only China and Russia come close to India in terms of the sheer number of skilled professionals. With a shortfall in skilled labour likely in the next four to five years in most of the developed economies, the demand for expertise from developing countries is expected to rise. This would give Indian professionals leverage in terms of work and wage returns.

Economics of Skill: Where are the Right People?

But despite the impressive numbers of the qualified professionals India produces every year, the available pool of talent is smaller than the total labour supply. The limitation arises from low employability and the competing demand from the domestic industry as the economy grows rapidly. Further, recent data reveals jobs in India are growing faster than the workforce: Off-farm jobs rose by 2.5 percent a year between 1998 and 2005 whereas the labour force grew only 2.0 percent. The slower labour force growth (as against the increase in the number of jobs) could lead to strong competing demand for labour from domestic companies. The high unemployment rate among professionals in a scenario of rising labour demand also suggests other factors affecting supply. NASSCOM, the country's apex association of software companies, has estimated that 2007-2008, demand for IT professionals in India will exceed supply.

A part of the reason then for high unemployment stems from the problem of 'employability'. Only a small fraction of the qualified labour force can be considered suitable for employment in companies operating in the global arena. The low employability could be attributed partly to the mismatch between the industry's requirements and the academic curricula of most of the professional colleges.

The huge demand for MBAs, for instance, from the handful of premier business schools contrasts strongly with the lack of job offers for those who graduated from places other than the Indian Institutes of Management and the second tier B-schools. So, while all the 2000-odd students who pass out of the Indian Institute of Management and 10 other premier business schools every year could be considered employable, only half the 84,000 graduates from the AICTE-approved Tier-

II business schools can be classified as fit to work in quality conscious and competitive international companies.

Experience has shown that reasons for poor employability range from lack of cultural fit, poor communication skills to inadequate proficiency in English. It was assumed that between 10-50 percent of the students who pass out with degrees and diplomas are likely to be considered suitable for employment with a globally networked company. The estimates therefore reveal that only over 500,000 out of the over 3 million educated workers added to the labour pool in 2005 could be considered employable in a world-class company.

Even out of this restricted set of people, it can be assumed that only about two people out of every 100 with the right skills set are likely to opt to work in the knowledge space. Currently, under that 0.1 percent of the total number of people employed in the public and private sectors are working in knowledge services outsourcing jobs. While the assumption that 2 percent of the employable force working in the knowledge services arena may seem steep, the high percentage takes care of the possibility of lateral movement from other industries.

A cursory look at the growth opportunities for the years 2009 and 2008 evidences steady headcount growth during 2009 with 25 percent predicting an increase in headcount and all the same 6 percent forecasting a decrease and 64 percent anticipating no change, with the resulting net employment at a favourable +19 percent these figures when Compared to 2008 it reveals a 17 percent weaker hiring plans thus, highlighting uncertain situations.

If India wants to remain a major player in the labour supply market, the government should focus on improving the quality of education and not merely the quantity of universities. Indeed, the government should consider relinquishing control over the higher education sector and allow private players, including foreign universities, a larger stake.

	Increase	Decrease	No Change	Don't Know	Net Employ-ment	Seasonally adjusted
	percent	percent	percent	percent	percent	percent
2nd Q 2009	25	6	64	5	+19	+25
1st Q 2009	22	4	63	11	+18	+19
4th Q 2008	50	2	34	14	+48	+43
3rd Q 2008	48	1	41	10	+47	+45
2nd Q 2008	37	1	54	8	+36	+39
1st Q 2008	43	1	45	11	+42	+46

Q = Quarter

After all, Harvard Business School alone awarded over 200 MBA Degrees, far exceeding the 1200-odd MBAs from all the Indian Institutes of Management. Perhaps, the government could consider setting up Special Knowledge Zones, along the lines of the Special Expert Zones (SEZs), to encourage the private sector to set up world-class institutions with more operational freedom. In the United Arab Emirates, for instance, educational institutions in special areas called 'Knowledge Villages' offer high quality education to local people depending on the industry needs.

In conclusion, it could be said that the limited labour supply may restrict the size of the knowledge services market, hence, the government needs to review its role in higher education. As for the industry, any plan to outsource, one should take into consideration the smaller subset of available resources. In the medium- and longer-term perhaps, greater private-public partnerships between industry, government and universities to improve both the quality and quantity of the labour pool could help India take advantage of any likely boom in the knowledge services industry.

References

Anderson, J.C., Gerbing, D.W. (1988), "Structural equation modelling in practice: a review and recommended two-step approach", Psychological Bulletin, Vol. 103, No.1, pp. 411-423.

Argote, L. (1982), "Input uncertainty and organizational coordination in hospital emergency units", Administrative Science Quarterly, Vol. 27, pp. 420-434.

Boles, J.C., Babin, B.J. (1996), "On the frontlines: stress, conflict, and the customer service provider", Journal of Business Research, Vol. 37, pp. 41-50.

Bowen, D.E., Lawler III, E.E. (1992), "The empowerment of service workers: what, why, how, and when", Sloan Management Review, Vol. 34, pp. 31-39.

Campion, M.A., Medsker, G.J., Higgs, C. (1993), "Relations between work group characteristics and effectiveness: implications for designing effective work groups", Personnel Psychology, Vol. 46, pp. 823-850.

Campion, M.A., Papper, E.M., Medsker, G.J. (1996), "Relations between work team characteristics and effectiveness: a replication and extension", Personnel Psychology, Vol. 49, pp. 429-452.

Chaston, I. (1998), "Self-managed teams: assessing the benefits for small service-sector firms", British Journal of Management, Vol. 9, pp. 1-12.

Ferrell, O.C., Skinner, S.J. (1988), "Ethical behaviour and bureaucratic structure in marketing research organizations", Journal of Marketing Research, Vol. 25, pp. 103-109.

Fornell, C., Larcker, D.F. (1981), "Evaluating structural equation models with unobservable variables and measurement error", Journal of Marketing Research, Vol. 18, pp. 19-50.

Hackman, J.R. (1987), "The design of work teams", Handbook of Organizational Behaviour, pp. 315-42.

Hair, J.F. Jr., Anderson, R.E., Tatham, R.L., Black, W.C. (1995) Multivariate Data Analysis with Readings.

Hartline, M.D., Ferrell, O.C. (1993) Service Quality Implementation: The Effects of Organizational Socialization and Managerial Actions on Customer-Contact Employee Behaviours.

Mathieu, J.E. (1991), "A cross-level non-recursive model of the antecedents of organizational commitment and satisfaction", Journal of Applied Psychology, Vol. 76, No. 5, pp. 607-618.

Mathieu, J.E., Zajac, D.M. (1990), "A review and meta-analysis of the antecedents, correlates and consequences of organizational commitment", Psychological Bulletin, Vol. 108, No. 2, pp. 171-194.

7

Training Needs Analysis (TNA) for HRM

Radha Iyer and Swagatika Panda

TNA is a process by which an organization's Human Resource Development (HRD) needs are identified and articulated. It is posited as one of the fundamental prerequisites of an effective training program (Moore and Dutton, 1978; Wexley, 1984). It is used in identifying an organization's goals and its effectiveness in reaching these goals, discrepancies or gaps between employees' skills and the skills required for effective current job performance, discrepancies (gaps) between current skills against the skills needed to perform the job successfully in the future including the conditions under which the training program will occur.

This information helps an organization to learn the kinds of training programs needed, who needs to be included in them, whether there are any roadblocks to their effectiveness and how they can be eliminated. Corporations spend billions each year to train and develop human resources. Evaluating the effectiveness of that cost is difficult: Much training is probably simply a reaction to discovered deficiencies. A realistic and practical strategic approach is needed to determine training needs to improve the investment (Capps, III, Charles J., Capps, Patricia J.).

To utilize most effectively both the training expenditure and resources, one must first determine exactly the location, scope, along with the magnitude of the training need. An effective training program is most likely after a meticulous needs analysis has been undergone. Once these needs are identified, it is very important to prioritize them so that it is very clear as to which programs or issues require attention and resources. Armed with the data obtained from needs analysis, the next step is to design an effective training program. Once the needs are identified and prioritized, they constitute the objectives of the training program, which in turn determines the outcomes.

Literature Review

The review of literature suggests the importance of analyzing training needs prior to conducting training has been emphasized by many writers (Wexley, 1984). In their seminal contribution to the literature on training needs analysis, McGehee and Thayer, 1961 as quoted in Moore and Dutton, 1978) suggested that assessment of training needs involves three types of analysis: organization, operational (task) and person analysis. Organization analysis was initially conceptualized by McGehee and Thayer as focusing on where in the organization training could be utilized, based on the organization's goals, climate and efficiency indices.

For the past thirty years, theoretical and empirical perspectives on the identification of training needs within organizations have been based upon this tripartite framework. More recently, this has been expanded to incorporate the identification of system-wide issues, the climate for training within the organization, the availability of training resources and external pressures (including economic, legal, political and social factors). Operations or task analysis entails setting performance standards or criteria, describing tasks to be completed, deriving optimal procedures for performing those tasks and specifying the requisite knowledge and skills for task performance.

Finally, individual analysis is used to identify personnel who need training, via performance appraisals, proficiency testing and other methods of measuring job performance. Self-assessment of training needs by managers has also been recommended by some authors (Ford and Noe, 1987).

Another study on needs assessment suggests that it helps

answering three questions: w*here* within the organization can and should training be placed, *what* should be the content of training in terms of what an employee must learn to perform the job effectively, and *who* within the organization needs training and of what kind in terms of skills and knowledge (McGehee and Thayer, 1961). Little research has been carried out with respect to organization Analysis in the three-fold approach suggested by McGehee and Thayer.

Often the impact of external environment on the organization too has not been taken into account. But at the same time, methodological sophistication in task analysis has continued to increase in recent years. (Wexley, 1984) proposed a new approach to person analysis for managerial jobs which focuses on observable behaviour rather than abstract skills and this approach has been the most preferred approach till date. But some researchers believe that the purpose of TNA is often targeted to the effectiveness of the organization (Chiu, Warren; Thompson, David; Mak, Wai-ming; Lo, K.L., 1997) while it should focus on individuals.

One of the studies stresses on person analysis, according to which, there are a variety of data sources and measurement tools available for the assessment of training needs. Few of the sources of training-needs assessment information include performance data (e.g., productivity, accidents, and customer complaints), work sampling, and job-knowledge tests. Another potentially useful source of information about individual training needs is the job incumbent. McGehee and Thayer (1961) stress that the incumbent is a key source of information about the skills needed to perform the job adequately. Morano (1973) maintains that employees are aware of their skill weaknesses and performance deficiencies and, therefore, are in the best position to determine their own training needs.

The use of self-assessments to determine training needs has become a strategy of growing importance for organizations especially for managerial positions (Burack, 1979). One major source of information about training needs is what scholars describe as the "pedagogical" approach or "supply-led" approach. This approach is largely trainer-driven and authority-oriented coming from the vested interests of trainers (Thompson, 1994). Ferdinard (1988) described TNA as a "rational process by which an organization determines how to develop or acquire the human skills it needs in order to achieve its business objectives"; hence, it is anticipatory in nature intending to meet long-term organizational objectives (Snape *et al.,* 1994). Delhaye (1992) has identified this with a "demand-led" approach.

Within the demand-led approach, the business-oriented approach is characterized by a top-down, finance-driven process (e.g. profit, growth) emphasizing more on the business outcome and less on employees' needs. Besides the business-oriented approach, the "demand-led" aspect of TNA has another counterpart–the process-oriented approach. While the business-oriented approach focuses on the whole organization, the scope of the process-oriented approach is mainly on a localized division or a department. Unlike the "demand-led" approach, the trainee-cantered approach is characterized by a bottom-up, self-development driven (e.g. performance, promotion) emphasizing more on employees' needs and less on the business outcome or work efficiency. The trainee-cantered approach often relies on self-assessment as the source of information.

Yet another research suggests that a case-study approach of TNA is an approach which combines the pooled judgments of practitioners with an in-depth study by training specialists (Moore, R.J., 1979).

Further literature reveals that the strategic ethical approach to training needs analysis uses personnel data already collected by most organizations (Charles J. Capps III). Common human resources methods currently used for performance appraisals, job evaluation techniques, and compensation practices provide the basic inputs. Human resource managers typically conceptualize employee rankings into thirds: top, middle, and bottom.

The view of needs analysis as description research centred on data-collection may need to give way to an action research approach. An action research approach means the investigator is involved with stakeholders in an ongoing process of defining present and future needs, anticipating change, implementing solutions and evaluating effectiveness.

An alternative approach suggested is to move away from the systems approach and be oriented towards responding to market demands and the future (Berger, M. 1993).

This approach has an edge over the traditional approach in ways like speed and ease of use, matching organizational structure with individual needs and focusing on outgoing as well as introspective needs.

Another approach to training needs analysis, the goal of the integrative approach (Hiebert, M. B.; Smallwood, W. N., 1987) is to use objective language and processes while thinking in the interpretive mode and concurrently moving management to recognize the value of new approaches.

The objectivist approach is most applicable when training skills can be clearly defined in behavioural terms and remains stable over time. The interpretive approach holds good when the environment is dynamic or when the training can't be described in behaviourally sub-divided terms.

An array of methods has been found for surfacing training needs from groups and organizations. There are variations and combinations of these methods used; but there are few of them that individually provide enough diversity and flexibility to work in most situations.

Taken together they become a "bag of options" from which a method (or a combination of methods) could be used to accomplish the assessment task.

The methods generally used are observation, questionnaires, key consultation, print media, interviews, group discussion, tests, records and reports, and work samples. These methods have their own advantages and disadvantages

(Steadham, 1980).

Concerned with focus on need analysis for an individual, a study review suggests that onsite observations provide more qualitative information when applied on a macro-organizational level while greater degrees of quantitative information are generated on a micro- or individual employee knowledge/skill level (McClelland, 1994).

The main challenges in this method are requirement of a highly skilled observer, limited scope of data collection and scepticism among the respondents regarding the transparency.

Again, focus group discussions serve as an important tool that is applicable in all fields where behavioural influence and its impact or outcome can be measured and subsequently analyzed (McClelland, 1994).

In this case, the main interferences are time and quantification of data collected.

Individual interviews involve direct interaction between the human resource development analyst and the individuals for whom the training is either being considered or for whom it is specifically intended, such that critical needs are identified and taken care of (McClelland, 1994).

Besides being time consuming, it is also difficult to quantify the results obtained and creates scepticism among the respondents.

A survey/questionnaire can provide accurate and relevant data through thoughtful design, testing, and detailed administration (McClelland, 1994).

The major challenges faced by adopting this method are that it's time consuming, makes little provision for free expression of unanticipated expression, is of limited utility in getting at causes of problems or possible solutions and suffers low return rates (mailed), grudging responses, or unintended and/or inappropriate respondents.

As mentioned above, one of the literature reviews informs that every method for needs analysis has its pros and cons and, thus, suggests an open-systems approach that involves two of the above-mentioned methods that are suitable for the organization such that the disadvantages of using any one method are minimized. Furthermore, it also suggests integrating organizational needs with individual needs, which is usually ignored, thinking individuals are, in fact, benefited (Chiu, W.; Thompson, D; Mak, W.; Lo, K.L., 1997). Lastly, it talks about an integrative approach for training needs analysis. This technique also takes into consideration the changes in the external environment, which is dynamic. Thus, this approach is expected to be a foolproof technique for needs analysis for any type of organization, either stable or undergoing any transition. But, this method is yet to be fully validated.

There are many formulations and techniques associated with needs analysis recommended by many researchers and theorists, but numerous others have commented on the infrequent application of these prescriptions by training practitioners. In a survey conducted in the USA by Saari *et al.* (1988), only 27 percent of companies had procedures for determining the training and education needs of their managers and, even in these companies, the focus was predominantly on lower-level managers. Similarly, a recent survey of European organizations by Holden (1991) showed that ad hoc and informal TNA methods, such as requests from line managers and employees themselves, were the most frequently used methods.

The fact that organizations are not going for systematic analysis of training needs has been strongly criticized by some researchers because this may lead to a focus on skills and knowledge which do not transfer to the work environment. In many cases, the failure of training to change individual behaviour and contribute to improved organizational performance has been attributed to weak or missing links between the training content and the actual needs and requirements of managerial personnel.

Finally, a study confirms that lack of information on conducting a TNA, management scepticism about the effectiveness of TNA, poor planning, no time to do a TNA and organizations following fads in training techniques (Schneier, C Eric; Guthrie, J.P.; Olian, J.D., 1988) are some of the common challenges that deter conducting an effective TNA.

Training Needs Analysis: Importance

Training needs analysis is recognized as one of the first important "before" contributions to training effectiveness (Salas and Cannon-Bowers, 2001). A thorough needs analysis takes into account the individual differences of trainees, the organizational climate and objectives, and the characteristics of the task/s to be learnt. This method is then used to determine both the method and content of training. In sum, training cannot be effective unless it meets the individual, organizational, and task needs as identified by needs analysis. The techniques identified from the literature review are those that are most frequently used and, thus, their pros and cons could be compared and the right method or methods could be used for effective needs analysis.

The Study

Recognizing the shift taking place in the strategic function of training and development a study was conducted, in 2008, on training needs analysis in various Indian organizations. In all, human resource (HR) executives from around thirty five organizations were surveyed. The questionnaire, which was supplied on demand, consisted of closed as well as open-ended questions ranging from methods used to suggestions for improvement. The responses were analyzed using SPSS. The data has been analyzed in the form of a pictorial presentation.

Results

The results state that except two organizations, all others followed some form of TNA. Performance management data, interviews and discussions are the most popular method for TNA, followed by manual observations. Most of the organizations did not use assessment centres, questionnaires, or peer review for TNA. Annual reviews and requisition forms are the least preferred methods among the lot. There are very few organizations that use methods like discussions, interviews with various stakeholders, individual employee feedback sharing, reference checks and customer feedback.

In most of the organizations, it is the staff department or the external consultants that initiate the process of TNA. In few of the organizations, it is also initiated by the clients, HR department or the top management team.

The survey also implies that the TNA process has changed a lot over the years. Many organizations did not have a TNA process in place and now most of them club it with performance appraisal. Those organizations which had TNA just as a namesake in the past, are conducting it more scientifically now. Many organizations have set up separate departments which can cater to a systematic TNA and few of them have gone an extra mile to take up new initiatives in TNA as well.

On-the-job performance is still, the most preferred operational data used for TNA followed by job description. But it was interesting enough to find that perception of the job holder regarding the job is still used less frequently.

The survey highlights the fact that most of the organizations follow the latest concept of quality control for TNA from operating problems rather than depending more upon downtime reports, quantity of waste and repairs. Late deliveries are also considered for TNA as timeliness is considered most important after quality.

While considering nominating an individual for a training program, supervisors are given a priority over self-requisition but in most of the organizations it is a combination of both. Sometimes the HR department, external consultant or even customers might be involved in deciding nominees for the training program. Supervisor's observation of the subordinate while at work and performance appraisal data are the most widely used tools for TNA. It is also interesting to note that some organizations have picked up individual development plans from development centres as a means for TNA.

Most of the respondents were aware of the fact that TNA is not just meant to be a form-filling exercise and a systematic TNA leads to an effective training program. They also suggested various ways of conducting a TNA like 360-degree feedback, competency mapping, more frequent performance reviews, and on-the-job observation of performance.

Conclusion

Learning and development are critical processes in all enterprises and, as noted by Guest (1986), cannot be left to chance. While training represents just one element of the learning process, considerable time, energy and financial resources need to be devoted to the TNA, as a precursor to an effective training programme. It is demonstrated that the organizations have moved drastically from traditional methods to contemporary methods of TNA. The organizations are increasingly perseverant in adopting even better methods of TNA, especially in uncertain situations.

References

Berger, M. (1993), "A market-led training needs analysis–is the training needs analysis outmoded?", *Industrial and Commercial Training*, Vol. 25, No. 1, pp. 27-30.

Burack E. (1979), "Self-assessments: A strategy of growing importance", *Training and Development Journal,* Vol. 33, Issue 4, pp. 48-52.

Capps, III, Charles J., Capps, Patricia J. (2005), The Human Resource Development Matrix: A Strategic Ethical Approach to Determining Training Needs; *Human Resource Planning,* Vol. 28, Issue 1, pp. 21-22.

Chiu, Warren; Thompson, David, (1999), Re-thinking training needs analysis, *Personnel Review*, Vol. 28, Issue 1/2, p. 77.

Ford, J. and Noe, R. (1987), "Self-Assessed Training Needs: The Effects of Attitudes toward Training, Managerial Level, and Function", *Personnel Psychology*, 40: 39-53.

Ferdinand, B. (1988), "Management training needs analysis (TNA)", *Industrial and Commercial Training,* Vol. 20, No. 5, pp. 27-31.

Hiebert, M.B. and Smallwood, W.N. (1987), "Now for a completely different look at needs analysis", *Training and Development Journal,* Vol. 41, No. 5, pp. 75-79.

Holden, L. (1991), 'European Trends in Training and Development", *International Journal of Human Resource Management, 2:* 113-31.

McClelland, S.B. (1993), "Training needs assessment", *Journal of European Industrial Training,* Vol. 17, No. 1, pp. 12-17.

McClelland, S.B. (1994a), "Training needs assessment data-gathering methods: Part 1–survey questionnaires", *Journal of European Industrial Training,* Vol. 18, No. 1, pp. 22-26.

McClelland, S.B. (1994b), "Training needs assessment data-gathering methods: Part 2–individual interviews", *Journal of European Industrial Training,* Vol. 18 No. 2, pp. 27-31.

McClelland, S.B. (1994c), "Training needs assessment data-gathering methods: Part 3–focus groups", *Journal of European Industrial Training,* Vol. 18, No. 3, pp. 29-32.

McClelland, S.B. (1994d), "Training needs assessment data-gathering methods: Part 4–on-site observations", *Journal of European Industrial Training,* Vol. 18, No. 5, pp. 4-7.

Moore, R. J.; "A case study approach to training needs analysis; Journal of European Industrial Training, 1994, Vol. 18, Issue 3/4, pp. 23-28.

Moore, M. L., Dutton, P., "Training Needs Analysis: Review and Critique", *Academy of Management Review*, July 1978, pp. 532-545.

Morano, R. (1973), "Determining Organizational Training Needs," *Personnel Psychology,* Vol. 26, pp. 479-487.

O'Driscoll M.P., Taylor, P. J., "Congruence between theory and practice in management training needs analysis; *International Journal of Human Resource Management*, December 1992, Vol. 3, Issue 3, pp. 593-603.

Salas, E and Cannon-Bowers, J. A., "The Science of training: A decade of Progress", Annual Review of Psychology, 2001, 52: 471-499.

Schneier, C.E., Guthrie, J.P. and Olian, J.D. (1988), "A practical approach to conducting and using the training needs assessment", *Public Personnel Management,* Vol. 12, No. 2, pp.

191-205.

Steadham, S.V. (1980), *Training and Development Journal*, January 1980, "Learning to select a needs assessment strategy", 30, pp. 56-61.

Wexley, K. (1984) 'Personnel Training", *Annual Review of Psychology,* 35: 519-51.

8

Managing Uncertainty Implications for HRM

D. Anil Kumar and M. Vinay Chandra Sai

The business environment marked by disruptive change has led organizations to acknowledge the need to redefine their mantras of effectiveness. A natural reaction in such tough times has been cost-cutting, and the human resources department stands first on the list. Tough economic times are not about financial meltdown alone, there is also the collateral damage that comes with it. Economic downturn brings different challenges for different functions. For the human resources function, the challenge lies in the ability of the organization to maintain healthy and competent bench strength without digging into the corporate wallet. HR managers have to try and prevent holes from forming in the talent bench.

Human Resource Management: Strategic Dimension

HR can deal with the changing circumstances by understanding the key drivers on the human performance dimensions. By virtue of their ability to determine what every person in the company requires in terms of input, they are ideally suited to both understand as well as implement this. They can thus, equip the managers to help cope with the new challenges and imbue them with the skills, knowledge and behaviour required to be successful in the changed situation. This will naturally place the HR manager in a new light and be seen for the value he offers to the business mangers to become more effective. The opportunity for HR to be strategic is brighter than it ever was. It is for the more clued in among HR managers to grab the opportunities and become absolutely relevant to the business. They now have the mandate to walk down the road less travelled and to shape organizations and find their place in the sun. This paper highlights the implications to HRM in uncertain situations. More specifically, the recruitment function of HRM in the face of volatile situations and the challenges there of are analyzed in this paper.

Managing Recruitment Function

The economic downturn has its negative impact on the recruiting function through hiring freezes as organizations are looking for budget cuts. Traditionally, when the economic cycle peaks and starts its cycle downwards, everything related to business and recruiting declines but this economic downturn is different. Instead of recruiting heading straight down, it will be volatile. The demand for talent management services will go radically down, then back up again in short spurts, and then down again. This volatility will require more planning than ever before from the recruiting function. Instead of planning for one consistent, long, downward spiral with associated layoffs and hiring freezes, organizations will need to prepare for spurts of growth and continuous hiring in some areas while layoffs occur in others. The reasons why hiring will continue are:

1. The first and perhaps most important cause of volatility will be the chaotic availability of credit and capital. The continued uncertainty related to financial markets will cause oscillations during which capital will be easier and then harder to get. This volatility will cause firms to grow and to hire in spurts.
2. A second cause of volatility is globalization. In a truly global business world, there will almost always be some degree of economic growth in emerging economies scattered around the world. As many major US companies now book a majority of their revenues abroad, pressure to keep corporate functions fully staffed will continue despite possible layoffs in production and client service groups.

3. A third reason volatility will plague the recruiting function is relentless consumer demand for new innovative products. Despite the downturn, consumer demand remains high.
4. Most recruiting efforts go wasted as recruiting managers witness a huge mismatch between the perceived competence of the recruit and the actual competence and they have to do the exercise all over again. Experts believe this is precisely where most resources-time, money and effort-get wasted and therefore this is also the point where resource economization can take place. Recruiting managers have to be aware and cautious about the possible traps that can hamper their ability to recruit right the first time. According to research, there are three basic recruiting traps that levy a heavy drag on a recruiting manager's ability to recruit right. These include:

- **Recruiting against Time:** Recruiting managers often recruit in a hurry under high pressure, without dwelling much on important recruit details and corporate requirements. In the rush to fill the empty chairs, recruiting managers lose perspective of the larger picture and make decisions based on availability of time and not availability of talent.
- **Recruiting on the Basis of the Resume:** Apart from recruiting in a hurry, recruiting managers also need to stay wary of resume recruiting and make a deliberate attempt to assess people on what they see and not what they read. Resumes can be extremely misleading, since most times they are not written by the person himself but by some resume management consultant. Achievements are exaggerated beyond comprehension to create an impression that often manages to do its job well. Such misleading resumes play havoc with organization's talent pool and only pollute it if anything.
- **Recruiting Purely on the Basis of Job Description:** Recruiting managers should be aware that job descriptions

represent only the technical aspect of the job. However, the soul of the job lies outside the technical pre-requisites and therefore it is important that recruiting managers take into account the intangible factors required to succeed in that particular job.

While recruiting managers, approach in a right way—internal recruiting is an extremely viable source of talent that works well. The crux of internal recruiting lies in benchmarking. Benchmarking provides recruiting managers with the right perspective about the existing talent within a given function, the top performer rating and the expectations tied to the established standards.

Advantages of Recruiting in Uncertain Situations

In uncertain economic situations many companies assumed that recruiting functions will not be necessary due to the availability of surplus of talent as a result of more and more firms engaging layoffs, consolidations, and the ceasing of operations. Many respected companies have already downsized recruiting. Despite all these, there are few positive things that can be observed in these bad times:

1. **Less Competition:** If the firm is not well known and doesn't have a strong employment brand, it can have less competition for talent. As the firms are reducing the recruiting budgets and the competitors' recruiting effectiveness is very low, we can get a competitive advantage. Candidates will be easier to sell as they will have very few options available.
2. **Availability of High Quality Candidates:** In the name of violatility, not only have organizations more number of candidates available but also they have the advantage of having quality candidates. In addition to the laid off individuals the survivors can be targeted.
3. **Weakened Employment Brands:** As the competitors make the mistake of conducting large scale layoffs, their employment brand will be weakened.

4. **Capability to Explode out of the Box:** If an organization can successfully defend its recruiting budget, it will have the capability of "exploding out of the box" immediately after the downturn is over. This capability will put it far ahead of other firms that have decimated their recruiting capabilities during this time. In order to have that advantage, the organization will need to calculate and then report the negative impacts of "disassembling the recruiting function" to their executives. That includes costs related to the delays in being able to resume hiring, the increased risk of losing top applicants, the lower quality of hires and the increased start-up costs related to reassembling the recruiting function.

Preserve the Talent

Recession is as natural to the economy as boom time, and it is the perception of corporate leaders that matters most in such testing times. While cutting costs is important, diluting internal talent resources and barricading flow of creativity can stifle organizational growth. The way a company treats its employees amidst gloom and doom impacts the loyalty quotient. Employers who harness internal talent in times of economic downturn can hope to see an army of loyal employees standing by them, while those who axe talent and get fidgety with employees fail to earn loyalty. When things are going well, people are 'too busy' or 'too successful' to take the time to pursue a learning initiative, leave aside apply the learning at the workplace.

Today, people are far more focused on developing their skills. A large number of people have grown through the organizational hierarchy as a result of their technical skill base, less so as a result of their conceptual and human skills. Now is the time to pause and implement a range of talent development strategies focused on these gaps as minds may be more open. Investment in talent development in these times has long term ramifications in terms of building company loyalty since the support and investment is available when it is most needed.

Motivation can do the Magic

Motivation plays a key role in the success of any organization. Companies need not leave any stone unturned in motivating their employees and keeping up productivity levels. In today's context, it is absolutely imperative to create an atmosphere of trust, understanding and cooperation between various groups within an organization to sufficiently motivate the employees. It is also necessary to provide a platform for them to discuss the impediments, both subjective and objective, to maximize team performance. Such an approach in organizations will help motivate the employees to develop action plans to circumvent the obstacles and focus on business propositions. In these tough times of having our competitors looking at our talented employees, to retain them, organizations need to give personal attention to the employees.

Alternatives to the Downsizing

Downsizing is a common strategy adopted by organizations to cut costs, during recession. Research proves that the primary objective of downsizing, of cutting costs, is not met often, since most companies rehire. To keep an organization afloat managements either have to cut costs or increase revenues. They choose the easy way and downsizing happens. But there are organizations that think otherwise. They use some creative ideas instead of downsizing to cut costs. HR should be aware of the alternatives to apply them to their company. Some organizations claim to have adopted techniques that could cut costs without resorting to downsizing.

1. At Charles Schwab the top management took a 50 percent pay cut as an example to the other employees.
2. Rhino Foods, an ice cream manufacturing company in Vermont, sought employees' suggestions on the issue. One strategy that proved successful was to lend employees to

their suppliers and other companies during off seasons. This way they cut costs without downsizing their employee strength.

3. Cisco is another company that does not believe in downsizing. During the depression its employees are allowed to work with non-profit organizations for 20-30 percent of their actual salary. Called the 'warehousing strategy', it helps retain employees even during tough times.
4. Similarly, Lincoln Electrical, Ohio, has not laid off any employees since 1930. During a sales slump they retrained their shop floor employees who were not more than high school graduates. They were expected to identify unexploited markets so that the company could leverage it. This is done now and Lincoln gets US$ 800 million as revenue from the market the employees identify.

Organizations must realize that the alternatives should be developed keeping in view the present and the future needs, which are changing rapidly. The success of options is based on the following two facts:

1. Everyone has to go through cost cutting strategies.
2. HR plays an important role in easing the strategies.

Sometimes organizations resort to reducing work hours by placing all the employees in flexible work arrangement. Others allow employees to share jobs and the benefits thereof. Wage reduction is strategy where employees face wage reduction irrespective of their position in the organization structure. The top management has the highest reduction followed by middle managers and lower level employees. When all the other alternatives fail to give expected returns organizations can find an alternative job for the laid off employees. AT&T adopted this option with a difference.

The organization advertised the availability of employees for other organizations. It paid off. Requests from various companies poured in to recruit the employees. Organizations can explore various other ways to resolve the problem. Some organizations do not downsize but wait for their employees to leave on their own. These positions are not filled immediately so existing employees can be placed there. Some others offer leave with benefits or part benefits to their employees. When they return from the leave they might be given the same or a different job position. Organizations also use employee buy-outs. The employees buy a business unit that is on the verge of closure and try to revive it on their own. Few organizations offer the company's equity in lieu of the salary cuts. Although this decision needs strong employee participation the reality is far from it. Employees are hardly involved in any kind of decision-making. Some of the Japanese companies use all the above alternatives. If one fails they use the next one.

Conclusion

The uncertain economic era has shown its impact on every organization. A good HR can use this situation even in a positive way. Many companies started freezing the hiring but missed many advantages of recruitment like less competition, availability of high quality employees, competitors losing their employment brands etc. In an economic uncertain economic situation recruiting becomes doubly challenging. Companies have little resources to spare while the demand and desperateness to survive increase creating a grossly skewed demand supply equation.

Thus, it is important that companies design their recruiting strategy in a way that helps them stay afloat even when the environment conspires against them. The onus of providing the organization with the best talent crop lies with human resources professionals. When the going gets tough and vacancies shrink, the responsibility to make a difference and keep the existing talent motivated and inspired also lies with them. HR leaders who understand this go out and prove HR's worth as a tactical asset.

We cannot deny the fact that an organization's greatest asset is its employees. Keeping the workforce intact during tough times is the biggest challenge companies are facing these days. Pats on the back, showing concern, giving personal attention etc are some of the methods that firms are adopting to beat the blues. Managers need to identify the key players of their work teams and understand why the teams are not working to their optimum levels. This understanding would help in identifying the missing links and prevent duplication and redundancy of any kind.

References

Dessler, Gary (2004), *Human Resource Management,* 10th ed. Englewood Cliffs, NJ: Pearson/Prentice-Hall.

Gueutal, Hal G., and Dianna L. Stone, (2005), *The Brave New World of eHR: Human Resources Management in the Digital Age.* San Francisco: Jossey-Bass, 2005.

Hamerman, Paul (2005), "HR and Administrative B2E: Maturing and Expanding." Business.com, Human Resources Outsourcing.

Losey, Mike, Sue Meisinger, and Dave Ulrich (2005), (eds), *The Future of Human Resource Management: 64 Thought Leaders Explore the Critical HR Issues of Today and Tomorrow.* New York: John Wiley and Sons.

9

Innovate or Evaporate: A Clarion Call for CEOs

A. Suryanarayana

The global economic recession while manifesting a deeper crisis in capitalism, confronts business leaders of the corporate world with a plethora of challenges. They, as the pioneers, visionaries, and innovators of the business world, can play a significant role in addressing them. Besides shaping the mindset of the managers, they also need to set a new direction to their organizations and employees as captains of the industry in declining markets.

They should be ready with a battery of strategic and innovative initiatives to be implemented in inhospitable markets in the existing hostile environment of economic downturn. Required change strategies should be structured according to the issues relevant to the global economic scenario from the point of view of specific functional areas. In this context, innovative strategies alone can best tackle the pressures triggered by the current economic turbulence. By broadly surveying the field of innovation management, this paper catalogues a slew of strategies to be adopted, talents to be acquired, honed, and applied by businesses to meet the challenges of a volatile business cycle.

Innovation: Need and Importance

Competition in global markets in virtually every product, service, industry, and market segment is fierce and will grow even fiercer. In order not only to endure but to prevail, organizations will find that bringing products to market that are *exact twins* relative to existing products is a strategy doomed to failure. Innovative differentiated products that create substantial additional value, relative to what customers can buy already, alone can succeed. The market place success is the sum total of strategy, production, marketing, finance, and an innovative idea. The business of innovation pervades the daily business of life and when implemented with skill, enriches and enhances our lives immeasurably.

To achieve this ultimate goal, organizations need skills, competence, and excellence in Innovation Management. In the Darwinian world of global markets, the companies able to innovate and manage innovation will be the survivors by being significantly better than their competitors. Winning innovation is a set of Russian 'Babushka' dolls, and that the 'idea', the innermost doll, is of no value unless wrapped in successive and successful 'dolls'—marketing, sales, service, strategy, production, etc., that together comprise a powerful, compelling business design.

Innovation ought to be a process that pervades every single part of the organization's value chain, as oxygen pervades our atmosphere. Vision, not greed, drives successful innovation. Innovation is fundamentally different for entrepreneurial start-up companies than it is for established organizations, which need to optimize their innovation portfolio, balancing mature products with *incrementally* new and *radically* new ones. Successful innovations create powerful feelings and emotions, and satisfy well-defined needs.

Innovation—the key to competitive growth and profit—rests on disciplined management of the innovation process, from idea inception to customer service. The ability to innovate is a vital core competency—one that you, as a leader, entrepreneur, or manager *must* possess, in order to build growing, profitable businesses. At the same time, *managing* innovation is one of the most *difficult* processes that one has to guide and shape. It is this combination of high risk and high return, mission-critical and Everest-size challenge that makes innovation and innovation management so challenging.

Reasons for CEOs to Innovate

CEOs as leaders and visionaries pioneer the innovation in organizations some of the reasons for CEOs to innovate are given below.

First, the need to innovate, *to energize existing people* and to attract new ones. If the organization's competitive advantage is driven by its great people—and in today's global world, nearly all successful organizations fit that description—then it must be innovative, because great people love to think up, develop, and develop new ideas. Organizations that do not innovate quickly lose their innovative people. They migrate to organizations that do welcome and encourage such people and allow their talents full expression. 'We innovate,' notes an IBM report, 'when a new thought, technology, business model, or service actually changes society (Global Innovation Outlook, 2004). Successful innovations are often a portfolio of new ideas, with some of them focused on the product and some focused on the value chain supporting the product innovation. That is why a pervasive spirit of innovation is so necessary and so valuable.

The second, powerful, and practical reason for innovation is to achieve high, sustained *growth, and profitability*. It is an empirical fact that companies that excel at innovation are also far more profitable than companies that do not. Innovation is one of the best ways to build market share which is directly related to *Return on Investment* (RoI). Innovation comes from empowered individuals and teams who break rules. To exploit their creativity, organizations need to deploy—produce, market, distribute, sell, service—them worldwide. Increasingly, this applies to small start up companies as well. Organizations that deploy globally from day one will have a competitive advantage over those that defer going global. This brings economies of scale (cost savings). However, size may destroy innovation. Creative persons tend to feel lost in large organizations, especially when 'scale' implies bureaucracy, discipline, and 'following the rules'.

The third key reason for innovating is simply *survival* in today's fiercely competitive global marketplace. Organizations that fail to bring to market innovative products that create value for their customers will quickly find their competitors have done so, and that their own existence is in danger. Today, innovation is an adaptive competence that is necessary for survival in global markets and for lasting in the long run. Wise companies attack their own mature products by introducing new, better ones. Innovation is not a luxury but a necessity for any organization. There are, however, certain myths and realities about innovation.

Innovation: Some Myths and Realities

1. It is sometimes believed that in innovation, the most challenging and difficult task is coming up with new ideas, which is generally *not so*. When people are empowered, inspired by vision, provided ample time and resources, and an appropriate environment, ideas proliferate like wild flowers in springtime. The main challenge lies not in ideation—producing ideas—but in winnowing wheat kernels from chaff, good ones from bad, and then in matching innovative business designs to innovative ideas for products and services. Bringing innovative products to market is risky. But refraining from doing so is even riskier. In this context, we should remember this wise business advice from poet Robert Frost:
   Two roads diverged in a wood, and
   I took the one less travelled by,
   And that has made all the difference.
2. Statistics on innovation are mostly depressing. Even with extensive market research, innovative products will fail more than nine times out of 10. Out of 30,000 new product launches in the United States, fewer than 3,000 achieve growth and profit.
3. Innovators improve their chances for success by becoming great listeners. They develop this skill by listening to the

four innovation voices viz., their products, customers, organization, and their own inner voice and make each of them an integral part of their own unique innovation system to achieve consistent innovation success far above the one-in-ten average. They learn how to amplify their signals when they are especially quiet and to mediate when the voices send conflicting messages. Recall that the high probability of failing in innovation is simply an average. It includes many innovators who do not use best-practice methods.

4. Great technology is *not* a sufficient condition for business success. Nor is great technology a necessary condition for business success. There is no superior technology or engineering in Barbie or Dell. But a creative, winning business design can be a sufficient condition for business success and profit. And the combination of great technology and a superior business model can prove virtually unbeatable.
5. Innovative companies should put a major part of their creative efforts and resources into the design of the business model—the value statement, pricing strategy, and cost structure—that accompanies their new products and services. Failure to do so is one of the key mistakes that cause many start ups, and long-established firms, to fail. Winning business designs can, like Barbie dolls, dominate their market for decades.
6. According to a Hebrew saying, smart managers know how to escape from tight spots that wise managers avoid. One may adapt this to read: Smart managers optimize trade-offs that wise and bold ones defy.
7. More and more organizations will find themselves locked in fierce competitive combat as more countries join the global economy. Banks, telecommunications, retailing, coffee shops all have global giants that replicate in many countries. The result of this competition is to create many winners—lower prices, better service, wider variety of

products—and some losers—those who worked in the present bankrupt businesses.

8. Innovation is a vital strategy weapon against marketplace incumbents who have leveraged scale economies, size, and learning with experience.
9. Learning curves are quite different from, though related to, scale economies; they are the foundation stone of many huge profitable global companies, such as Intel. The other facet of the scale and/or scope, or 'volume and/or variety' issue is related to the basic behavioural question as to how do organizations learn and how can the core competency of learning confer a vital strategic advantage. Learning curves, like heroes, *are made and not born.* We have to remember that those who fail to build steep learning curves and then fail to race them down rarely survive to tell the tale.
10. The fundamental logic of capitalism is a remarkably powerful system for translating the wants and needs of consumers into signals that create the very products and services to satisfy those needs. Large rewards accrue to managers and entrepreneurs who are skilled at understanding customer needs, wants, and preferences and in meeting them even when market research and the customers themselves initially react negatively to their innovations.
11. One of the many paradoxes that have innovation at their core is the clash between Pablo Picasso and Jim Collins—the need for free, unfettered creativity, together with the need for focused, systematic discipline—and the overriding imperative to make these two qualities not only co-exist but fall in love and marry.

Some Practical Tools for CEOs

Innovative leaders should have high-level collaborative mindset and be skilled at cooperative teamwork.

Competing successfully in global markets will

increasingly require the kind of high-level collaboration mindset that made Edmund Hillary the first to reach the summit of Everest. Indian entrepreneur Narayana Murthy, founder of the global software giant Infosys, puts it as follows.

The development of a product or service might typically be split among countries, with experts in America defining the customer requirements; the British defining the product attributes; the Australians defining the technology architecture; the Indians doing the software development; the Germans or the Japanese doing the manufacturing; and the Taiwanese doing the packaging. This new business model will distribute high-quality jobs around the world and deepen international collaboration (Murthy, 2005).

Increasingly, innovators will be asked to cultivate an Eastern yin-yang philosophy of performing an action and its opposite at one and the same time. In Darwin's language, collaboration is an adaptive attribute that makes organizations more competitive, hence fit to survive. Increasingly, it will be those most skilled at cooperative teamwork that will compete best and grow geometrically. One reason why collaborative teamwork dominates the latest globalization is that increasingly, innovative products comprise portfolios of diverse technologies, each requiring a different kind of expertise. Few organizations can command world-class expertise in every technology. When technologies converge into innovative products, collaboration is vital for survival.

Develop strategies for the entire value chain by getting the innovation engine in the organization into 'cruise mode'.

The key learning from the Tata Motors story of making the people's car project a reality is that when an impossible target has been set, innovation must take place across the entire value chain. There are no 'holy cows' that cannot be questioned. 'Mission impossible' will soon be a 'mission reality' for Tata Motors. The CEO Ratan Tata got everyone in his organization to think innovatively, and do whatever it takes to get the innovation engine in the organization into 'cruise' mode.

Innovation-driven management should recognize the imperativeness of creating an organization that is willing to learn

Given the nature of its business, which changes rapidly, the Top management at Infosys Technologies recognizes that creating an organization that is willing to learn is at the core of its business. In this sense, the ability of its employees to learn both on the job and through formal learning programmes is central to its success. The software industry is characterized by a lot of 'churn' of its employees. Creating, capturing, and deploying knowledge is a vital skill Infosys has mastered. It has done this through elaborate and structured processes. Rapidly moving down learning curves and quickly changing 'horses' from existing learning curves to new learning curves that relate to technologies and services in the distant horizon, is a skill that is vital for the company's continued growth. Learning curves are made, not born. The Infosys story amply illustrates that indeed.

Warren Buffet, the 75-year-old legendary head of the US$ 133 billion holding company Berkshire Hathaway, 13th on the US Fortune 500 list in 2005, was once asked when he planned to retire." Two years after my death,' he replied. 'Plans I put in place will last for two years after I am gone.' Does Buffet love what he is doing? There is no question. He is a constant innovator and original thinker (Marsteller, 2005). CEOs generally indicate that they think of leaving their jobs due to stress, pressure, and uncertainty and also on account of boredom and lack of challenge. On the contrary, in this context, it is believed that a lower proportion of CEOs consider quitting dynamic, innovative, creative, and learning organizations.

Instead of becoming "local", innovative firms think local and then apply their local insights on a global scale.

'Think global, act local' (deploy globally, adapt locally) has become a cliché. But, Gurucharan Das, a former Proctor and Gamble top manager, the reverse is also true;

'International managers must also think local and then apply their local insights on a global scale...reemploying communicable ideas in new geographies...'—One of Das' innovations was to introduce Vicks Vaporub in India in small 5 gms. tin priced at 10 cents each, it was cheaper to buy four of them than the larger 19 gram tin. 'The trade thought we were crazy,' notes Das. But it was a wise local adaptive innovation. The same strategy was successful for shampoo. Tiny one-dose sachets sold very well to those who could not buy a whole bottle. Even package size can sometimes be a major profitable innovation (Das, 1993).

Creative CEOs strive for building into their teams a good balance of vision, discipline, and managerial skill.

Google's three-word credo is: 'Do not be evil,' though few know precisely what those words really mean. Brin and Page the Google's co-founders started off with their vision: "Use the Internet to make nearly all information accessible to everyone all the time." They brought in a veteran manager, Eric Schmidt, who is the Google' CEO today. Together, the three provide a good balance of vision, discipline, and managerial skill (Ignaties, 2006).

Innovation conscious companies constantly look for vulnerabilities in their business models and get their funnels of innovation flowing!

There is a powerful lesson in it for all CEOs. In the case of Ingersoll-Rand Ltd. (IRL), the innovative change in business model encompassed their entire way of doing business, and resulted in a totally different business model vis-à-vis the traditional business model that they had followed for decades and their competitors continued to follow. The IRL case study shows that when it was pushed against the wall, it innovated the entire business model. That led to a change in nearly all aspects of its 'going to market strategy.'

Leaders driven by innovation culture are adept at Platform Leadership i.e., building a powerful concept for collaborative competitive strategy.

Annabelle Gawer and Michael Cusumano have built a powerful concept for collaborative competitive strategy which they call Platform Leadership (Gawer and Cusumano, 2004). Platform leadership is the ability of a firm to drive innovation around its particular platform at the broad industry level. The platform is located functionally at the heart of a variety of other products. Platform leaders operate within an ecosystem of firms. They set in motion a rapid pace of innovation not only on their own product, but on the array of complementary products that function in conjunction with their own, resulting in virtuous cycle of interactions.

The Head of the Intel Architecture Lab, Craig Kinnie describes that his mission is to '… grow the innovation, which is occurring in the ecosystem that is creating opportunity for all the actors in the ecosystems in which Intel can participate' (Gawer and Cusumano, 2002). Both technological convergence and platform leadership often require implementing a strategy of acquiring, or merging with, other firms with complementary technologies and skills. Such collaboration, within an existing old industry or with a burgeoning new one, demands skill in integrating the people, resources, skills, and knowledge of two firms.

Innovation-centric enterprises appreciate the payoffs from customer retention rather than enticing competitor's customers

Most CEOs know that it costs on average 11 times more to acquire a new customer, than to retain the loyalty and business of an existing one. Why do so many companies then spend endless millions of dollars trying to acquire their competitor's customers, rather than truly satisfy their own? CEOs of great global companies know how to do three things: create customer loyalty, measure it continually, and act to retain it. They understand the simple rule stated by Andy Taylor, CEO of Enterprise Rent-a-Car: "The only way to grow a business is to get customers to come back for more and tell their friends. This is the ultimate collaboration."

Inventive top management believes in contingency

planning based on scenario analysis as against conventional forecasting.

Some CEOs ask, 'What will happen to us?' This is forecasting. Other CEOs ask, 'What will we do, if x, y, or z happen?' This is contingency action planning based on Scenario Analysis. The problem with forecasting is that even if it is accurate, which is rare, it fails to prepare organizations to take action. Identifying risks in scenarios is important. However, it is equally more important to find ways to measure those risks. The growing pervasiveness and magnitude of uncertainty compels every CEO to acquire a toolbox that turns uncertainty into quantitative risk and then helps manage that risk.

Companies that are skilled at innovation management succeed in creating powerful and innovative Unique Value Propositions.

Good managers create winning products; Great managers create whole new industries (S. Mittal, 1994). The best way to predict the future is to create it (Peter F. Drucker). Powerful innovative Unique Value Propositions (UVPs) can create entire new industries. Two examples are Walkman and iPod. Walkman's UVP is—"we let you listen to your favourite stereo music anywhere, anytime without disturbing anyone else. The only product to rival its global conquest was iPod, whose UVP is "cool-looking device, ultra-simple—spin one wheel to scroll your songs, select the one you want, use the wheel to set volume—and presto."

Understand fully the fundamental logic of capitalism is an imperative in successful innovation.

The fundamental logic of capitalism is that it is a remarkably powerful system for translating the wants and needs of consumers into signals that create the very products and services to satisfy those needs. Successful CEOs are those who are skilled at understanding customer needs, wants, and preferences and in meeting them to reap large rewards even when market research and the customers themselves initially react negatively to their innovations and reap large rewards.

Successful business leaders are those who have the talent to innovate and give serious rejuvenation and invigoration to their innovation culture.

One of the most important talents that the top executives need to have is the talent to innovate—the talent to energize their existing people and to attract great new ones. In today's global world, the competitive advantage of nearly all successful organizations is driven by its great people. For this, they must be innovative as great people love to think up, develop, and implement new ideas. Organizations that do not innovate quickly lose their innovative people. They migrate to organizations that do welcome and encourage such people and allow their talents full expression. Organizations where innovation resides solely among R&D engineers are often boring, bureaucratic places to work and rarely sustain growth and profit. Innovation ought to be a process that pervades every single part of the organization's value chain, as oxygen pervades our atmosphere. CEOs who strongly endorse this idea drive behaviour throughout the organization, from R&D to the assembly line, through the customer service centre and down to the mailroom and warehouse.

The oft repeated phrases in an organization go like this....In your organization, can you imagine a warehouse worker calling up the CEO and saying, boss, why do we need a parts warehouse anyway?, and explaining how much money could be saved by just-in-time parts deliveries like the company down the block? And a CEO who will take the call and listen? If you cannot, your innovative culture needs some serious renovation. For the CEOs of such companies, the ultimate goal of innovation is sustained competitive advantage that necessarily requires sustained innovation.

Effective innovators resolve the paradox of clash between culture of discipline and creativity.

One of the many paradoxes that have innovation at their core is the clash between Pablo Picasso and Jim Collins—the need for free, unfettered creativity, together with the need for focused, systematic discipline—and the overriding imperative to make these two qualities not only co-exist but fall in love and marry. Great CEOs score 10 out of 10 on both culture of discipline and creativity despite the fact that these two dimensions are like wolf and lamb. The Bible, says, 'The wolf and the lamb shall lie down together. "But...they won't get much sleep," commented humorist Woody Allen. Neither will managers trying to reconcile creativity and internal discipline. Judging by Collin's data, few managers fully succeed.

Innovation flourishes when companies cultivate the habit of 'listening'.

Ideas can sprout anywhere and everywhere, but the question is: Does senior management listen? If no one with the power to implement listens seriously who will bother to express those ideas? If new ideas are shot down as soon as they are born, a second idea will rarely follow the first. However, if every new idea gets a serious hearing no matter who proposes it, one day just such an idea may transform your organization and brighten the future. Global giant IBM's new CEO Lou Gerstner is prime example. He championed the idea of a junior IBM employee who showed six ways IBM could leverage the web. And IBM built a powerful, profitable, and fast-growing new business, without which its future would have been bleak (Kinntie, 2002).

Innovators with business acumen have the intuition to abandon ideas destined to fail.

Marketing expert Robert McMath has 80,000 new products in his New Products Showcase and Learning Centre in Ithaca, New York. There are a lot more 'fizzlers' (failures) than 'sizzlers' (successes), he notes. "When about everything that needs to go right does go right", new products succeed. He claims you are a success as a new product developer if you abandon ideas destined to fail (Hamel, 2005).

Companies that develop and deploy adaptive competence alone survive in hostile markets.

CEOs best adapted to their environments, and best able to change in response to changes in that environment, are most likely to survive. This adaptive competence is necessary for survival in the turbulent global markets. Due to fierce Japanese competition and commoditization in Intel's key product memory chips, Intel's profits plummeted in the year 1985. Intel President Andrew Grove, together with CEO Gordon Moore, decided to shut down the entire memory chip business. They did this by doing what is called 'getting on the balcony' (stepping outside a subjective perspective). Grove asked Moore, what he would do if they got kicked out and the Board brought in new CEO. Get out of memories, said Moore. "Why not walk out the door, come back, and do it ourselves," asked Grove. Grove said that at that moment he had a hard time getting those words out. 'Face the brutal facts' is a key skill of great CEOs (McMarth and Forbes, 1998).

Firms that want to manage innovation profitably should be able to drive changes by reinventing their companies.

When in trouble, CEOs must decide to reinvent their companies by initiating a series of concerted actions. They have to seek to leverage the existing strengths of the companies that do not require large cash outflows. They develop intense inward focus to improve its performance without getting distracted. Any journey towards international competitiveness must be set out with the personal commitment and change-oriented leadership of its top management, with an intense focus on the 3Cs: Change (i.e., to mutate and improve furiously), Cost (i.e. ruthlessly cutting of wasteful expenditure), and Customers (i.e. strive relentlessly to build relationships and influence consumption. All this has to be anchored in the code of conduct, which provides a strong ethical value base and more compass for each employee in the company.

Leaders who believe in innovation culture also sincerely believe in creating a culture of total transparency.

The willingness of the top management to create total

transparency and subject its own performance to discipline and the scrutiny of the entire organization would help greatly in bringing about a mental transformation in the workforce. They should break down company's strategy into its component elements and track performance across the organization starting from the managing director. The KRAs for the top managers are to be cascaded down, using the Balanced Scorecard tool for strategy translation, communication, and implementation. In this manner, strategic alignment across the organization is achieved.

Innovation management is all about striving for world-class operations at world's lowest costs.

Once the CEOs ensure that its operations are world-class and that its costs are amongst the lowest in the world, they turn their energies towards the customer. The top management should find ways to ensure that the enthusiasm of the employees involved in implementing whatever initiatives they had initiated was sustained. Appropriate reward and recognition mechanisms have to be put in place to ensure the development of true meritocracy in the company.

Managers possess and demonstrate a discipline of *not* diluting the sense of urgency and purpose for onward march in Innovation Management.

After initial successes, CEOs should continue to press ahead, and ensure that the sense of urgency and purpose is not diluted and continue their forward momentum with even more acceleration. The Price-Value-Cost dynamic is clearly a moving target, and no company can afford to rest on its past laurels.

Successful innovators are those that create powerful feelings and emotions, and satisfy well-defined needs.

Pierre Omidyar, founder of the eBay, made the company one driven by a simple, yet powerful vision. He successfully transformed the company from a start up to an established company in the past decade retaining its innovative energy while adapting constantly to its complex environment, meeting competitive challenges and customer needs. In the process, the company has changed many peoples' lives. It proves that while good CEOs improve our lives, great ones fundamentally change how we lead our lives—how we work, spend, save, consume, travel, and enjoy leisure. Successful CEOs create powerful feelings and emotions, and satisfy well-defined needs. A key principle of this CEO from the start has been to treat small and big customers in precisely the same way—with direct access to him (Tedlow, 2005).

Leaders with a passion for innovation are always obsessed with making their managers to ask the right questions rather than knowing the answers.

Former Intel CEO Andy Grove was famous for rebuking his managers for not asking the right questions. If you do not ask the correct question, Grover noted, then by definition, the answers will be irrelevant; knowing the questions is more important than knowing the answers. How can CEOs tell the difference between a winning business idea and a disastrous one? Much is at stake when they select ideas for implementation. Many radically new ideas seem at first sight to be ridiculous; that is why great CEOs insist on never rejecting any idea at once. And many ideas that sound wonderful at first hearing turn out to be disasters (Meller, 2006).

Companies that rank very high on innovation ladder ponder over ways and means to get their customers to love their products through transformational experiences.

Many global CEOs lose sleep wondering how to get customers all over the world to like their product enough to buy it. But in today's competitive markets, the real question is: how do you get customers to love your product? In a product ladder, at the bottom are commodities, standardized undifferentiated products where competition is based solely on cost and price; next, goods, which are differentiated, often through branding; then services, and then, transformational experiences—services offering a memorable and delightful experience that we love and remember them.

Great CEOs should aim as high as possible on the Experience Economy ladder through innovation.

The higher the product is in the commodity (where the material is the offering)-to-transformation (where the individual is the offering) ladder, the higher the profit margins and the stronger the customer loyalty. Great CEOs should aim as high as possible on the Experience Economy ladder through innovation by finding ways to push their products up the ladder and resist this commoditization. Experiences (where the encounter is the offering) and transformations create an emotional bond with customers—the basis of enduring customer loyalty and powerful global brands. People want to buy things they have an emotional connection with. For CEOs, the eternal question is, 'How can our goods (where the products are the offering) and services (where the process is the offering) be kept from sliding down the ladder, becoming commoditized, and how can we push them up the ladder by shaping them into memorable customer experiences?' said Tedlow (2005).

Innovation is also about being able to gain a competitive edge by anticipating Government Legislation.

Changes in government regulation create superior opportunities for CEOs. By anticipating the legislation, they gain a decisive competitive edge on competitors who only react to the legislation after it was passed. Teva Pharmaceutical Co., headquartered in Israel, is one of the world's largest generic medicine companies. Teva CEO Eli Hurvitz spotted an opportunity when the Hatch-Waxman Act was passed by the US Congress in 1984, encouraging generic drugs as a way cut the soaring cost of medicines for consumers. Teva quickly aligned its competencies with the generic business model and in two decades became the world's largest supplier at a time when for years other drug companies scorned the low margins inherent in the generic business (Pine and Gillmore, 1999).

Pioneers in innovation management appreciate the advantage of listening to their customers as against their inner voices or even their products themselves.

For the first Lego Toys, carpenter Ole Kir Christiansen listened to his inner voice. His son pioneered interlocking Lego bricks, in part, by listening to the product itself. The grandson of the founder, retired as CEO in 2004; his skill lay in listening to Lego's customers. Today's Lego managers, when upgrading a Lego robit kit, Mindstorm, listen to their customers in interesting, and novel ways. They also listen to the Lego organization while adapting its innovation system to its culture, history, and personality (Gladwell, 2005).

Businesses manage to become adept in the art of innovation by learning the art of becoming original thinkers and developing the will to take courageous decisions independently.

CEOs need three things to be original thinkers. (1) A tremendous amount of information. (2) Willingness to pull the ideas, because they are interested. (3) Ability to get rid of trash ...one cannot think only of good ideas...one must be able to throw out the junk immediately. Though many psychologists view creativity as some kind of innate ability, great CEOs, on the contrary, view it largely as a decision. Great CEOs are creative largely by the dint of their decision to go their way. They make decisions for which others either lack the will or even the courage to make by daring to define the problems in ways different from those in which their colleagues define them.

Among the crowd, the 26-year old Chuck House, an engineer, with Hewlett-Packard defied company co-founder and CEO and won the HP 'Medal of Defiance' when his product achieved tremendous success in annual sales with no redesign and made high profit margins. Then, what are the key success factors? A creative, defiant individual; a strong team; a champion; House's one-on-one market research with user; House's perseverance—and rank insubordination; defying the crowd; a sponsor in the form of House's manager; and an organization culture that tolerated such insubordination (Pinchot, 1985).

Conclusion

Successful innovation occurs when an invention, related to a product, service, or process in some part of the organization's value chain, is joined with business design, which in turn is implemented with discipline and skill through innovation management. Innovation management is the process of creating and implementing a business design surrounding a creative idea, with the goal of transforming an invention into an innovation, and ultimately to achieving sustained competitive advantage, leading to growth and profit, in the marketplace.

To build profitable, in-demand products from appealing new ideas, it is necessary to manage the innovative process—that is, wrap an innovative business design or model around a product or service innovation, and then manage that process, down the value chain to the ultimate consumer. That is why in the term 'innovation management', the noun 'management' is as important as, or more important than, the adjective 'innovation'. 'Successful strategy is 10 percent formulation and 90 percent implementation, Collins (2001). Surely this lesson was learned the hard way from the key management discipline of competitive strategy. Michael Porter's powerful 1980 book Competitive Strategy created a new management discipline with the same name (Porter, 1980).

All the 'most admired' companies share a common skill. They identify innovative business ideas that create unique value and become experts in the next two crucial stages. After 'innovate' comes 'deploy' (usually globally), and 'adapt'. Facility in innovation requires operational efficiency (deploy widely) and customer intimacy (adapt to local markets and segments) in order to achieve growth and profit.

CEOs should succeed in developing an innovative

business idea, and be able to apply the innovation tools to build an innovative business design well aligned with this idea, to generate growth and profit. Combining the strategies and concepts of innovation with tools of innovation management gives innovators the best chance of building competitive, growing and profitable brands, product lines, and business.

References

Adi Ignatius, (2006), 'In Search of the Real Google', Time, 20 February, p. 28.

Annabelle Gawer and Michael A. Cusumano, (2002) Platform Leadership: How Intel, Microsoft, and Cisco Drive Industry Innovation Cambridge, MA: Harvard Business School Press.

Annabelle Gawer and Michael A. Cusumano, 'What does it take to be a Platform Leader: Some recent lessons from Palm and NTT DoCoMo?', Working Paper, 2004, p. 1.

B. Joseph and James H. Gilmore (1997) "Beyond Goods and Services: Staging Experiences and Guiding Transformations', Strategy and Leadership, May-June.

B. Joseph Pine and James H. Gilmore, (1999), The Experience Economy: Work is Theatre and Every Business a Stage (Boston, MA: Harvard Business School Press.

Based on Gary Hamel, (2005), 'Waking up IBM', Harvard Business Review, July-August 2000, and Jay Galbraith, Designing the Customer-centric Organization: A Guide in Strategy, Structure, and Process, San Francisco: Jossey-Boss.

Burton Marsteller, (2005), Forester Magazine, Issue 1, p. 37.

Gifford Pinchot III, (1085), Intrapreneuring, New York: Harper, pp. 23-30.

Global Innovation Outlook: 2004, Armonk, NY: IBM, 2004, p. 3.

Gurucharan Das, 'Local memoirs of a global manager', Harvard Business Review, March-April 1993.

James Collins, (2001) Good to Great: Why Some Companies Make the Leap…and Others Don't New York: HarperCollins.

Maital Shlomo and Seshadri, (2007), Innovation Management: Strategies, Concepts, and Tools for Growth and Profit, New Delhi, Response Books, p. 71.

Malcolm Gladwell, (2005), Blink: The Power of Thinking without Thinking, Boston, MA: Little Brown.

Murthy, 'Global Corp, 2005', The Economist: The World (2005).

R. Foster, Innovation: The Attacker's Advantage (1986) New York: Summit Books.

R. Tedlow, (2005) 'Lessons in Leadership—The Education of Andy Grove', Fortune, 28 November 2005 (also on Fortune.com).

Richard S. Tedlow, 'The Education of Andy Grove', Fortune, 12 December 2005, p. 34.

Robert M. McMarth and Thom Forbes, (1998) What Were They Thinking? Marketing Lessons You Can Learn from Products that Flopped New York; Three Rivers Press.

Some information on eBay is available online at http://www.internet-story.com./ebay.htm and on the CNN Money Website at http://cnnmoney.com.

10

Urban Development Projects through Public-Private Partnerships (PPPs)

Aditya Sriram, Aniket and Harish S. Vangala

Need for PPPs in Urban Development

Urbanization is both a resultant condition and a determinant of economic growth. Migration from towns and villages to cities is inevitable as well as absolutely essential to sustain parts of our 60 percent population currently engaged in agriculture related activities (and contributing to a meagre 17 percent of the GDP) in manufacturing and the service sector. Hence, it can be intuited that urban areas in India will continue to play the role of key drivers of the manufacturing and services-led economic growth. Thus, urban development in India has been identified as an important sector by our policy makers and there is a consensus on the urgent need for reforms and investment.

The urgency for overhauling the cities is more relevant in times of global economic slowdown where restoring the growth of different sectors through large scale infrastructure projects is a very plausible solution. However, at present, there still exists a gap in the urban infrastructure investments and funding. In addition to the shortfalls in the urban infrastructure development, severe inefficiencies hamper the delivery of basic urban services, especially in water supply and sanitation. Lack of empowerment of local governing bodies and ambiguous distribution of funds and responsibilities between different tiers of government organizations make the implementation of urban development plans worse. All these challenges call for alternate, more efficient frameworks for strategizing and implementation of urban development frameworks, Public Private Partnerships (PPPs) being the most promising one.

PPPs enable governments to overcome their budgetary and borrowing constraints and raise finance for high-priority public infrastructure projects. Second, PPPs allow the costs of the investment to be spread over the lifetime of the asset and thus can allow infrastructure projects to be brought forward by years compared with the pay-as-you-go financing typical of many infrastructure projects. Third, PPPs have a solid track record of on-time, on-budget delivery. Fourth, PPPs transfer certain risks to the private sector and provides incentives for assets to be properly maintained. Fifth, public-private partnerships can lower the cost of infrastructure by reducing both construction costs and overall lifecycle costs. Sixth, because satisfaction metrics can be built into the contract, PPPs encourage a strong customer service orientation.

Finally, because the destination, not the path, becomes the organizing theme around which a project is built, public private partnerships enable the public sector to focus on the outcome-based public value they are trying to create. Thus, PPPs are seen as a sustainable financial and institutional mechanism resulting in improved delivery of public services and at the same time, promoting public sector reforms.

Also, since the private sector is a vital stakeholder in the urban growth story, it is natural that they are involved in meeting the funding gaps and ensuring more efficient implementation of urban infrastructure projects. The PPPs are an institutional response to the increasing "complexity and fragmentation of community life" for improvement of urban governance. The stakeholders of PPPs include the civil servants of state and ULBs, civil society, non-government organizations, political executives, private sector, financial intermediaries, and the urban poor.

The framework of PPP for urban development could generally be based on any of the models such as service contracts, operation and management contracts, lease contracts, Build–operate–transfer (BOT) and similar arrangements, concessions and joint ventures. These models cover the complete spectrum of complexity of risk transfers between the public and private sector. Based on the nature of the project, PPPs have evolved in different forms with increasing private sector risk, responsibility and financing starting at the low risk to high risk as follows: service contracts (low risk); management contracts; leasing; joint ventures and partnerships; build-operate-transfer, concessions; and finally, build-own-operate and divestures (high risk).

PPP in Urban Development: Impact Analysis

The Government of India (GoI) has recognized the important role PPPs can play in accelerating infrastructure development. As a result, it has announced policy initiatives and measures to create an enabling environment. These include setting up of committees like the PPPAC (Public Private Partnership Appraisal Committee) to ensure proper planning of PPPs; provision of financial assistance from the Government in form of Viability Gap Funding; preparation of model documents (Concession Agreements, RFQ and RFP documents etc.) to streamline the bidding process and implementation; implementing capacity building programmes at regional levels; and improved information dissemination by creating databases and capturing the best practices.

With an aim to encourage reforms and fast track planned development of identified cities, the GoI has launched in 2005 the Jawaharlal Nehru National Urban Renewal Mission (JNNURM), a reform-based, part-grant driven program of ₹ 50,000 crore (US$ 11 billion) outlay over a seven-year period. Many of the JNNURM-supported reforms are expected to create favourable governance and institutional framework for private sector to feel more confident to venture into the urban sector. The JNNURM is so designed to enhance private sector participation and provide an impetus to PPPs. JNNURM achieves its objectives in two ways: (i) part-grant financing by the JNNURM (which is likely to increase the bankability of a number of large urban infrastructure projects) and (ii) the financing gap/needs to meet the project costs.

A number of PPP projects have been already implemented or are being implemented in the urban development area. A total of 78 PPP projects are under various phases of implementation (as on October 28, 2009). One of the major PPP projects implemented in the country was the water supply and sewerage project in Tirupur, Tamil Nadu. It was implemented through a Special Purpose Vehicle promoted by the Government of Tamil Nadu and Infrastructure Leasing and Financial Services Ltd. (IL&FS). It involved the largest private investment in the water infrastructure of the country. It provided for a new sanitation network covering over 60 percent of Tirupur which included low cost sanitation for slums along with a dedicated water supply for the industries in the area which resulted in higher economic growth and creation of jobs and poverty reduction.

This project is a very good example of how PPPs can help leverage the state investment. In this project an investment of ₹ 550 million helped raise about ₹ 10,000 million for the project. The Phase II Sardar Patel Ring Road is also an interesting case of a successful partnership; it envisaged four laning the existing ring road using the BOT model. The private sector was involved in all technical inputs like planning, feasibility studies and surveys. The public authority (Ahmedabad Urban Development Authority) developed land through a town planning scheme mechanism rather than a coercive land acquisition method. The authorities organized extensive public consultations in all villages falling en-route this ring road. They emphasized the financial gains due to appreciation of land prices. Such personal interactions were instrumental in ensuring smooth transfer of land ownership. The project highlights the importance of a strong political and administrative leadership which gives due consideration to concerns of all stakeholders.

It is important to remember that PPP projects are complex to execute and implement. There are many cases of failure in India and it is imperative to learn from them. One of the bitter experiences in PPP was in the Karur Toll Bridge construction. It was a toll bridge (< 1 km.) to be constructed over a period of two years. The concessionaire in this case was ECCI and the model adopted was DBOT. It was the first toll bridge to be contracted out by an ULD and involved provision of funds from TNUDF and a stable regulatory framework by way of an amendment to the TN State Toll Act. However, damage to the bridge approach road during rains gave pretext to Government to terminate the contract without any compensation to the concessionaire. It is crucial to ensure the inclusion of proper dispute resolution mechanisms in order to make sure arbitrary decisions are not taken by the public authority.

Based on our analysis of the above and several other pertinent PPP cases, we discuss some challenges facing PPPs in urban development in the next section.

Challenges

Even though the magnitude of challenge of urban development is huge, the existing municipal laws are inadequate to enable Urban Local Bodies (ULBs) to implement necessary projects of scale. Though the 74th Amendment to the Indian Constitution enacted in 1992 enables the devolution of powers to the urban local bodies, the extent of its implementation has been unimpressive. The Amendment evolved a framework for the States to transfer some 18 functions to the urban local bodies (ULBs) areas that are vital to the growth of cities, from urban planning to regulation of land use. The States were also empowered to pass on the authority to raise revenues through taxes. It can be argued that urban local bodies are currently powerless to raise resources. But that need not be the case if the States are pressured into implementing the 74th Amendment provisions.

Another serious challenge impeding private sector

participation in urban development projects include the perceived political risks. There is a general lack of transparency at the third tier of government in the decision making process. As a result, projects at the municipal level represent significant risk to private companies because the outcome of a project bid depends more often than not on factors other than market forces. Moreover, most of the urban services like water have been traditionally viewed to be "public", i.e. charging users for such services was deemed unethical. However, governments have failed to realise that such services are resource constrained and have an economic utility. As a result the irrationally low user tariffs make some projects non-bankable and require greater support from general revenue for operations and maintenance (O&M). Considering the weak financial health of most ULBs, urban sector projects are deemed to be of high risk.

There is no proper regulatory or policy enabling framework of PPPs at the urban government level. This makes it unclear for private investors to understand the clauses and provisions of the project. There is also a lack of standardized documents and procedures needed to streamline identification and implementation of PPP projects. Given the variations in the formats, bidding procedures, agreements, and overall execution of the PPPs among the various agencies, there is a need for standardized prequalification and bidding procedures and guidelines for ensuring efficiency, predictability, and ease of approval process. An appropriate legislative framework for PPPs, with necessary amendments to municipal laws, is needed to ensure clarity of entry conditions, contractual structures, and incentives and concessions.

A key impediment to successful commercialization of projects in urban sector has been the absence of rigorous project development. Many of the projects made available for bidding by governments have been inadequately structured and hence unsuitable for PPP. A project development facility that provides project sponsors the resources to procure consultancy and expert services for conducting pre-feasibility studies and assessments is required. Moreover, there is a deficiency in the public sector capacity to successfully execute PPPs. The private sector has highlighted its concerns about the absence of a robust pipeline of bankable PPP projects. This is attributed to insufficient capacity within the PPP-sponsoring public entities to identify and implement deals and execute PPPs.

Recommendations

It is necessary to ensure an environment which aims to foster efficiency and transparency in the bidding process, ensures sanctity of contracts, encourages competition, and promotes market-driven tariffs, and separates regulatory and adjudication authorities. To this effect, we recommend the following strategies.

Choosing the Right Model To encourage PPPs, it is important to develop 'bankable' or financially-sustainable models at a project level following a full life-cycle approach for partnerships that confers adequate attention to all phases of a PPP—from policy and planning, to the transaction phase, and then to managing the concession. Many PPP models are feasible only when tariffs or user fees meets the full recovery of the cost of service including O&M and depreciation. In the urban sector, full cost recovery is not immediately possible in areas such as water supply and sewerage due to a variety of factors, including the essential nature of the services and poverty. Governments should not only adopt PPP models that bring in private investments but also allow services to be subsidized through output-based-aid, which use explicit performance-based subsidies to deliver basic services. The level of certainty the public sector possesses about its infrastructure and service requirements should also be a key determinant in the choice of model.

This includes certainty about the external environment, including the policy environment, as well as the capacity of contract performance standards and realities and incentives to higher outputs. A high level of certainty suggests that the government can shift substantial control and risk to the private sector. At the same time, several new models such as Bundling, Integrator, Incremental and Competitive Partnerships can also be explored.

Capacity Building of ULBs: There is insufficient expertise and experience at the ULB level to execute PPP projects. Hence, capacity building of ULBs is an area of key focus. Even though each sector of urban development sector will require specific skill-sets, general understanding of project structuring, contractual provisions and risk transfer can be utilized in all areas. ULB level capacity building should focus on improving the awareness of select city officials and political executives in commercial and operational issues impacting PPP development. Commercial and operational issues are likely to include understanding the true cost of operations, user charge structures, alternative revenue generation possibilities (such as carbon emission credits, recycling, etc.), credit ratings, debt leveraging, development of key performance criteria such as loss level reductions.

An assessment should also be carried out to match sub-sectors (e.g. raw water treatment, water distribution, wastewater treatment, solid waste collection, landfills, sewerage network, collections of garbage, metering, collections of tariffs, bus rapid transport systems, mass rapid transport systems, traffic management systems, and others) to the most achievable PPP modalities for that particular city or ULB given a host of considered criterion. Interactions including visits with selected municipalities or PPP projects can be planned under this component.

Risk Audit of PPP projects Legal, regulatory and policy issues that might prohibit private sector (including foreign) investments (funds and/or strategic and operational interests) flowing into the urban sectors or sub-sectors should be identified, and where possible, mitigating strategies should be laid out. On the funding side, analysis to identify key obstacles to the provision of long tenure competitive finance to urban projects as well as potential collaborators for funding bankable projects and probable lending criterion should be explored. Based on an agreed PPP impediment audit and mitigation framework, the sub-sectors and urban projects that are amenable to PPP structuring would be identified for immediate support. Workshops and training programs should be supported for awareness building of PPP impediments, and for evolving time-bound executable mitigation road map with support of all stakeholders, especially the private sector.

Model PPP Projects: In an attempt to create some good models, demonstration projects should be identified and implemented subject to all regulatory approvals. It is recommended that all the stakeholders work in developing bankable project models that will be sustainable on their own, without recourse to guarantees from the state or central governments and will be able to attract private sector investments. Issues such as tariff reforms, alternative revenue lines, leveraging JNNURM grant funds for good debt/equity structures, creation of special purpose vehicles or incorporated entities, amongst others, should be structured in the development of the project. PPP modalities should be considered in the structuring with the intention of bidding out the projects to private sector.

Value Generation from Underutilized Assets: It is recommended that ULBs identify and unlock value from these underutilized assets (e.g.: land, buildings), and use it to help pay for new infrastructure. It shall encourage greater bidder competition because there is less risk associated with payback to the private partner, thus increasing the success rate of PPPs.

Policy Implementation and Policy Changes: Some of the medium term policy changes happen to be ideas in conflict at present. These include empowering the local governing bodies with more funding and responsibility to implement urban projects. Creation of city-states will also help channel the flow of funds from the cities back to the source to meet the gap in funding. At the same time, effective ways for wealth creation and distribution through other sources can be facilitated.

The states should be pressurized to implement the 74th Amendment so as to empower the ULBs with added responsibilities and resource-raising powers. Constitutionally, the municipality is not barred from tapping global sources for funds; the States are. Similarly, the ULBs can borrow from banks and raise bonds, as Bangalore and Ahmedabad have done.

To ensure that the ULBs are capable of executing PPP projects, which might have huge investment requirements from the public partner, some measures need to be followed. This includes clear division of functional responsibilities and linkage among different levels of government to ensure upward and downward accountability and to enable the SFCs (State Financial Corporations) in their constitutional task of devolution of funds to ULBs.

Conclusion

PPPs involve risk sharing between public and private partners resulting in efficiency, equity, greater value creation and distribution. Our study examines some successful and unsuccessful cases of PPPs in urban development and their impact assessment. The key challenges were identified as inadequate devolution of necessary powers to the local governing bodies, lack of transparency at lower tiers of the government, unavailability of standardized frameworks at the grassroots and insufficient project development. Based on the study, we recommend that PPP models (comprising the underlying characteristics of a PPP contract) should evolve on a case-by case basis. All of the existing models, shall, however, be used as reference.

Other urgent changes are required in terms of capacity building of ULBs, mitigation strategies for any existing framework preventing private participation and creation of certain exemplary PPP projects.

Initiatives on the government side to optimize the use of the existing resources such as land, for generating additional revenues and for use in infrastructure development shall also greatly increase private participation. Lastly, empowering local bodies such as the municipal corporations through legislation, enforcing the 74th Amendment and creation of city states leading to better linkage among different levels of government will be crucial in long term sustainability of urban development projects through PPPs.

References

Bonu, Sekhar (2007), Opportunities and Challenges for Public-Private Partnerships, New Delhi, Excel.

Centre for Organization Development (2009), Public Private Partnerships-An Indian perspective, Kharagpur Consulting Group Report.

Deloitte Research (2007), Closing the Infrastructure Gap, Deloitte Research Report.

Department of Economic Affairs (DEA) and Asian Development Bank, (2006), Facilitating Public Private Partnership for Accelerated Infrastructure Development in India, a Report.

Government of India: Detailed Information on PPPs (http://www.pppinindia.com).

Infrastructure Challenges in South Asia–The Role for Public-Private Partnerships, an ADB presentation to South Asia finance ministers in 2008.

Kumar Sasi and Prasad C. Jayasankar (2004), Public-Private Partnerships in Urban Infrastructure: Kerala Calling, New Delhi, Response.

Peter Farlam (2009), The South African Institute of International Affairs Nepad Policy Focus Series. A Report on Assessing Public-Private Partnerships in Africa.

Report of Ernst and Young on Public Private Partnership in Urban Infrastructure (2009).

World Bank Infrastructure Governance Roundtable, UK, PPP Forum (worldbank.org website).

11

Challenges Facing Indian Business Schools

B. Savitha

B-schools play a crucial role in shaping the attitudes and behaviour of business leaders through business education, research, management development programs and training. On the ground, the spiralling global crisis has exposed the gap between the theory and practice of successful business management. It has turned the focus on the need to make management education more responsible. The crisis has initiated discussion and doubts about the educational efficacy of B-Schools the world over.

The current economic slowdown has proved that outstanding business administration becomes crucial for business leaders to guide their companies on the right path and with the right tools. Several stakeholders are raising questions about different factors that have contributed to the crisis (Davis and Hogarth, 2008). In order to find solutions to emerge out of the current meltdown and to avoid future instances akin to this, B-schools have been placed under scrutiny to assess the quality of management education that is provided to future managers.

The economic downturn has also been a period of reflection and introspection for B- Schools. They are engaging in dialogue with various stakeholders to better orient themselves to developing abilities of students that will deliver value to business and society. B-Schools are being forced to choose between doing business as usual and devising an agenda that will result in a value addition to their students and businesses.

Management Education Landscape in India

India is a major player in the Asian management education market. India is the second largest provider of MBAs in the world after the United States of America while it still largely catering to domestic demand. Management education in India has witnessed phenomenal growth in last twenty years. From just around 100 B-Schools in 1998, the number stands at an impressive 1800 colleges producing around 1,70,000 management graduates. There is a tremendous rush for management education in our country. There are about half a million students appearing for admission tests seeking admission into an MBA programme. The prestige attached to the degree, the employability, and the image of B-Schools has contributed to the growth of management education in our country. The management education market is valued at ₹ 30 million and is growing at the rate of 12 percent (Gill, 2008).

The growth of management education in India has brought along with a number of challenges. B-Schools are important suppliers of managerial talent. The role of B-Schools in developing and nurturing managerial talent that can thrive in an uncertain economic environment has gained significant importance. With popularity of MBA education rising, the danger of losing its relevance is imminent if it cannot respond to the evolving needs of the business community.

Challenges Faced by B-Schools in India

Some of the challenges faced by B-Schools in are as under:

Restrictions Owing to Regulatory Framework: The B-Schools recognized by the AICTE, or affiliated to various universities are required to follow a syllabus prescribed by the regulatory authority. They do not have the freedom to design the curriculum to meet the needs of business that recruit their graduates. Private B-Schools have managed to set up campuses abroad but management institutes funded by the government are not able to so because of the shortage of faculty and the problem of complying with guidelines relating to reservations in recruitment of faculty. The paucity of resources and the regulatory restrictions has hampered the opening of campuses abroad.

Lack of Dynamic Curriculum Development: Dynamic curriculum development is not possible in a scenario controlled by restrictions on curriculum development. The need to design curriculum to enable students to be exposed to real world applications needs to be addressed. The B-Schools in India will have to evolve a system of sharing their course content with each other in order to improve the quality of management education.

Shortage of Talented Faculty: Another crucial factor posing a serious problem to management education in India is the quality of faculty. Quality and qualifications of faculty are reflected in the teaching and the courses. Though management education has turned into a money-spinner, the faculty who impart the knowledge are still a neglected lot. There is an acute shortage of management teachers primarily owing to poor pay scales that match industry pay packages. Teaching is a profession of last resort. Qualified faculty will be able to see future needs better and can develop courses to meet them. In several rankings conducted in the country, most schools have found to have good physical and academic infrastructure, a majority lagged behind in outcomes, such as skill tests imparted in graduating students, research output, collaborative studies, training and consultancy. There are around 2000 B-Schools in India, out of which only 200 are capable of imparting good training and education (Business Today, 2010).

Lack of Research Focus: Poor faculty performance and lack of research orientation is one area where performance levels have been very disappointing. The downturn took a toll on the B-Schools itself.

- In 88 percent of the B-schools surveyed, not a single faculty member was sent to participate in an international conference.

- In 68 percent of the schools, the faculty development expenditure did not exceed ₹ 10 lakh.
- In 91 percent of the schools surveyed, not a single paper has been published in any international journal by their permanent faculty in the last academic year (Business Today, 2010).

Quality of Student Intake: While management education is a preferred path for most graduates owing to the successful career prospects and growth up the corporate ladder, one of the challenges faced by B-schools is ensuring quality of its incoming class. While the expectation is that the B-schools produce excellent managers, the hardship faced by them is that the aptitude of students who enter the MBA program is most often far from desired. Lack of communication, inability to keep pace with the demands of management education and failure to gain a good conceptual understanding of all functional areas inhibit the overall quality of MBAs (Bhata, 2002).

Overcoming Challenges Faced by B-Schools: B-Schools have a responsibility to prepare their students for a new business system so that public needs are met. While some challenges can be overcome by policy level changes that are external to the operating environment of B-Schools, some challenges are well under the jurisdiction of B- Schools.

Knowledge Development: Business schools need to equip students with skills that stay with them throughout their careers. They need to enable their students to achieve exceptional performance levels on a continuous basis. Effective performance is the result of actions. The determinants of action in business settings are conceptual knowledge, domain knowledge and action skills.

- Increase the depth of conceptual knowledge by constant curriculum revision to strengthen content to keep in tune with latest developments. Incorporate case studies relevant to Indian Scenario rather than providing students with canned options of western case studies. In doing so, they also need to maintain balance theory and real world applications.

- Widen Pedagogical spectrum across disciplinary and functional boundaries to equip students to become multi-functional managers.
- Supplement curriculum with experiential learning and leadership development and prepare future managers to meet global challenges not only of the US.
- Enable acquisition of domain knowledge by facilitating learning of both action and insight skills and these will facilitate the acquisition of domain knowledge through business experience.

Workforce Development: There is a need in business schools to develop critical thinking in their students. B-Schools should not only teach basics but also there is need to convince students to be sceptical and to challenge conventional thinking. There is widespread feeling among many in the industry and academics that today's financial crisis was caused not by just greed but by lack of confidence among the B-Schools graduates to ask the tough questions. The need of the hour is that the management education of today must instil a confidence in people to do new things and not just hang on to job because it pays well.

B-Schools should be able to nurture innovation and creativity. They should be providers of intellectual and moral leadership and should be able to lead and manage change towards sustainability and sustainable development. Further there is an imperative need to develop an Indian Breed of Managers who can tackle the problems that are unique to the Indian Business environment.

Talent Management: B-Schools in India are not attracting nearly enough teachers to meet the growing demand. There exists a demand and supply mismatch that is bound to have profound impact on the future of the education sector and of the country. The mismatch between demand and supply of faculty talent appears to be more of a supply side problem. The B-School faculty talent pool is eroding currently owing to non-entry of qualified faculty, attrition and mobility. Further there is a geographical imbalance among management institutions, as the supply is not evenly distributed across the country.

While most B-Schools do a good job of developing their students, they are less successful at helping their faculty and staff improve their skills. The very tools used to develop students are not easily available to the institution's faculty. Most colleges have in place some mentoring of junior faculty but few have fully realized strategies for talent growth and development.

B- Schools will have to look at talent management from a holistic perspective—not only recognizing faculty talent and selecting talent, but hiring faculty talent, retaining those same faculty, developing those faculty, keeping them engaged and, at the appropriate time, redeploying and transitioning.

A good talent management strategy forecasts what kind of talent is needed and planning to meet that need. Further, there is a critical need for an integrated talent management strategy that identifies internal inefficiencies that B-Schools have to overcome and implement innovative practices that will support an effective talent supply chain.

One key element of any effective talent strategy for B-Schools is to identify critical workforce segments–those high-value faculty who can be difficult to replace. It doesn't mean that the other segments can be ignored but special attention needs to be given to those who are critical to replace.

The dearth of qualified and efficient teachers will have adverse spiralling effects on the future of our generation of managers. Faculty jobs world over have become a profession of last resort. The B-Schools joined by many other sectors globally faced with a shrinking talent pool.

B-Schools will have to work on reclaiming their lost faculty–those faculty who have been lost to other lucrative positions due to the rigidity, internal inefficiencies, imbalances and management education sector's inability to dynamically evolve with the growing Indian economy's demands. The responsibility of reclaiming B-School's lost talent does not fall only institutions but on collectively on all stakeholders that are involved.

Strategic Partnerships: B-Schools need to enter into strategic partnerships with one another. They need to utilize the expertise of faculty across schools. They need to provide students with different learning styles. Industry academic partnership will help students of B-Schools to understand the changing corporate dynamics. It will also help to bridge the gap between the classroom and the real world. They need to bring in real time learning.

However, the image of a B-Schools is greatly dependent on three critical factors namely- the faculty, the students and the alumni. In the west, these three factors have combined well and have contributed to the growth of management education. The alumni who have made it big fund the B-Schools. In India however, this is yet to take off on a serious note. This is probably why privately funded B-Schools in India are able to secure a higher ranking when compared to B-Schools such as the IIM's that are dependent on government grants.

Role of Stakeholders in Talent Reclamation: B-Schools significantly contribute to society and are a key linking factor that connects all vital branches of the economy. The success of the Indian B-Schools is of crucial importance to ensure the knowledge supremacy that India's labour force is known for. In order to ensure that B-Schools are successful, all stakeholders need to perform their role efficiently. Identified below are a few key stakeholders and their role in ensuring success of the B-Schools.

- The Central Government represented by the Human Resource Development Ministry that establishes the public policy to encourage a climate that would be conducive for development of the Management education sector.
- The Governing bodies such as AICTE that draft

regulations and ensure seamless enforcement of the regulations across the nation.

- State Governments and local bodies that offer strong statutory support and compliance to policies drafted at the central level.
- Universities that can encourage academic mobility, recruitment strategies and faculty development practices at the university level.
- Heads of B-Schools who implement the policies drafted and are responsible for B-School branding and institutional image.
- Faculty who have the responsibility of creating a desire among others to pursue a career in management education and raise standard of the talent pool.
- Students of B-Schools who create the challenge for raising the standard of faculty teaching standards and later as alumni.
- Other B-Schools both domestic and international that create a competitive educational climate and raise the overall standards of education.
- Alumni and corporate sector provides a 360^0 feedback and provide faculty with insights and training on emerging trends in the corporate world.
- Colleges that provides a steady stream of inputs into management institutes.

Conclusion

Business cycles are an essential part of the evolution of the corporate sector and in turn educational institutions. Imperative is the need for B-schools to reinvent themselves and prepare a knowledge base that will provide the necessary tools for managers to proactively address challenging times. Though in the middle of a crisis, this is the most opportune moment for all of us involved in the business of education to engage in self-reflection.

References

Babu, T.D. and Jayabal G. (2005), "An analytical study of teaching methods at affiliated B-Schools in Hyderabad and Secunderabad", Journal of Services Research, Vol. 5, April 2005-September 2005, pp. 101-122.

Bennis W. G and Toole J, (2005), "How business schools lost their way" HBR, May, pp. 96-104.

Bhatta C.P., (2002), "Interfacing business education with cultural wisdom: new insights" Integrating World Markets, School of Management Studies, Allahabad, pp. 5.25-5.38.

Cheryl Kerr, Cathryn Lloyd (2008), Pedagogical Learning's from Management Education-Developing Creativity and Innovation. Journal of Management and Organization, Vol. 14, pp. 486-503.

Education at B-Schools–A look at what lies ahead, Business Today, Business School compendium, pp. 4-6, (2010).

Gill, N. (2008), "The Cosmode-BW Survey-what separates the best Indian B-schools from the rest, Business World, September 23.

Harry, L. Davis and Robin M. Hogarth (2008), Rethinking Management Education, selected paper no. 72.

Iyer, V.R. and Gopalakrishnan P. G. (2004), "Higher Education in a Liberalized Economy", University News, Vol. 42, No. 01, January 05-11, pp. 7-13.

12

Open Innovations in Turbulent Times: The Role of University-Industry Interaction

Mohd. Moiz

As the global economy slowly slides into recession, organizations face new challenges and opportunities. Innovation is the life blood of a business and in today's interconnected world; it's impractical for companies to suspend their innovation initiatives until the worst of the storm blows over. To do so is to risk being well behind the curve when the economy does recover, and losing precious ground to competitors who found creative ways to keep their innovation initiatives moving during the darkest days of the downturn. In these uncertain and challenging economic times, many employees are seriously concerned about the security of their jobs. In addition, companies are making severe cutbacks in R&D. The danger is that these two factors in combination will stifle creativity and innovation to such a degree that many organizations will lose their strategic track.

It may be difficult to convince all the stakeholders, but a recession is exactly the time to invest in innovation, as it will lead to the greatest competitive advantage. In economic downturns, real leaders translate uncertainty into opportunity by taking actions that are somewhat counter-intuitive. Studying past downturns illuminates clear signs of hope. First, many great companies were formed in years featuring a downturn .Most companies lose opportunities in a slowdown because they cut too much or cut the wrong things. They panic and focus on the short-term. They survive in the short term but in the long-term they lose out to companies that had more foresight and focused on innovating for the long-term.

Companies only survive long-term if they keep on changing and evolving as times and tastes change.

While it is tempting to cut resources, slow down product launches, and refocus only on the core, companies that continue their commitment to innovation are more likely to reap great rewards. And not only is innovation more critical in a down economy, it is also more valuable. A British study of 1,000 businesses showed that over the last 30 years, innovation investments in a recession generated a 24 percent return on capital while cost cutting only garnered 0.6 percent. The issue is not whether we should innovate in a recession, but how we can do it most effectively. One of the techniques for doing so is to develop open innovation business model.

Many firms have failed to pass through the tough times even though they have many innovations on their R&D shelves. It is not that innovations alone will help firms to tide over in the crisis, but the firm should have proper business model to commercialize those innovation .It is important those innovation are taken to market. If firms develop innovations that are not profitable they may well go out of business. Millions of innovative companies have gone out of business precisely because they focused on innovation rather than on profitability.

Time to market is very crucial in these uncertain times. It can be tough to go it alone. By creatively employing the talents, insights, and ideas of those outside your own firm, firms can forge important connections for good times or bad. An example is Thread less, the hot, community-cantered online and brick and mortar apparel store. It has created an entire open source model where it never has used any in-house "designers" to create its products. Businesses that find ways to continue to foster innovation in their systems and cultures despite the hard times will come out ahead in the end. Since the world economy started to slide into recession, there have been a huge number of articles reminding that companies that continue to invest in innovation during a recession and find themselves well placed to benefit from the economic upturn when it happens.

However, in recessionary times there are also huge pressures on R&D budgets. So a key question facing many companies is how to innovate successfully in a recession. One of the solutions in such situations is embrace open-source innovation. Look for opportunities beyond your firm's walls to continue R&D, but at a lower cost and lower risk. Companies can do this by Partnering with other firms who provide complementary products and services. This is another way to share costs and risks, and maintain your R&D momentum through the downturn. Open innovation is one model of the business which gives leverage to the firms in times of recession.

Open Innovation: The Emerging Model

Continuous innovation is a necessity for organizations to remain competitive. For the organizations to prosper, grow and sustain a high profitability innovation is the main driver. It is observed that many organizations are not able to reap the benefits of the internal innovation due to many factors. In the organizations new technologies which were invented and patented were lying in the shelf. When Procter & Gamble surveyed all the patents it owned, it determined that about 10 percent of them were in active use and that many of the remaining 90 percent patents had no business value of any kind. When Dow chemical's conducted an extensive analysis of its patent portfolio starting 1993 they found that about 19 percent of Dows patents were in use in one of Dow's own business, while further 33 percent had some potential defensive use or future business.

The remaining patents were either being licensed to others (23 percent) or simply not being used in any discernable way (25 percent). So it seems wasteful to create and develop a large number of technologies and then utilize only a small fraction of the technologies. And especially when the economy is in recession it is natural for the companies to cut back on the R&D expenditure. This will hamper the innovation capacity of the organization and in the long run the organization many not survive the market when the market is bounced back.

As it is now clear that innovation is necessary to remain competitive, the main research question now is that how to innovate and how innovation processes can be managed. A recently proposed and popularized model for the management of innovation is based on the need for companies to *open up their innovation processes* and combine internally and externally developed technologies to create business value. The most important benefit of open innovation to companies is that it provides a larger base of ideas and technologies.

Companies look at open innovation as a close collaboration with external partners–customers, consumers, researchers or other people that may have an input to the future of their company. The main motives for joining forces between companies is to seize new business opportunities, to share risks, to pool complementary resources and to realize synergies. Companies recognize open innovation as a strategic tool to explore new growth opportunities at a lower risk. Open technology sourcing offers companies higher flexibility and responsiveness without necessarily incurring huge costs. Open innovation is a powerful concept that in recent years has come to the forefront of the management of innovation.

Different names are used to describe it, for instance P&G, the highest profile user of the idea, call their programme "Connect and Develop". Chesbrough coined the term in his seminal book, open innovation published in 2003. It is true that most companies have been doing some aspects of open innovation long before 2003. Chesbrough innovation was to create and publish a common language for the people and the companies to describe to the world and each other what they do. This common vocabulary has enabled people to examine and implement ideas much more quickly and coherently than was the case before Chesbrough wrote up his observations.

Closed innovations pertained for most of the 20th century. In closed innovation concept, ideas were developed within the corporate R&D labs and sold to the market place. However the world has changed over the last few years, making open innovations both more essential and easier to undertake.

The concept of open innovation is that by looking outside their own boundaries, companies can gain better access to ideas, knowledge, technology and markets than would be the case if they relied solely on their own recourses. This is shown systematically in the following diagram.

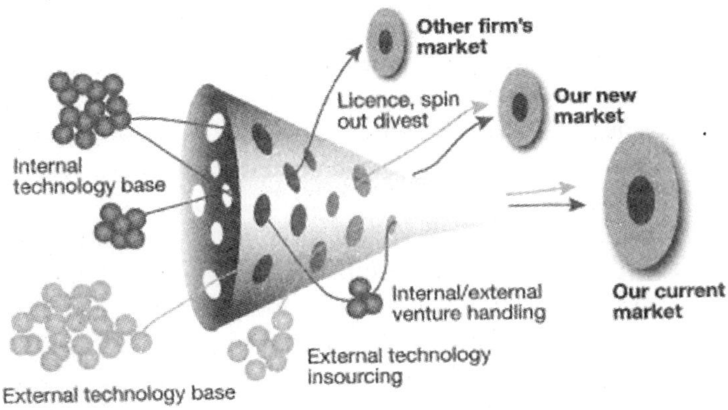

Source: Dr. Treve Willis, Oxford Innovation.

Open innovation describes a process by which companies actively pursue externally generated knowledge and bring it to business, and allow internally generated knowledge to flow outwards, in order to increase the rate of innovation in the business. This is distinctly contrast to older, closed models of innovation in which new technological knowledge was developed internally, in corporate research and development (R&D) laboratories and retained within the business. The closed innovation model which was once a source of real competitive advantage is increasingly seen as slow and insular.

Because of increasing complexity of innovation,

globalization and increasing mobile knowledge workers it is becoming difficult for the companies to maintain specialist knowledge base. In open innovation models, companies look for the external opportunities to exploit unused technologies through licensing or other arrangements. In practice, there are many open innovation models covering a broad spectrum of activity.

These range from the idea of open sources intellectual properly at one end, where intellectual property assets are made freely available to anyone who can make use of them to develop new products and services to models where new IP is openly traded into and out of the company using formal mechanisms such as licensing and technology transfer agreements or strategic alliances. Knowledge based economies are increasing reliant on the exploitation of knowledge of all kinds for business growth and wealth generation. In the present globalised world much of the knowledge business needs is sitting beyond its organizational boundaries.

New ways of working are essential if the companies want to able to access and make use of that knowledge. Traditional closed models of innovation will not generate competitive advantage when much of the knowledge required is outside the organization. Open innovation is essential for companies to remain competitive in an increasingly complex, uncertain and changing environment. Under the concept of open innovation research results are able to traverse the firm's boundaries. Other companies that are able to utilize a technology can license it, creating a win-win situation. Similarly, the firm may be able to license the technologies created by other firms.

Role of Web 2.0 Tools in the Process of Open Innovation

The growth in the information technology and the opening up of global markets have facilitated the diffusion of information and further encouraged open innovation, not only by facilitating desirable information flows but by increasing the difficulties in preventing information from spreading.

Companies are using more Web 2.0 tools like wikis, blogs, social networks, and mash-ups to open up their innovation process. These new tools include blogs, social networking applications, RSS, social networking tools, and wikis. The three year Web 2.0 Global Survey Result from McKinsey showed that 69 percent of the respondents have benefited from the application of Web 2.0 technologies.

"When asked respondents about the business benefits their companies have gained as a result of using Web 2.0 technologies, they most often report greater ability to share ideas; improved access to knowledge experts; and reduced costs of communications, travel, and operations. Many respondents also say Web 2.0 tools have decreased the time to market for products and have had the effect of improving employee satisfaction." Open innovation in SME-networks enabled by Web 2.0 applications can foster the exchange of creativity and innovative ideas within a network of SMEs and hence catalyze new forms of innovation processes among its participants. It's fast becoming a Web 2.0 business world.

Ideas and collaboration are the fuel for innovation. The early adopters of Web 2.0 philosophies and approaches are gaining competitive advantage by fostering innovation and responsiveness to customer and marketplace trends and by simplify communication and collaboration among members of the extended value chain. Web 2.0 technologies can help accelerate time to market by improving the usability of enterprise assets. Web 2.0 is about using the Internet creatively, as a platform to foster innovation, speed and simplicity.

Role of University-Industry Interactions in Innovations

In order for countries to be prosperous the countries in the globalised economy, must be a leader in innovation. Innovation adds value to the business, allowing adaptation to new challenges and promising sustainability in the face of changing market demands and growing environmental and economic pressures. Innovation is thought of as the successful application of new ideas or knowledge and in this context universities must be seen as key resources for the generation of new knowledge that can prime innovative commercial activity. Universities produce effective research and this extensive knowledge base should be harnessed for economic benefit. Indeed in the 21st century universities will be the drivers of economic prosperity in the same way that textile mills were at the outset of industrial age. This comment may be particularly pertinent with the increasing trend for the companies to adopt open innovation models under which they are looking to external organizations to feed their R&D pipelines.

Universities have, of course always been synonyms with ground-breaking research and discoveries. However, historically, a lack of structured interaction between universities and industry has often led to ideas diffusing out of institutions in an unmanaged manner. Although this is one route for dissemination, it has been recognized that a more formal proactive approach to the transfer of knowledge from academic environments to industry is more likely to lead to successful collaborations, mutual benefit and long term sustainable relationships. While teaching and research remain at the heart of every university, realizing the social and economic benefits of this core activity is vital to ensuring the future prosperity of the nation.

Effective knowledge transfer will allow universities to play a critical role in future innovation ecosystem. The ability to commercialize knowledge at an accelerated pace induces firms to identify new sources of knowledge production and this can be achieved by participating in a broader collaborative effort. Industry university relationships emerge not as a substitute to corporate R&D but as a complementary activity. As a consequence, we see the emergence of new and more flexible "triple helix" models of knowledge generation with an increased orientation towards the exploitation of publicly funded research, often with new revenues for the universities usually thorough intellectual property right (IPR) licensing.

The output from the academic research is diffused to the non academic through patents, licenses and practical applications which has a positive contribution to economic performance the nation. Research by Adams et al. (2001) suggests that collaboration with academics has more complementary than substitute character in relation to company–internal R&D activities and that university collaboration has a positive impact on the ratio: numbers of patents awarded per R&D spend. So an important source of knowledge and ideas to open innovation processes of firms are universities. The industry university collaborations can build dynamic capabilities and can generate lower transaction cost with less risk than alliances between firms.

The relationships with universities are a vehicle to build up new skills and to develop knowledge .Small scale industries which are more concerned for their survival, can gain cost efficient access to university facilities to advance technologies that support their core. By supporting academic R&D companies can gain access to up to date knowledge in new fields of science and technology and obtain access to potential new scientific employees and can get answers to specific scientific problems that their internal R&D labs cannot develop as efficiently.

University–industry linkages can play a crucial role in technological innovation for the developing countries. Manufacturing and service companies can gain access to appropriate and cheaper technologies and become more competitive in the world market place. Industry university research consortia can provide an effective means of pursuing research on next generation technology. It seems clear that university research and research consortia can offer an important source of breakthrough innovation. Students from universities with industry ties are better prepared for industry jobs.

Challenges to Open Innovations

There is a general assumption that though open innovation increases the potential creativity in the innovation process, it also increases the complexity involved in managing the process. The complexity becomes higher both because of the increased number of actors involved, and the fact that the organization is no longer itself in control. An open innovation process demands that managers can handle both the inside and the outside of the organization. For any organization effective leadership play an important role in the process of innovation. There should be support from the top level leadership to effectively carry out the firm's innovation process. What kind of leadership style (e.g. transformational, transactional, controlled schizophrenic, political) is needed in open innovation and how this is influencing the members of the innovation process is still a big question.

Motivation is play an important role in the process of innovation. The interesting question to be answered is what keeps motivating people to generate and contribute in an open innovation approach. It is important to tackle NIH syndrome. Open innovation may increase the risk of leakage of proprietary knowledge and involuntary spill-overs.

Other potential disadvantages are the extra costs of managing co-operation with external partners, the loss of control, the adverse impact on the flexibility of the company, the dependence and possible over-dependence on external partners, and the potential opportunistic behaviour of partners. Intellectual property theft is typically identified as the most important risk of global innovation networks. Unique knowledge may be revealed to external partners who could later become competitors or who could make better use of the fruits of the venture or the know-how.

Working closely with external partners can create uncertainty about how the benefit of technology collaboration is to be appropriated. SMEs may be confronted with larger risks in collaborating with larger companies because of their typically smaller resources and limited expertise in intellectual property rights (IPR) issues. The effective management of intellectual property (IP) is therefore crucial, not only in identifying useful external knowledge but especially to capture the value of a firm's own IP rights. In the past, IP management was often relatively closed since intellectual property was mainly created and used internally, and intellectual property protection was used to prevent or block off competitive moves.

Conclusion

Innovation has become a key factor for the economic success of countries and a prerequisite for sustainable development. In a complex and highly competitive global market, companies have to innovate and develop commercially viable products and services faster than ever. To meet these new challenges, companies adopt new approaches to their innovation strategies and processes. Confronted with increasing global competition and rising research and development (R&D) costs, companies can no longer survive on their own R&D efforts but look for new, more open, modes of innovation.

Companies' innovation activities are increasingly international, and they are embracing "open innovation"– collaborating with external partners, whether suppliers, customers or universities, to keep ahead of the game and get new products or services to market before their competitors Companies are also found to be more active in licensing and selling results of their own innovation to third parties. Uncertainty and recession often forces companies to cut R&D, but as they should refocus on the core. But innovation need not go by the wayside. By placing certain assets and projects outside the walls, companies can actually preserve opportunities for overcoming uncertain situations and future growth while they shore up the fortress. Anyone not working on innovative projects today is simply rearranging chairs on the deck of the Titanic.

References

Allen, T. (1977), Managing the Flow of Technology: Technological Information within the R&D Organization, Cambridge, MA: The MIT Press.

Argyris, C. and Schon, D. (1978) Organizational Learning: Theory, Method and Practice. London: Addison.

Wesley, Technology Transfer and the Dissemination of Technological Innovation.

Bekkers, R., Duysters, G. and Verspagen, B. (2002), Intellectual property rights, strategic technology agreements and market structure: the case of GSM. *Research Policy,* 31, 7, 1141-1161.

Blumenthal, David, Michael Gluck, Karen Seashore Louis, Michael A. Stoto, and David Wise (1986), 'University-Industry Research Relationships in Biotechnology: Implications for the University', *Science,* 232 (4756), 1361-1366.

Chesbrough, H., 2003a, Open Innovation: The new imperative for creating and profiting from technology, (Harvard Business School Publishing: Boston, MA).

Chesbrough, H., 2003b. "The Era of Open Innovation", *Sloan Management Review,* Vol. 44, #3, (Spring):35-41.

Chesbrough, H., 2003c. "Open Innovation: How Companies actually do it," *Harvard Business Review,* Vol. 81 (7), July, pp.12-14.

Chesbrough, H., Vanhaverbeke, W., and J. West, 2006, Open Innovation: Researching a New Paradigm, Oxford University Press.

Cohen, W. M. and Levinthal, D. A. (1990), Absorptive capacity: a new perspective on learning and innovation. *Administrative Science Quarterly,* 35, 128-152.

Cohen, Wesley M and David A. Levinthal (1989), 'Innovation and Learning: The Two Faces of R&D', *The Economic Journal,* 99(397), 569-596.

Collins, Steven and Hikoji Wakoh (2000), 'Universities and Technology Transfer in Japan: Recent Reforms in Historical Perspective', *Journal of Technology Transfer,* 25, 213-222.

Dedrick, J. and J. West, 2004, "An exploratory study into Open Source platform adoption," IEEE Proceedings of the 37th Hawaii International Conference on Systems.

Debackere, K. and R. Veugelers. (2005), 'The role of academic technology transfer organizations in improving industry science links'. *Research Policy,* 34(3), 321-342.

Gerlach, M., 1992. Alliance Capitalism, (University of California Press: Berkeley, CA).

Henderson, Rebecca, Adam B. Jaffe, and Manuel Trajtenberg. (1998a), 'Universities as a source of commercial technology: A detailed analysis of university patenting, 1965-1988', *The Review of Economics and Statistics,* 80(1), 119-127.

Hall, Bronwyn H., Albert N. Link, and John T. Scott (2001), 'Barriers Inhibiting Industry from Partnering with Universities: Evidence from the Advanced Technology Program', *Journal of Technology Transfer,* 26, 87-98.

Mansfield, Edwin (1991), 'Academic research and industrial innovation', *Research Policy,* 20, 1-12.

Mansfield, Edwin (1998), 'Academic research and industrial innovation: An update of empirical findings', *Research Policy,* 26, 773-776.

Narin, Francis, Kimberly S. Hamilton, and Dominic Olivastro (1997), 'The increasing linkage between U.S. technology and public science', *Research Policy,* 26, 317-330.

Nooteboom, B. 1999, Inter-Firm Alliances: Analysis and Design, (Routledge: London).

Porter, Michael, 1990, The Competitive Advantage of Nations, Free Press: New York, NY.

Sakkab, Nabil, 2002, "Connect and Develop Complements Research and Develop at P&G", Research-Technology Management, Vol. 45, (2):38-45.

Schumpeter, J.A. (1934), *The Theory of Economic Development,* Cambridge, Mass., Harvard University Press.

Siegel, Donald S., David A. Waldman, Leanne E. Atwater, and Albert N. Link (2003), 'Commercial knowledge transfers from universities to firms: improving the effectiveness of university-industry collaboration', *Journal of High Technology Management Research,* 14, 111-133.

Teece, David J. (1986), 'Profiting from technological innovation: Implications for integration, collaboration, licensing and public policy', *Research Policy,* 15, 285-305.

Von Hippel, Eric (1988), *The Sources of Innovation.* New York: Oxford University Press. Von Hippel, Eric, 2005. Democratizing Innovation, (Cambridge, MA: MIT Press) Yin, R., 1988. Case Study.

Zucker, Lynee G., Michael R. Darby, and Jeff S. Armstrong, (2002),

'Commercializing Knowledge: University Science, Knowledge Capture, and Firm Performance in Biotechnology', *Management Science,* 48(1), 138-152.

13

Corporate Governance and Investor Protection in Uncertain Situations

Harish S. Vangala

The debate on corporate governance in India draws heavily on Anglo-American experience, literature and practice. The Globalization and growing capital market with active presence of Foreign Institutional Investors, banks, mutual funds, and general public has reshaped Indian business and placed huge premium on transparency in corporate dealings. Indian corporate sector regulators too, have been quick to assimilate and apply international practices based on the latest available knowledge.

Banaji and Mody (2001) described corporate governance in India as a phenomenon of global consistency, since the governance norms illustrate a careful adoption of best practices elsewhere, therefore reflecting international convergence of CG standards. This view of global consistency ostensibly justifiable in the current internationalized context as few powerful institutional investors straddle diverse international markets and seek for regulatory and business regimes that minimize risks to their investments. Investor protection thus, turned out to be crucial from regulatory standpoint to check managerial expropriation and to align interests of the agents (managers) and principals (shareholders).

At the outset, it is befitting to explain the uniqueness of corporate governance problem in India which may not fully subscribe to widely accepted view that contemporary capitalism is characterized by a conflict between shareholders and management. Banaji (2006) explained that general view on agency problem has to be drastically modified when applied to markets like India, where shareholding remain concentrated in the hands of family business groups who control the management of 'their companies.

These controlling or 'dominant' shareholders do not face a problem of accountability in the same way that shareholders in the Anglo-American markets do because they are also the managers in the companies they control. In this sense the classical agency problem holds no ground in the majority of Indian companies.

However, a vast majority of these companies are public corporations i.e. listed on the local stock exchanges, so here issue of governance becomes, as Varma (1997) described, potentially a conflict between two categories of shareholders: non-controlling and controlling or minority and dominant. It has also been time and again observed that in India (like in many countries), expropriation of minority shareholders and creditors by controlling shareholders is extensive. The controlling shareholders or managers expropriate the returns on investment that actually belongs to other investors who bare the risk of financing the firm. Thus, Corporate Governance reforms in India, to a large extent, aims to set of mechanisms through which outside investors protect themselves against expropriation by the insiders.

Corporate Governance Regulations and Investor Protection

As the cornerstone of liberalization, the idea of corporate governance does not work in abstract but as a parallelogram of forces, in which the regulatory mediation is a crucial and intrinsic for investor protection. The regulations after 1998 reflected both state-based and market-based approach to uphold fundamental rights of shareholders and to enhance management oversight thereby protecting investors. Corporate governance practices for investor protection are central in Company Law reforms and SEBI regulations.

Company Law and Investor Protection: The Indian company law provides that shareholders may seek government intervention to enforce their ownership rights. The courts in this connection can wand up the concerned company if it is equitable and just rather than letting the value of minority shareholders be flittered away by the enrichment of dominant shareholder.

Minority shareholders might as well approach courts if the company affairs have being conducted in a manner prejudicial to the interests of the company or its shareholders.

Company law provides for regular accounting information to be supplied to the shareholders along with a report by auditors. It also requires that company must furnish all material facts to shareholders in case of special resolutions on which shareholders approval is needed.

These disclosure practices as Varma (1997) observed does not by itself provide the means to block the dominant shareholders. However, disclosure enhances investor awareness and preparedness in terms of managing investment risks. It is another prerequisite for the minority shareholders to exercise means available to them.

In addition to this, the minority shareholders can approach company law tribunals in case of certain wrongdoings like violation of fundamental shareholders' rights, vote for directors, share transfers, to participate in shareholder's meetings, to receive dividends, insider trading and self dealing by the management, substantial acquisitions and mergers etc.

Securities Regulation and Investor Protection: Securities and Exchange Board of India (SEBI) has taken a number of initiatives to enhance management oversight, audit function, board procedures, disclosure and reporting standards, compliance certification etc to positively improve corporate governance practices and thereby to create better investor protection regime.

The SEBI recently has mandated Indian companies as part of listing agreements to provide timely information regarding financial and non-financial aspects of the company to the general investors. The disclosure practices have significantly improved in the sense that companies not only provide financial performance but also about strengths, competitive position in the given industry, opportunities and threats etc. alongside, SEBI also has set conditions for internet based trading that is to be followed by stockbrokers working with several stock exchanges in India.

These conditions relate to operational integrity, system capacity, signature authentication, client-broker relationship, contract notes, trade confirmation, risk management, network security protocols and interface standards. SEBI has also directed stockbrokers to display information related to investor protection on their websites.

Alongside, SEBI also proposed tougher disclosure norms to discipline defaulting companies, which are not complying with the listing norms.

SEBI also implemented Clause 49 of listing agreements in 2006 based on recommendations of the quadrilateral of Indian corporate governance reports (CII Desirable Code-Kumar Mangalam Birla Committee-Naresh Chandra Committee- N.R. Narayana Murthy Committee) that placed a huge premium on 'transparency and accountability' in Indian corporate practices. These reports adhere to the regime of internationally best practices like board procedures, accounting standards, financial reporting, disclosure and transparency, responsibility to shareholders and other stakeholders.

The SEBI also vested with more powers for investor protection and has power to ask fraudulent companies pay compensation to the investors. SEBI can not only fine the company and de-list it from the bourses but also debar the directors and attach the assets of these fraudulent companies. It has also tightens investor complaint norms for Mutual Funds. Along with this, the 'Disclosure and Investor Protection (DIP) guidelines' ere amended to enhance streaming lining of Initial Price Offerings (IPOs), to give more clarity on provisions relating to minimum promoters' contribution for the purpose of public issues etc. SEBI also intervened to tackle the dominant shareholder by imposing pricing rule on 'preferential allotments'.

Another decisive initiative for investor protection has come in the form of setting up Investor Education and Protection Fund which SEBI started in October 1 of 2001. The fund was started with an initial corpus of ₹ 700 crore which, will be invested for providing investor education through multimedia publicity, seminars and conferences. It will also be used to take care of the distressed individual investors. The Fund enhances Investor protection in India as it protects the interest of small shareholders and enables them to make well-informed choices in view of repeated stock market crashes. The amounts in unpaid dividend accounts of companies, application money received by companies for allotment of any securities and due for refund and matured deposits of companies will be credited into the fund. Only amounts that have remained unclaimed and unpaid for seven years from the date of payment will form part of the fund.

SEBI enacted prohibition of 'insider trading regulations' in 1992 that effectively deal with the menace of insider trading. These regulations prohibited dealing in securities by insiders on the basis of certain price sensitive information. SEBI also has set the tone for introducing a market for corporate control i.e. framing rules for orderly conduct of takeovers. SEBI regulations on 'substantial acquisition and takeover provisions' are based on UK city code on takeovers and mergers, incorporated ways and means to deal with 'inter-se transfers, buyback of shares and creeping regulations'.

The SEBI also favoured a separate legislation for protection of small investors. However, this is highly contested by several academicians, legal experts and finally scrapped by finance ministry in the view of administrative as well as financial constraints. This is an unfortunate move so for as small and retail investors are concerned who in reality forms an integral part, paramount importance for the development of any country.

Challenges to Investor Protection in Uncertainty

The challenges to promoting a good investor protection regime in India faces problems at two different levels i.e., at the firm level and at the extraneous (extra-firm) level. The most striking and commonly agreed challenges of investor protection and corporate governance in India have been the widely perceived (a) independence of board, (b) accounting practices, (c) insider trading, (d) shareholder activism and last but not the least (e) lack of enforcement mechanisms.

Independence of Board: Boardroom independence has become convenient shorthand for whole range of issues about how outside directors are able to manage companies accountably and serve the interests of shareholders. These issues generated considerable interest over past few years for quite obvious reasons that have been somewhat addressed by the capital market regulator and other interested parties. The concerns are again raised with the recent fallout of a largest Indian software firm wherein independent directors with prestigious positions has skewed towards promoters who are indeed minority shareholders of the company. The fiasco happened due to independent directors supporting high risk strategies and insider's greed that explicitly contradicts their role as stewards of corporation with fiduciary responsibilities to shareholders. However, the question of director's independence is not new to India because there have been several instances where directors in family managed firms failed to provide critical review and independent thought.

As an idea, the independent director is independent of management and free of any business or other relationship that could materially interfere with the exercise of their unfettered and independent judgment. But in practice, though independent directors have been elected by shareholders but they were chiefly selected by nominations committee headed by the executive directors of the company. Therefore, independent directors are generally at the behest of management and seldom looked upon themselves as who had a responsibility not to the promoters but to the outside investors and shareholders.

Accounting Practices: The greatest challenge of investor protection in India is the feeble (creative) accounting practices and abysmal disclosures standards. Som (2006) described that the absence of detailed reporting of related party transactions and having no requirements to report in the balance sheet about the investments and loans made by the company to its subsidiaries and associate companies have led to weak investor protection. Alongside, the absence of segmental reporting limits the data required by securities regulators, which give executives considerable leeway to interpret the rules. As a result, the investors may not receive authentic information about sales, profitability metric, depreciation and amortization, capital expenditures etc. for each significant business segment of the company in which they invested.

In the wake of recent IPO scams and biggest Indian corporate governance scandal that clearly illustrated evidences of cosmetic accounting by the companies and inadequacies of the existing system to detect fraudulent practices. The auditor's independence yet again highlighted and overhauling of audit rules became the priority for regulators. However, this will not answer the claims of more than three million retail investors and minority shareholders whose returns on investments had only remained in calculators and personal computers.

Insider Trading: The much celebrated insider trading prohibitions does not necessarily mean that they have effectively led to minority shareholder protection in India. The frequent incidents of insider trading fundamentally undermined investor confidence in fairness and integrity of capital markets and benefited the privileged few while making common investors suffer. The malafide intentions of insider trading can be seen in the numerous case laws like–Hindustan Level Ltd. (HLL) v. SEBI in 1996, Reliance Industries Ltd. v. SEBI in 2001, Dilip Pendse (Tata Finance Ltd.) v. SEBI in

2001, Rakesh Agarwal (Bayer ABS Ltd.) v. SEBI in 2003, Samir Arora (Alliance Capital Mutual Fund Ltd.) v. SEBI in 2003. The instances of insider trading and self dealing in securities can also be noticed in the very recent scandal, where employees and big lenders have sold their ESOPs and equity shares a few days before the acceptance of guilty by the defamed promoter.

A point to bear in mind, that most instances of insider trading have nothing to do with the dominant shareholder. Varma (1997) accorded that many of them involve small trades by junior employees who come to know of price sensitive information. A recent example to this is Pyramid Saimira theatre-a Chennai-based entertainment group. The company's scrip saw wild fluctuations on 23rd December 2008 due to a fake letter from SEBI. In the process few people made huge money at the cost of thousands of retail investors.

Shareholder Activism: The shareholders activism is viewed as representing a continuum of response to corporate performance. The proponents argue that companies with active and engaged shareholders are more likely to be successful in the long-term than others, where as critics say that it is disruptive and in it's extreme form leads to an extortion scheme that weaken strong companies. However, many unanimously agreed (till recently) that in India it is practically non-existent. Som (2006) had stated numerous reasons for the lack of shareholder activism in the Indian equity market. In India promoters typically retain control of companies by owning a small, yet significant, ownership stake in companies. Shares are not owned by promoters and his family and friends are widely dispersed, making it difficult for minority shareholders to voice their concerns. Therefore, even though there are laws empower shareholders controlling 10 percent of equity, the dispersed nature of ownership of shares makes it difficult for minority shareholders to take more active role in the management of the company.

Similarly, the institutional investors like insurance

companies, mutual funds and banks though have significant stakes in Indian companies but are historically have not been the activist shareholders (Banaji, 2000). They had exercised control over firms through the nominee directorships, but the intent was only to protect the interests of the Indian (shareholding) public, not to exercise operational control over firms. As a result, in India there is no large institutional investor engaged in shareholder activism through its investment decisions like Calpers in the United States.

Lack of Regulatory Enforcement Mechanisms: Although laws in India are generally comparable to those in the UK, the judicial system is seen as inadequate to handle the volume of cases being brought to trail. Som (2006) criticized verdict delays and cost of litigation that span over ten to twenty years after the incidences have occurred.

Despite incorporating several positive features at the level of securities market and the regulatory authority, their implementation has proven to be challenging. This is partly because SEBI has insufficient powers to police violations of regulations. SEBI trots out a very lame excuse in case of recurrent IPO scams, saying that it cannot inspect the books and it is responsibility of merchant bankers to ensure that the contents of the prospectus are true. One does not and cannot buy this argument as protecting small investors is SEBI's responsibility and it should not shirk in discharge of the same.

That apart, there are a couple of serious issues of minority shareholder rights which have not got caught the attention of regulators. The first and foremost among them is preferential issuance of equity warrants to promoters. Equity warrant is an instrument allowing the subscriber the option to buy shares in a company at a pre-specified price at or before some future date. In the last few years, a number of listed companies have issued equity warrants to promoters which basically done to shore up the promoter's holding. These warrants have fundamentally denied minority shareholders participation at the same level as the promoter shareholders. In addition to that, the promoters, while subscribing to the warrants, essentially get an option from the company to pay only 10 percent of the equity warrant's value which is a major breach of trust and faith on minority shareholders.

Similarly, no piece of regulation drafted by SEBI has been subjected to sharper criticism than the takeover regulations. The takeover regulations have been criticized both in general terms for skewing the balance in favour of incumbent management (mostly promoters) and indeed making hostile takeovers more difficult. Banaji (2006) perceived the very existence of the code as a watershed in the history of Indian business, and to protect the interests of dominant corporate lobbies who are otherwise worried by the prospect of hostile takeovers.

Conclusion

The recent corporate governance problems at DLF in case of open market buyback offer, de-merger proposal of Macmillan India, delayed disclosure on ownership of Solex pharmaceuticals at Ranbaxy and massive accounting scandal at Satyam computers have undeniably, shook the investor confidence on Indian capital markets. However, a positive trend, in the midst of these transgressions is growing shareholder activism and investor awareness which restored confidence and managed uncertainty.

The recent episode of shareholder activism in Satyam Computer's acquisition plans which has literally forced Satyam computer services to call off its US$ 1.6 twin deal to acquire Maytas Properties and Maytas Infra, controlled by the son's of the company's chairman. This has subsequently resulted in exposing several wrongdoings at the company and generated heightened interest among several interested parties with regard to investor protection. Another instance of shareholder activism in India, can be seen in case of government's decision to part 30 percent of PBT at Gujarat Mineral Development Corporation for socio-economic development. Although state government proposal passed in the AGM, disappointed shareholders have approached high court of Gujarat to claim their right over unpaid dividends.

Likewise, shareholders of Bajaj objected the modus operandi of ownership and share transfer between the disputed Bajaj brothers. The shareholders sought Mumbai high court intervention to critically examine the unfair treatment towards retail investors. The shareholders opposition to the delayed disclosure in case of Solex pharmaceuticals has made the beleaguered promoters of Ranbaxy to reveal ownership issues-who are otherwise, maintained a 'no comment stand' all the while.

The shareholder activism however, may be a positive trend but it should combine with a regulatory re-look at rules governing corporate governance to ensure better investor protection. The need of the hour is to change regulatory mind set from 'best practices' to 'next practices'. The best practices in reality will only lead to mediocrity in haste. Contrary to that, the next practices approach by definition mean 'amplifying weak signals'. The regulators have to amplify weak signals in investor protection, be it legal provisions for quorum at the Annual General Meetings or takeover code or insider trading prohibitions or lack of independent audit function or weak surveillance mechanisms, thereby prefer either 'self regulatory system' or introducing a new 'rule based approach' with effective enforcements. The current politically correct box-ticking approach also needs to transform to an enlightened ethical leadership model for equitable treatment of investors and protection of minority shareholders rights.

References

Banaji, J. (2000), 'Investor capitalism and the reshaping of business in India', Queen Elizabeth House (QEH), working paper 54.

Banaji, J. and Mody, G. (2001), 'Corporate governance and the Indian private sector' Queen Elizabeth House (QEH) working paper 73.

Banaji, J. (2006), 'Thwarting the market for corporate control:

takeover regulation in India', unpublished conference paper, Queen Elizabeth House (QEH), available: http://www.qeh.ox.ac.uk/dissemination/conference-papers/banaji.pdf/ (accessed 24 May 2008).

Institute of International Finance (2006), Task force report on corporate governance in India: an investor perspective, Washington: IIF Equity Advisory Group.

Joshi, V. (2004), 'Corporate governance: the Indian scenario', New Delhi: Foundation Books.

Reed, M. A. (2002), 'Corporate governance reforms in India', Journal of Business Ethics, Vol. 37, pp. 247-268.

Som, S. L. (2006), 'Corporate governance codes in India', Economic and Political Weekly, Vol. 41 (39), pp. 4153-4160.

The World Bank (2004), Report on Observance of Standards and Codes, Washington: the World Bank group, available: http://www.worldbank.org/ifa/rosc_cg_ind.pdf (accessed 7 June 2007).

Varma, R. J. (1997), 'Corporate governance in India: disciplining the dominant shareholder', IIMB Management Review, Vol. 9 (4), pp. 5-18.

14

Corporate Governance in India

S.C. Vetrivel

Good corporate governance helps an organization achieve several objectives. Some of the more important ones include:

1. Developing appropriate strategies that result in the achievement of stakeholder objectives.
2. Attracting, motivating and retaining talent.
3. Creating a secure and prosperous operating environment and improving operational performance.
4. Managing and mitigating risk and protecting and enhancing the company's reputation.

The corporate governance literature in the US and the UK focuses on the role of the Board as a bridge between the owners and the management (Cadbury, 1992; Salmon, 1993; Ward, 1997). In an environment in which ownership and management have become widely separated, the owners are unable to exercise effective control over the management or the Board. The management becomes self perpetuating and the composition of the Board itself is largely influenced by the likes and dislikes of the Chief Executive Officer (CEO). Corporate governance reforms in the US and UK have focused on making the Board independent of the CEO.

Many companies have set up a Nominations Committee of the Board to enable the Board to recruit independent and talented members. There is now increased recognition of the role that the Board could play in providing a strategic vision to the company. The Compensation Committee of the Board has been strengthened to exercise greater control over CEO compensation following widespread complaints that top management pay is disproportionate to performance. There is also a great deal of discussion in the literature on the role of the Board in firing non performing management and in managing the CEO succession. Perhaps the most powerful and well established of the Board committees is the Audit Committee. Apart from acting as a deterrent against financial improprieties and frauds, the Audit Committee also enables the Board to keep a pulse on the financial health of the company.

Turning to the Indian scene, one finds increasing concern about improving the performance of the Board. This is doubtless an important issue, but a close analysis of the ground reality in India would force one to conclude that the Board is not really central to the corporate governance malaise in India. As elaborated at length in this paper, the central problem in Indian corporate governance is not a conflict between management and owners as in the US and the UK, but a conflict between the dominant shareholders and the minority shareholders. The Board cannot even in theory resolve this conflict. One can in principle visualize an effective Board which can discipline the management.

At least in theory, management exercises only such powers as are delegated to it by the Board. But, how can one, even in theory, envisage a Board that can discipline the dominant shareholders from whom the Board derives all its powers? Some of the most glaring abuses of corporate governance in India have been defended on the principle of "shareholder democracy" since they have been sanctioned by resolutions of the general body of shareholders. The Board is indeed powerless to prevent such abuses. It is indeed self evident that the remedies against these abuses can lie only outside the company itself.

It is useful at this point to take a closer look at corporate governance abuses by dominant shareholders in India. The problem of the dominant shareholder arises in three large categories of Indian companies. First are the public sector units (PSUs) where the government is the dominant (in fact, majority) shareholder and the general public holds a minority stake (often as little as 20 percent). Second are the multinational companies (MNCs) where the foreign parent is the dominant (in most cases, majority) shareholder. Third are the Indian business groups where the promoters (together with their friends and relatives) are the dominant shareholders with large minority stakes, government owned financial institutions hold a comparable stake, and the balance is held by the general public.

The governance problems posed by the dominant shareholders in these three categories of companies are slightly different. Against this background, this paper highlights corporate governance practices and abuses by dominant shareholders in India. More specifically, the governance problems in the Public Sector Units (PSUs), the MNCs and the Indian business companies are discussed in detail in the paper. The role of the regulator and the capital market as outside forces is also included.

Public Sector Units (PSUs)

The governance structures of PSUs date back to the days when they were typically wholly owned by the government and were merely an extended arm of the state. These structures allowed the administrative departments in the concerned ministry to exercise virtually complete control over the functioning of these enterprises. It is now evident that these structures are incompatible with the efficient and successful operation of the PSUs in an increasingly competitive and deregulated economy. These issues are discussed extensively in literature (Vittal, 1997).

It is interesting however to observe how totally irrelevant the Board really is in the governance of the PSUs today. The Board has no role to play in any of the areas where US and UK reformers have sought to strengthen the Board. The Board has very little say in the selection of the CEO or in the composition of the Board. The government as the majority shareholder takes these decisions through the concerned ministry with the help of the Public Enterprises Selection Board. The Board cannot fire the CEO nor can it vary his compensation package. As far as audit is concerned, again the dominant role is that of the Comptroller and Auditor General (CAG).

There is very little that an Audit Committee could add to what the CAG does. In many PSUs, the Board may still be powerful on paper because the delegation of financial and operating powers to the CEO is very limited. Many operating decisions have to be brought to the Board for decision making. This does not however make for an effective Board because it pushes the Board into "managing" rather than "directing". There is a clear difference between directing and managing, and the Board's legitimate function is directing (Balasubramaniam, 1997). The current governance structure allows the Board to play a highly obstructive role if it chooses by opposing the CEO operational matters. What it does not allow the Board to do is to play a meaningful strategic role since all strategic decisions are taken by the dominant shareholder through the concerned ministry.

Multinational Corporations (MNCs)

Government regulations require most MNCs in India to operate through subsidiaries which are not 100 percent owned by the parent. In the 1970s, the government enacted a law limiting foreign ownership in most industries to 40 percent while allowing 51 percent in a few high technology areas. This law was liberalized in the 1990s and now 51 percent is permitted in most industries while 74 percent or even 100 percent ownership is allowed in some cases. These regulations have created severe corporate governance problems in several key areas as may be seen from the examples below.

In the 1970s, MNCs were forced to issue shares to the Indian public to comply with the law. The controls that then existed on pricing of public issues meant that these issues were at substantial discounts to the market price. In the 1990s when the law permitted higher foreign ownership, these MNCs raised the foreign stake by issuing shares at very deep discounts to the market price. This obviously meant a large loss to the minority shareholders. One particular case where shares were issued to the parent at less than one-tenth the market price was analyzed in detail by Barua and Varma (1993a and 1993b).

They calculated that the net gain to the foreign parent after compensating for the loss that it suffered in the 1970s (together with interest thereon at market rates of interest) amounted to over US$ 200 million. This and other similar share issues by MNCs were made with the explicit consent of the shareholders in general meeting. The parent companies with their dominant shareholding were able to get the resolutions passed with impressive majorities. In fact when the government introduced regulations to prevent such preferential issues, the MNCs protested against what they called an assault on "shareholder democracy". Another corporate governance problem arises where the foreign parent has two subsidiaries in India in one of which it holds a higher stake (say 100 percent) while in the other it holds a smaller stake (say 51 percent). The manner in which the MNC structures its business in India between these two subsidiaries is riddled with problems as far as the minority shareholder is concerned. There have been allegations in some cases that the most profitable brands and businesses have been transferred from the long established 51 percent subsidiary to the newly formed 100 percent subsidiary at artificially low prices. This implies a large loss to the minority shareholders of the 51 percent subsidiary who have after all contributed to in equal measure to the investments that were made in the past to build up these businesses to their current dominant position.

Yet another problem is the payments that parent companies increasingly demand for all the services that they provide to their subsidiaries. One well-known example involves a company where the parent has recently started collecting royalties for the use of a brand. In this case, India is actually the principal market for this brand and the Indian company had assiduously cultivated the brand through decades of advertising paid for in part by the minority shareholders. Minority shareholders could only watch in dismay as the royalties knocked off a sizeable chunk of the earnings of the company.

Indian Business Groups

The situation in this category of companies is more complex than in the PSUs and the MNCs where there are clearly defined dominant shareholders. In the Indian business groups, the concept of dominant shareholders is more amorphous for two reasons. First, the promoters' shareholding is spread across several friends and relatives as well as corporate entities. It is sometimes difficult to establish the total effective holding of this group. Second, the aggregate holding of all these entities taken together is typically well below a majority stake. In many cases, the promoter may not even be the largest single shareholder.

What makes the promoters the dominant shareholders is that a large chunk of the shares is held by state owned financial institutions which have historically played a passive role. So passive have they been that in the few cases where they did become involved in corporate governance issues, they were widely seen as acting at the behest of their political masters and not in pursuance of their financial interests. So long as the financial institutions play a passive role, the promoters are effectively dominant shareholders and are able to get general body approval for all their actions.

This allows the promoters to play all the games that dominant shareholders play in PSUs and MNCs—structuring of businesses and transfer of assets between group companies, preferential allotments of shares to the dominant shareholder, payments for "services" to closely held group companies and so on. But there are a number of new games too. Over several decades of the command economy, a large parallel black economy has developed in India where transactions are carried out in cash and are not recorded in the books of accounts. Some industries were at one stage so strongly permeated by the black economy that it was almost impossible to carry on business without using black money.

Though there have been several honourable exceptions, many Indian business groups have succumbed to the lure of black money. The literature on black money views it primarily as a means of cheating the government of its legitimate dues. But the fact that it is not accounted for in the company's books means that it is also cheating the minority shareholders. Quite often when a company makes losses in its books, the true picture of the business is much healthier because of the profits pouring in the form of black money.

It is a standard joke among bankers in India that there are many financially sick companies but no financially sick promoters. The situation in some of these business groups is strongly reminiscent of what the father of economics, Adam Smith, wrote over two centuries ago about the rampant corruption in the East India Company: "Frequently, a man of great fortune, sometimes even a man of small fortune is willing to purchase a thousand pounds share in India stock merely for the influence which he expects to acquire by a vote in the court of proprietors.

It gives him a share, though not in the plunder, yet in the appointment of the plunderers of India...Provided he can enjoy this influence for a few years, and thereby provide for a certain number of his friends, he cares little about the dividend, or even the value of the stock upon which his vote is founded" (Smith, 1776, Book V, Chapter I, Part III, Article 1st). Tax reforms coupled with economic liberalization have tilted the balance away from black money transactions. This is partly because tax rates are now lower, and partly because increasing scale economies make it more difficult to operate with the informal organizational structures and financial arrangements that black money entails. It is to be hoped that tax reforms, deregulation and competition would gradually reduce the role of black money to the point where it is confined to isolated cases of corruption.

Another important corporate governance issue is that of mergers and restructuring of companies in the same group. There have been several instances where the valuation of two group companies for the purpose of merger has been perceived to be biased in favour of one of the companies. It has been alleged that in many of these cases, the promoters had secretly built up large positions in this company as a cheap means of acquiring shares of the merged company. The amorphous nature of the promoter group makes it very difficult to verify these allegations. Mergers are subject to approval by shareholder bodies of both companies as well as judicial review. But shareholder democracy is an empty defence against the dominant shareholder. In addition to the problems of these three shareholders, the regulators also face a number of difficulties with respective CG abuse by the shareholders.

The Regulatory Dilemma

Regulators face a number of difficulties in tackling the problem of corporate governance abuses by the dominant shareholders. In many cases, it is difficult to decide how far the regulator should go in interfering with the normal course of corporate functioning. Some of these problems are highlighted below.

Shareholder Democracy: A much talked about regulatory dilemma is that of balancing the rights of minority shareholders against the principle of shareholder democracy. On closer examination, this regulatory dilemma is not as serious as it might appear at first sight. In many ways, the very term shareholder democracy represents a misguided analogy between political governance and corporate governance. Unlike political governance, corporate governance is primarily contractual in nature, and corporate governance is at bottom a matter of enforcing the spirit of this contractual relationship.

It is important to bear in mind that the relation between the company and its shareholders and the relation between the shareholders *inter se* is primarily contractual in nature. The memorandum and articles of association of the company constitute the core of this contract and the corporate law provides the framework within which the contracts operate. The essence of this contractual relationship is that each shareholder is entitled to a share in the profits and assets of the company in proportion to his shareholding. Flowing from this is the fact that the Board and the management of the company have a fiduciary responsibility towards each and every shareholder and not just towards the majority or dominant shareholder.

Dilemma of Micro-management: Corporate governance abuses perpetrated by a dominant shareholder pose another and far more difficult regulatory dilemma. Regulatory intervention would often imply a micromanagement of routine business decisions. In a competitive world, highly complex business decisions have to be taken quickly and smoothly. Subjecting a large number of these decisions to the process of regulatory review would make a travesty of a free economy. In the name of ensuring that corporate decisions are taken in the best interests of the company as a whole (rather than just the dominant shareholder), the regulator would end up running the company by remote control. The company would then effectively become an extended arm of the state.

Regulatory intervention must perforce be confined to a few clearly defined prohibitions and restrictions that require minimal exercise of regulatory discretion. This approach carries with it the danger that broad prohibitions would also stand in the way of many legitimate business transactions. Some examples of these issues are discussed later in this paper.

Regulatory Response: Company Law

The primary protection to minority shareholders is laid down in the company law. Some of these provisions are the regulatory equivalent of an atom bomb—they are drastic remedies suitable only for the gravest cases of mis-governance.

Protection of Minority Shareholders: Company law provides that a company can be wound up if the Court is of the opinion that it is just and equitable to do so. This is, of course, the ultimate resort for a shareholder to enforce his ownership rights. Rather than let the value of his shareholding be frittered away by the enrichment of the dominant shareholder, he approaches the court to wind up the company and give him his share of the assets of the company. In most realistic situations, this is hardly a meaningful remedy as the break-up value of a company when it is wound up is far less than its value as a "going concern". It is well known that winding up and other bankruptcy procedures usually lead only to the enrichment of the lawyers and other intermediaries involved.

Company law also provides for another remedy if the minority shareholders can show that the company's affairs are being conducted in a manner prejudicial to the interests of the company or its shareholders to such an extent as to make it just and equitable to wind it up. Instead of approaching the Court, they can approach the Company Law Board (now proposed to be renamed as the Company Law Tribunal). The Company Law Tribunal which is a quasi-judicial body can make suitable orders if it is satisfied that it is just and equitable to wind up the company on these grounds, but that such winding up would unfairly prejudice the members.

In particular, the Tribunal may regulate the conduct of the company's affairs in future, order the buyout of the minority shareholders by the other shareholders or by the company itself, set aside or modify certain contracts entered into by the company, or appoint a receiver. The Tribunal could also provide for some directors of the company to be appointed by the Central Government, or by proportional representation. The Tribunal normally entertains such complaints only from a group of shareholders who are at least one hundred in number or constitute 10 percent of the shareholders by number or by value.

The powers given to the Company Law Tribunal are perhaps more effective remedies than the power of winding up which is vested in the Courts, though one may wonder whether these powers are too sweeping. However, their scope is limited to very extreme cases of mis-governance where it is just and equitable to wind up a company.

Special Majority: Another safeguard in the company law is the requirement that certain major decisions have to be approved by a special majority of 75 percent or 90 percent of the shareholders by value. This may not be an effective safeguard where the dominant shareholders hold a large majority of the shares so that they need to get the approval of only a small chunk of minority shareholders to reach the 75 percent level. Even otherwise, it may not be a sufficient safeguard if the process of conducting shareholder meetings is not conducive to broader participation by a large section of the shareholding public. The Indian system does not allow for postal ballots. Effective participation by small shareholders is possible only if there is a cost effective way of waging a proxy campaign. This would enable dissenting shareholders to collect proxies from others and prevent measures which are prejudicial to the minority shareholders.

Information Disclosure and Audit: Company law provides for regular accounting information to be supplied to the shareholders along with a report by the auditors. It also requires that when shareholder approval is sought for various decisions, the company must provide all material facts relating to these resolutions including the interest of directors and their relatives in the matter. Disclosure does not by itself provide the means to block the dominant shareholders, but it is a prerequisite for the minority shareholders to be able to exercise any of the other means available to them. Disclosure is also a vital element in the ability of the capital market to exercise its discipline on the issuers of capital.

Regulatory Response: Securities Law

Historically, most matters relating to the rights of shareholders were governed by the company law. Over the last few decades, in many countries, the responsibility for protection of investors has shifted to the securities law and the securities regulators at least in case of large listed companies. In India, the Securities and Exchange Board of India (SEBI) was set up as a statutory authority in 1992, and has taken a number of initiatives in the area of investor protection.

Information Disclosure: As discussed above, the company law itself mandates certain standards of information disclosure both in prospectuses and in annual accounts. SEBI has added substantially to these requirements in an attempt to make these documents more meaningful. Some of these disclosures are important in the context of dealing with the dominant shareholder. One of the most valuable is the information on the performance of other companies in the same group, particularly those companies which have accessed the capital markets in the recent past. This information enables investors to make a judgment about the past conduct of the dominant shareholder and factor that into any future dealings with him.

Promoters' Contribution and Lock in: Another aspect of the SEBI regulations is that in most public issues, the promoters (typically the dominant shareholders) are required to take a minimum stake of about 20 percent in the capital of the company and to retain these shares for a minimum lock-in period of about three years. At first sight, it might appear to deal with a problem closer to the US and UK predicaments where the management has only a minuscule stake in the company. This however is not so at all. The SEBI regulations provide an exemption to those companies where there is no identifiable promoter group, that is to say, no dominant shareholder. In other words, if these regulations were copied by US and UK regulators, they would not make much of a difference to most of the companies in those countries as these companies would typically fall in this category of not having an identifiable promoter group.

Pricing of Preferential Share Allotments: Another area in which SEBI has intervened to tackle the dominant shareholder, is the pricing rule that it has imposed on preferential allotments. Company law itself provides that new issue of shares must be rights issues to existing shareholders unless the shareholders in general meeting allow the company to issue shares to the general public or to other parties. As has been pointed out earlier in this paper, the requirement of shareholder approval is quite meaningless when there is a dominant shareholder. Many dominant shareholders (both Indian and foreign) responded to the liberalization of the Indian economy by making preferential allotments to themselves at a small fraction of the market price. In 1994, SEBI issued new guidelines on preferential allotment that prohibited preferential allotments at a price lower than the average market price during the last six months.

In short, this example shows very well how regulatory interventions designed to discipline the dominant shareholder always run the risk of attempting to micro-manage the affairs of the company. This is a dilemma that simply will not go away.

Insider Trading: Securities regulators around the world have framed various regulations to deal with the problem of insider trading. The existence of regulations does not necessarily mean that they are enforced. In South Africa, for example, a recent report on insider trading pointed out that in the quarter century that the insider trading law has been in existence in that country, there has not been a single prosecution (King, 1997). The situation is not very much better in many other countries. However, in the United States and the United Kingdom there have been a large number of well publicized and successful actions against insider trading.

Most instances of insider trading have nothing to do with the dominant shareholder. Many of them involve small trades by junior employees who come to know of price sensitive information. In a few instances, insider trading may be indulged in by directors and other senior employees. In the context of this paper, however, the interesting cases are large scale trades by the dominant shareholder. Market gossip has long speculated on the prevalence of such trades in the build up to large mergers especially between group companies. Some promoters have merged small companies in which they have a large stake into a larger more widely held company at a swap ratio which is highly unfavourable to the widely held company. These allegations have been difficult to prove in most instances as the promoters can act through numerous friends, relatives and other fronts. When SEBI recently initiated action for insider against a large multinational in a somewhat different situation, the action proved to be highly controversial and the ultimate resolution of this case remains uncertain.

Takeovers: Instead of directly exploiting all the privileges that his controlling block gives him, the dominant shareholder can choose to sell his entire holding to somebody else. In a well functioning market for corporate control, he can expect to get a premium over the price equal to the present value of all the privileges that the dominant shareholder can enjoy in future. The take-over regulations in India require that a slice of this cake be shared with other shareholders. The acquirer of a controlling block of shares must make an open offer to the public for at least 20 percent of the issued share capital of the target company at a price not below what he paid of the controlling block. Of course, if more than 20 percent of the shareholders want to sell at that price, the acquirer is bound to accept only 20 percent on a pro-rata basis.

Discipline of the Capital Market

Corporate governance is such a burning issue for regulators that it is often forgotten that the capital market by itself exercises considerable discipline over the dominant shareholder. Minority investors may rarely attend shareholder meetings where the dice are loaded against them, but they are continuously voting with their wallets. They can vote with their wallets in the primary market by refusing to subscribe to any fresh issues by the company. They can also sell their shares in the secondary market thereby depressing the share price. A cash rich company with no foreseeable need for additional funds can be relatively unconcerned about this kind of action by minority shareholders. Even in this case, however, the dominant shareholder (unless he holds a clear 51 percent) faces the risk of being ousted in a take-over battle. A depressed share price makes the company an attractive take-over target. A well functioning market for corporate control makes this threat more real.

The most powerful impact of voting with the wallet is on companies with large growth opportunities that have a constant need to approach the capital market for additional funds. For these companies, shareholder disenchantment can be very expensive. In fact, in equilibrium, the price at which such companies can raise funds from the public will reflect the true worth of the business less the present value of all privileges that the market expects the dominant shareholder to extract in future. If these market expectations are fulfilled, the minority shareholders have little cause for complaint since they end up getting what they paid for. The market may be fooled once or twice, but pretty soon they can form a fair idea of the nature of the dominant shareholders and what they are likely to do.

It is quite common for investors in India to value a scrip using a standard financial model (like the price-earnings model, dividend discount model or discounted cash flow model) and then to subtract a "management discount" of 15 percent or 20 percent depending on the particular management group involved. This management discount reflects the present value of all future losses to the minority shareholder from governance abuses by the dominant shareholder. This impact is further strengthened when the minority shareholders are large institutions (both domestic and foreign) who, in a sense, act as the gatekeepers to the capital market. When they vote with their wallets and their pens, they have an even more profound effect on the ability of the companies to tap the capital markets. Indian companies that opened their doors to foreign investors have seen this power of the minority shareholder in very stark terms.

These investors can perhaps be fooled once as easily as any other intelligent investor, but the next time around, the company finds that its ability to tap the international markets with an offering of Global Depository Receipts (GDRs) or other instrument has practically vanished. In the mid-1990s, company after company in India has woken up in this manner to the power that minority shareholders enjoy when they also double up as gatekeepers to the capital market. The role of gatekeepers is quite crucial when a company accesses the capital market infrequently. When a company comes to the market for the first time, there is no track record on the basis of which the market can assess the damage that the dominant shareholder is likely to do. In well-developed capital markets, large investment banks perform the gate keeping function of making a judgment about the company and its management.

Conclusion

The structural characteristics of the Indian corporate sector make the corporate governance problems in India very different from that in say the US or the UK. The governance issue in the US or the UK is essentially that of disciplining the management who have ceased to be effectively accountable to the owners. The solution has been to improve the functioning of vital organs of the company like the board of directors. The problem in the Indian corporate sector (be it the public sector, the multinationals or the Indian private sector) is that of disciplining the dominant shareholder and protecting the minority shareholders.

A board which is accountable to the owners would only be

one which is accountable to the dominant shareholder; it would not make the governance problem any easier to solve. Clearly, the problem of corporate governance abuses by the dominant shareholder can be solved only by forces outside the company itself. This paper has discussed the role of two such forces–the regulator (the company law administration as well as the securities regulator) and the capital market. Corporate governance abuses perpetrated by a dominant shareholder pose a difficult regulatory dilemma in that regulatory intervention would often imply a micro-management of routine business decisions. The regulator is forced to confine himself to broad proscriptions which leave little room for discretionary action. Many corporate governance problems are ill suited to this style of regulation.

The capital market on the other hand lacks the coercive power of the regulator. What it has however is the ability to make business judgements and to distinguish between what is in the best interests of the company as a whole as against what is merely in the best interests of the dominant shareholders. The only effective sanction that the market can impose against an offender is to restrict his ability to raise money from the market once again. Denial of market access is a very powerful sanction except where the company is cash rich and has little future needs for funds.

In short, the key to better corporate governance in India today lies in a more efficient and vibrant capital market. Over a period of time, it is possible that Indian corporate structures may approach the Anglo-American pattern of near complete separation of management and ownership. At that stage, India too would have to grapple with governance issues like empowerment of the board. Until then, these issues which dominate the Anglo-American literature on corporate governance are of peripheral relevance to India. This assumes all the more significance in certain situations across the world. Companies across the global in general and in India in particular need to keep these issues in mind while dealing with corporate governance.

References

Bajaj, R., Chairman, (1997), *Draft code on Corporate Governance,* Confederation of Indian Industry.

Balasubramaniam, N. (1997), "Towards Excellence in Board Performance", *The IIMB, Management Review*, January-March, 67-84.

Barua, S.K. and Varma, J.R. (1993a), "FERA in Reverse Gear; MNCs Strike Gold", *Economic Times*, November 12, 1993.

Barua, S.K. and Varma, J.R. (1993b), "MNCs Must be Subjected to SEBI Acquisition Code", *Economic Times*, November 17, 1993.

Cadbury, A., Chairman, (1992), *Report on the Financial Aspects of Corporate Governance.*

King, M. E., Chairman, (1997), *Report on Insider Trading.*

Pound J. (1993), "The fight for good governance", *Harvard Business Review,* January-February, 76-83.

Pozen, R.C. (1994), "Institutional investors: reluctant activists", *Harvard Business Review,* January-February, 140-149.

Salmon, W.J. (1993), "Crisis prevention: how to gear up your board", *Harvard Business Review,* January-February, 68-75.

Smith, A. (1776), *An Inquiry into the Nature and Causes of the Wealth of Nations*, Modern Library Edition, New York, Random House, 1937, 1965.

15

Managing Uncertainty through Self-help Marketing (SHM)

B.K. Swain

SHM: An Introduction

Over the last few years, successful experiences in providing finance to small entrepreneurs and producers demonstrates that poor people when given access to responsive and timely financial services at market rates, repay their loans and use the proceeds to increase their income and assets. This is not surprising since the only realistic alternative for them is to borrow from informal market at an interest much higher than market rates. Community banks, and credit groups operating at grass root levels around the world have shown that these micro-enterprise loans can be profitable for borrowers and for the lenders, making micro-finance one of the most effective poverty reducing strategies. Through proper implementation and effective marketing strategies, micro-finance has the capacity to rejuvenate the economy of a country.

In this perspective, we may observe that SHGs have contributed substantially to the economic growth of their members in all the four southern states of India. The members' incomes have increased to manage their domestic expenses effectively as well as enable them to make a surplus to increase the scale of operations of activities undertaken by self-help groups (SHGs). Though most of the members are aware that without large scale marketing of their products, their ongoing occupation would be in danger, yet few groups are fortunate to link their business with the available marketing channel. Due to low level of output and lack of brand support, even their long standing market connection often dismantled because of demand fluctuation as well as due to disruption in supply channel.

In this scenario and as an exception, the SHGs in several blocks in the district of Coimbatore have evolved a new technique called Self-help Marketing (SHM) strategy to dispose their products by first catering to the needs of their group members and federations. By giving first priority and preference to the demands of their co-members, the urgent need of selling their products for earning a minimum base level of income has been mitigated to a great extent. Moreover, the needs for marketing the products through engagement of salesperson have also been reduced to a great extent as co-SHG members do not require any description or explanation about the nature and quality of the products. Presently, there are several products which are marketed through this SHM strategy. Against this background the paper highlights how the concept of self help marketing can be used to manage uncertain situations in India. Around a dozen of those products are discussed below, giving a fair idea about the concept of SHM.

Manure from Domestic Wastes

By using effective micro-organism technology, manure from domestic wastes is produced by several SHGs in the Periyakottai Panchayat of Udumalpet Block. By using this technology, the members are capable of filtering organic material separately from ordinary domestic wastes. Twenty five members of two SHGs are engaged in this activity and are able to produce more than ten tons of natural manure per day. Initially, the products were not sold quickly and the stocks were piled up for more than a fortnight. Subsequently, the group members approached other SHGs members who are engaged in vegetable gardening, horticulture, paddy cultivation etc. and requires substantial amount of manure for their fields. Observing the quality of natural manure and educated by the local extension officials about the uses of natural manure to protect their land from ill-effects of chemical fertilizer, the adjoining groups came forward to lift the manure from these two groups, who are actively engaged in this activity. Within a few days, a stage finally arrived wherein these two groups were unable to supply manure and cater to the ever growing demands for natural manure of several groups in the district. In turn, the existing groups had welcome many others groups to join this activity and produce sufficient manure to meet the ever growing demands of the other SHGs group members in particular and the farming community of the district in general.

Local Brand Electronic Stabilizers

Three SHGs in Udumalpet Block are involved in production of "I CARE' local brand Electronic Stabilizers. Few days of professional training to these group members has helped to enter in this hi-tech electronic industry. Though most members in the local federation posses TV and refrigerators in their houses, in turn it is very difficult on their part to purchase costly branded electronic stabilizers to protect their electronic gadgets from electronic supply fluctuations.

This local 'I CARE' brand has created a small revolution as costs of these products are too low and there is a warranty for a long period of around three years. Through SHM strategy, some rebates are invariably provided to these SHG members and the brand has emerged as a highly competitive product due to intensive marketing support by the DRDA functioning in the district. The members of Annai Therasa SHG and Malligai SHGs of Udumalpet Bank have escalated their level of operations for making these stabilizers and each member now earns at least more than ₹ 2000 per month by putting only part-time effort.

Fast-food Service Outlets

About forty self-help groups are involved in the fast food services in the district, which require around ₹ 40,000 of investment per canteen. As the members are trained to prepare food in hygienic manner, there is an upsurge in demand of their tiffin business by the local inhabitants in their respective areas. Needless to add, much marketing effort is not required for mobile canteen except the members have to adhere to their scheduled operating schedule and maintain the quality of food material sold to the general public. The members of all these forty mobile canteens in the district are happily engaged in selling their products to the locals who constitute majority of members from other SHGs operating in this operational area. Each member of these forty SHG now able to earn more than ₹ 100 per day by dedicating only half-a-day of labour for the group activity.

Stone Quarry Mining

Nineteen SHGs run quarries in the District of Coimbatore. Running a store quarry is indeed a bold decision taken by these SHGs and they have proved that this is the most right decision. After linking the supply of chips for construction of concrete roof houses under Indira Awaas Yojana, the groups are hard pressed to meet the demands of several beneficiaries helped under these low cost housing schemes meant for people living at the grass root level.

Mostly the members worked in the morning hours up to 10 a.m. and left to their homes to complete their household chores. Despite putting part-time labour, the group members able to earn more than ₹ 3,000 per month as the cost of stone chips have increased upward recently due to overall increase in constriction work.

The inter-linking of supply through SHM strategy have benefited the members most as they have no idle days and often required to work in the evening hours to meet the demands of other SHG group members.

Community Bio-gas Plants

These are the most creative business constructed and

maintained by number of groups. It not only help in un-interrupted supply of bio-gas for cooking purposes', but also reduces the expenses incurred towards acquiring fuels like kerosene oil, firewood and ordinary coal for cooking purposes. Now-a-days, due to depletion of forest area as a whole, it is very difficult for the local tribal as well as other people under BPL to arrange fuel for their cooking activities. As most of these people keep cattle for farming activities and sell milk in the local market, providing a small quantity of cow dung to the general pool for running a bio-gas plant is not a problem for them.

Hence, effort to run a community bio-gas plant by these groups is itself a commendable job for getting un-interrupted fuel supply for cooking purpose. The beneficiaries have nothing to lose except just to supply a small quantity of cow-dung to the bio-gas plant for getting the gas. Moreover, alternatively there is a provision that if a person does not maintain cattle, then a nominal amount is required to be paid in the month end.

The groups running diary plants usually have more supply of gas and they are marketing these extra gases to other communities and villages located adjacent to their own community. This has not only augmented extra income for these SHG members, but also provided self-sufficiency and hassle-free supply to meet their domestic fuel consumption.

Tailoring and Dress-making Units

Tailoring is a usual and normal activity which is being pursued by many SHGs. But making tailoring a most profitable activity, depend upon the quantum of dress materials ordered by external agencies. There are several textile mills operating in the district headquarters of Coimbatore. Every day these factories throw several tons of cotton wastages in their backyards. The group members collect these materials, sort them, clean them and coloured them to prepare dress materials for the workers of these cotton mills. The refinement and designs they make while preparing these dress materials, is praiseworthy. No one can imagine that quality dresses for workers, usually shirts and trousers are made from these wastages just lying in the backyard of these cotton mills.

Most of the dress materials are not required to be marketed in far-off areas. Even local populace consisting of BPL residents of slum areas and other group members are regular customers of these local materials sold cheaply throughout the year. The concept of SHM is truly imbibed by these group members.

Mango Pulp-making Machine

A single machine has provided sustainable livelihood to more than six SHGs consisting of more than eighty individual members in the district of Coimbatore. This has been proved that providing infrastructure facility is one of the appropriate steps to augment the income of the people remaining under BPL. The mango-pulp making machine is not only handy but easy-to-operate type machine which has given sustainable livelihood to the members for more than six self-help groups. The soft drinks are made hygienically and stored in local made bottles, which are not only tasty but also quite cheaper as compared to other similar brand products like fruity or maaza bottles available in the market.

Earlier the sales were low and it was discouraging the group members as they were not able to get the right price for their products. Subsequently, they decided to adopt the strategy of SHM and supply the products to other group members even at a break-even price to keep their units running. This has paid-off and now other group members are purchasing these delicious drinks, which are available very cheap compared to similar products in the market, especially for distribution in their social functions and village meetings.

Masonry Training for Construction Work

This is not a field where women would have tried their

luck in the past. But, with sincere effort of government functionaries and similar support from officials of some NGOs, women members of some SHGs have gone through a month long masonry training to construct standard latrines in the villages. As 50 percent subsidy is available to the family which wants to own latrines in their backyard under 'Nirmal Gram Puraskar' scheme, many villagers are interested to avail this benefit as provided under the subsidy scheme. Now there is a huge demand for masonry work including hallow-block and pan making to make the scheme a grand success throughout the country.

These women members, after undergoing the necessary training, are first taking up the activities for constriction of latrines in the houses of other group members and members enrolled in their federation. This activity has not only keeping them busy for a long time but also providing good income beyond their expectations. Supporting income on supplying pans and hollow-blocks also helping these members to engage in this activity for longer period and presently this activity has tremendous scope to be picked up by most of the self-help groups. In few months, there is bright scope for more groups to join in this activity.

Paper up Manufacturing

This is easy and can be made by not-so-educated group members. The local demand for paper cups have increased tremendously both during marriage and festival seasons as well as during summer seasons for meeting the demand of local ice-cream companies. The groups operating in the Udmalpet Block have roped in and supplying different sizes of cups to Aavin, an ice-cream company operating in Coimbatore with networks in other districts and towns of Tamil Nadu. The paper cups machine is capable of producing different sizes of cups with different thickness. It can satisfy the needs of different types of customers. Thus, it directly benefits the members to cater to the needs of all type of clients.

But the group members still interested to meet the needs of their local group members first by satisfying their requirements of paper cups for distribution of tea in district federation meetings as well as paper cups for providing water during innumerable social functions. The groups have also planned to make paper plates for eating snacks which have huge demand in the city of Coimbatore. The demand has outreached the supply to such an extent that members have to often work overtime to meet the supply targets fixed by the ice-cream company and the local traders.

Bricks Making

This is a time consuming activity. During the whole process, the group members requires to sustains themselves by borrowing money for consumption purposes from their group funds, however, it is a highly rewarding activity. The cost of bricks has increased three hold during the last five years because of booming construction work. The members received substantial amount at the end of this activity, especially after disposing quality bricks to high class contractors.

Recently, they have exposed the avenue of self-help marketing by approaching the BPL members of various groups who are undertaking constriction of their houses under Indira Awaas Yojana (IAY). It appears, the demand level is so high, that the present eight groups who are engaged in brick making may not able to meet the demand for few years to come. Hence, it is advisable that more groups are encouraged to take up brick making activity in a large scale, at least to meet the major chunk of the local demand.

Fish Processing

This activity has a bright future not because of the fact that long coast of Tamil Nadu produces a robust supply of marine fish, but encouragement of many banks on providing loans for pisciculture and encouraging taking up this activity as one of the major profession. Now, it is not possible to dispose all the fish caught, either in the local market or at far-off markets because extra money and energy required for faster movement of fish, which is a perishable product.

It is a better idea to process the collected fish and preserve it through canning for a longer period. Moreover, canned fish is more in demand by the foreigners who visit the country, as they are comfortable with this type of preserved food. A country like Japan stored around 35 percent of its fish through effective processing technique for future uses.

However, the SHGs are very new to the processing techniques, but this activity is not prohibitive from any angle. The groups in Coimbatore purchase fish from local market, procure and canned through preservative as well as try to dispose as much as possible in the local market. Though initially not very successful, subsequently the group members tried to convince the federation to process the fish produced by other groups and share the benefits by disposing the final products in major towns. The federation has new supported the idea and helped the groups even to supply un-tinned processed fish among other group members who want to purchase this item available locally. It appears the activity has a fair chance to grow rapidly and leave a good surplus in the hands of the members.

Tractor Operations

Tractors operated by the SHGs in agricultural activities in the Udumalpet Block of Coimbatore district. Initially, the group members able to acquire a tractor through bank loan by paying the margin money to the bank. With their dedicated efforts and by making the tractor available for hire in their own village as well as in nearby villages for transport and ploughing activities, the members were able to repay the loans within three years and managed to purchase another new tractor to carry out their activities at a higher scale.

The requirement of the tractor to meet the local demand is so high that hardly any idle hours lapsed during the last two years. Obviously the members charge slightly lower than their competitors possessing tractors in these villages, yet other group members prefer to avail this facility because of affinity towards the federation and the group members. The tractor activity is again a bold decision for these BPL members, and the way they are meeting the demand in the local villages, it appears that it is one of the most profitable business proposition for these BPL members.

Conclusion

The activities highlighted in the paper evidenced that sufficient demand from the local area has been created through other SHG and Federation members. It also proves the fact that it has solved the problem of marketing the products and services and mitigated the hardships to a great extent. It appears, the concept of SHM may be one of the most important strategies in India, as meeting the demand of internal population would be easier and always approachable by the group members so that, the uncertain situation could be averted. As SHG activities hover around the BPL population, meeting the needs and requirements of own fellow members is itself a novel strategy. No doubt, the income of other fellow group members should be such that they should have the purchasing power to create demand for the product, but now in the beginning stage it is comfortable to market a major share of the local products among the disadvantaged people.

Specifically focusing on poor, it can be rightly observed that providing marketing avenues for a large section of self-help groups is essential to create the challenges and utilize the opportunities arising out of empowerment process undergoing in many developing countries. Even to avoid spatial and regional imbalances, delivery of products through self-help group (SHG) making the poor empowered, need to be expanded at a faster rate uniformly throughout the country. Indirectly, this proposition is also a blessing in disguise for bankers who are too worried to increase their advance portfolio searching for creditworthy clients among the masses.

References

Arthur, J.B. (1992), "The link between business strategy and industrial relations systems in American steel mini mills", Industrial and Labour Relations Review, Vol. 45, No. 3, pp. 488-506.

Arthur, J.B. (1994), "Effects of human resource systems on manufacturing performance and turnover", Academy of Management Journal, Vol. 37, No. 3, pp. 670-87.

Aryee, S. (1991), "Creating a committed workforce: linking socialization practices to business strategy", Asia Pacific Human Resource Management, pp. 102-112.

Baird, L., Meshoulam, I. (1988), "Managing two fits of strategic human resource management", Academy of Management Review, Vol. 13, No.1, pp. 116-28.

Becker, B., Gerhart, B. (1996), "The impact of human resource management on organisational performance: progress and prospects", Academy of Management Journal, Vol. 39, No. 4, pp. 779-801.

Cappelli, P., Singh, H. (1992), "Integrating strategic human resources and strategic management", Research Frontiers in Industrial Relations and Human Resources, pp. 165-192.

Cunningham, J.B., Debrah, Y.A. (1995), "Skills for managing human resources in a complex environment: the perceptions of human resource managers in Singapore", The International Journal of Human Resource Management, Vol. 6, No.1, pp. 79-101.

Huang, T.C. (1998) "The strategic level of human resource management and organizational performance: an empirical investigation", Asia Pacific Journal of Human Resources, Vol.36 No.2 pp59-72.

Huselid, M.A. (1995), "The impact of human resource management practices on turnover, productivity, and corporate financial performance", Academy of Management Journal, Vol. 38, No. 3, pp. 635-672.

Kelly, J., Gennard, J. (1996), "The role of personnel directors on the board of directors", Personnel Review, Vol. 25, No.1, pp. 6-24.

Lundy, O., Cowling, A. (1996), "The emergence of strategic human resource management", Strategic Human Resource Management.

MacLachlan, R. (1996), "Job-hopping or 'industrial espionage", Personnel Management, Vol. 2, No. 14, pp. 15-16.

Massey, R. (1994), "Taking a strategic approach to human resource management", Health Manpower Management, Vol. 20, No. 5, pp. 27-30.

Wright, P.M., Snell, S.A. (1991), "Toward an integrative view of strategic human resource management", Human Resource Management Review, Vol. 1, No. 3, pp. 203-225.

Youndt, M.A., Snell, S.A., Dean, J.W., Lepak, D.P. (1996), "Human resource management, manufacturing strategy, and firm performance", Academy of Management Journal, Vol. 39, No. 4, pp. 836-866.

16

Recession Marketing: A New Mantra for Indian Marketers

R. Sreenivasa Rao and G.V.S. Ravindra Babu

The contemporary organizations evidence a gloomy atmosphere across the world. The worst possible fear felt by the policy makers has finally come true. The great global financial crisis in eighty years has weakened the world's major economies, with many of them heading for recession. The US economy has finally slipped into recession and the economy is estimated to shrink 2.6 percent in the fourth quarter of 2009, primary stroked by worsening credit conditions.

Moreover, the unemployment rate has increased from 6.1 to 6.5, and it is likely to reach 7.5 percent by the end of 2009. Japan's economy has shrunk 0.1 percent, sending the world's second biggest economy into recession for the first time in several years. Unemployment in UK is expected to rise to almost three million in 2010 and the economy will contract by almost two percent. Germany, the largest euro economy, has shrunk 0.5 percent in 2009 the third quarter as its main source of growth – exports dropped and it could no longer rely on household demand to power the economy. Italy has officially slid into a recession as the euro zone's third biggest economy has shrunk 0.5 percent in 2009. Hong Kong and Singapore economies are also suffering from worst ever slow down in the several years. 'Sub-prime financial crisis' developed in USA has created havoc not only in America, but all over the world. Several countries are experiencing the severe blows of recession. India is no exception to this situation thus leading to uncertainty across the country.

Like virulent virus, the recession is likely to create a

deliberating effect on the investors, employers, industrialists and the whole Indian economy. Several Indian big and small companies have already felt the mighty blow of the economic turmoil. Thousands of small businessmen might see their market virtually evaporating and lakh of workers might lose their jobs. Several organizations all over the world including India have already started issuing 'Pink Slips' to their employees.

Certainly, the life will never be the same for those investors, employees and businessmen who were devastated by the tidal wave of recession that has already hit the country. The fear is now palpable as the pall of gloom hangs over the economy.

Consequences of Worst Ever Global Financial Crisis

Due to the 'Sub-Prime financial crisis' developed in USA, several financial organizations, investment banks and insurance companies in America either faced the insolvency or are on the way to insolvency. Since these organizations have spread their activities in Europe and South East Asia, several countries in these areas are going to be hit adversely. It would create harsh effect especially on those banks and companies which have taken part in 'Securitization of home loan in USA. On the whole, this recession is going to affect adversely the great super power USA and its supporting nations like UK, France etc. at the same time, this might increase the significance of China, India, Brazil and few other developing countries in the world power balance, as it has been observed in the G-20 summit held at Washington on 16th November 2008. Leaders of the Group of Twenty (G-20), at their summit held in London on April 2, 2009, made important progress in coordinating a global response to the crisis. The summit's outcome showed a clear concern with the serious development dimension of the crisis. Agreements reached at the summit have laid a good foundation for follow-up.

Indian Prime Minister Dr. Manmohan Singh has expressed

that the financial crisis has exploded into a systematic crisis, which has choked normal credit channels and triggered a worldwide collapse in stock markets around the world. He also said that the country should aim to sustain an economic growth rate of 9 to 10 percent per annum sustaining high rate of growth is the primary challenge in the next decade. India's economic growth fell to 6.7 percent during the last financial year (April-March) after expanding at about 9 percent for three consecutive years during 2005-07. The fact that our savings rate are as high as 35 percent of our GDP suggests that what is saying is a realizable goal According to former Financial Minister Mr. P Chidambaram, "The financial meltdown will not spare any sector of the economy. But monetary measures, counter-cyclical measures and enlightened measures by the companies themselves can get over this painful period of adjustment, and in about 6-9 months, we should be back to our growth rate."

The crisis increases the urgency of bolstering multilateral cooperation in trade. A quick and successful conclusion to the Doha Round of trade negotiations would help to ease protectionist pressures, keep markets open, and strengthen the rules-based multilateral trading system. It would also provide a much-needed boost in confidence to the global economy at a time of high stress and uncertainty.

Truly speaking, it is difficult to predict exact time period within which such recovery would be possible. At the moment, it is essential for the Indian businessmen to accept the fact that recession is going to hit all the areas of economy and it is necessary to adopt suitable marketing strategies to become successful in such grave situation.

The main aim of marketing is to create customer delight preferably by building value-laden relationship with chosen customers. The outdated, yester years strategies of Indian marketers would lead them to darkness. Rather than to combat the unprecedented hurdles, marketers should equip themselves to face the varying dimensions, challenges and opportunities they would face in the near future. They will have to tune up to global economic crisis adversely affecting Indian economy.

It is conventional wisdom that during recession, companies scale down their operations and try to protect their core business. However, by using some special marketing strategies according to the nature of recession it is possible to achieve the desired success. Such marketing strategies adopted during recession period are referred as Recession Marketing strategies

Basically, it is essential to remember that approach of consumers during recession is totally different from it is during the boom period. Their primary need is to get delighted, and hence they are ready to purchase high priced premium products. But during recession, they are uncertain depressed and always eager to get definite value for the money they spend. They preferred low priced products and may accept reasonable or comparatively low quality. During boom, consumers have open ended budget, and they are ready to conduct trails for novel product ideas. How ever, during recession, they have fixed budget, and cautious approach while purchasing the products.

During slow down of economy, it is observed that consumers may stop using products all together or switch on to a low priced substitute. They may not purchase a reputed brand, but may purchase the product in generic or commodity form. Lower price, discounts and concessions etc. are likely to be more influential than brand loyalty. In nut shell, consumers emphasis is on value for money with or with out sacrificing quality aspect.

Recognizing the consumer mentality, Indian marketers will have to re-write the recession dictated objectives and decide the marketing mix accordingly. Some of the objectives are as follows:

1. Convince the consumer to maintain and increase the consumption level of not just the product, but also of a specific brand.

2. Persuade non-user to use the brand, overcoming their natural barriers against experimentation, when budgets have to be protected.
3. Retain the loyalty of customers to the product and brand.
4. Advance the consumer's purchase decision which he might be postponing.

Recession Marketing Strategies

To achieve the above referred objectives, marketers may use certain demand boosting recession specific marketing strategies. Some of them are discussed below.

Price Related Strategies: Emphasis on lower price and offer of discounts, concessions etc. indicates the easiest and direct route which may be adopted by marketers during the recession. With its new campaign 'Save Money, Live Better', the giant retail organization Wal-Mart has managed to survive and thrive, even though US economy faces the recession phase. During the slow down of 1996, to quote just a single example, Baron Electronics Company a high growth rate for its Akai brand TV set as it surprised the consumers by launching it as a premium product with (comparatively) a lower price.

In nearest future, several electronics and FMCG companies will have to offer lesser prices, huge discounts and concessions on regular basis. 'New for old' exchange schemes would become common not only for consumer durables like TV sets and refrigerators, but even in case of shirts and trousers, furniture and foot wares (as observed in the slow down of 1996 in India). Creation of new low price segment, to accommodate customers looking to move below their present price level, would be common sight in coming days. Various types of novel sales promotional schemes would be observed in the sphere of Indian service sector in coming days. On the whole, Indian consumers would witness a tremendous battle among businessmen with the major weapon in the hand-price.

Competition Oriented Approach: During boom, focus is

usually on expanding the market size. However, this is quit difficult in recession period. Hence, focus is on grabbing market share from competitor and increase the product usage occasion. In the nearest future, a marketing warfare might be seen for a small piece of loaf in several areas of Indian consumer market. Rigorous efforts will have to be made by the market leaders and followers to defend and attack the market share respectively. This can be done emphasizing the plus points of our products on the backdrop of minus points of competing products.

Chase New Markets: Another rule of recession marketing –If your costumer is not responding as per your expectations, take your product elsewhere i.e., from urban to rural area, from domestic market to foreign market. Companies will have to either launching their existing brands in the rural or foreign markets, or design altogether new brands to suit the expectation of concerned buyers. Considering the low cost of production, it would be possible for Indian businessmen to export in several countries. At present, our 15 percent exports are to USA, whereas 23 percent are to western European nations. In nearest future, this proportion is likely to be reduced. Hence, efforts will have to be made to find out new markets for our products.

In this period of global crisis, it can be argued that considering the cheap and skilled manpower, obtaining outsourcing business would be easier for Indian businessmen. Foreign companies that struggled to justify outsourcing in good times now would find it easier to move jobs to low cost destinations like India citing savings.

When the atmosphere is favourable, you can sell from chair. But when the circumstances are tough, it is essential to go out and approach your prospect. In this context, direct marketing is an effective strategy of recession marketing will have to be used to convert the planned purchases of consumers into impulse buying. Various forms of direct marketing such as network marketing, telemarketing, online marketing etc. can be and should be considered by Indian marketers to increase and retain sales.

Recession Brand Strategies: In future, Indian marketers will have to closely monitor their brands. If the brand is found to be loosing its strength during recession, attempt will be necessary to realign the value to recession driven need. Where the brand would reach the commodity status, efforts will have to be taken to use promotion based on price. Where the consumers would switch over to cheaper substitutes, brand extensions should be offered in cheaper segments. 'Me-too products' or 'Copy-cat brands' may survive in the boom period, but it is almost impossible for a new comer to win hearts of recession hit consumers without a strong USP (Unique Selling Proposition). Considering the same, new products will have to launch with strong differentiating attributes to achieve desired success.

Relationship Marketing from CRM to CEM: During recession obtaining single new customer is a very difficult task, so the efforts should be made to retain all present customers. This is possible with '*Relationship Marketing*' or 'Customer Relationship Management' (CRM), which involves creating, maintaining and enhancing relationship with customers. Here, the aim is customer loyalty and focus is on long term relationship, long term value and satisfaction to customers.

The term relationship marketing can be of great use, during recession, to all the organization in India, whether from manufacturing sector or service sector. Just to identify a single area–retail sector in India, one may imagine different types of CRM strategies. In the matrix of CRM strategies to be followed in the retail sector, emphasis is given on specific components depending on situation–whether low or high involvement of the customer and the customer and low or high retail service offered.

From CRM to CEM: The industry wide interest in CRM is created out of a need to curb alarming customer addition.

Retaining customer is far less costly than gaining one from competitor by offering very attractive (and hence costly) switching option. Customer retention and customer perceived value can be improved by managing customer interactions under the wider perspective of total Customer Experience Management (CEM). Customer experience refers to the various interactions with a brand through the sales and service process and product usage.

CEM means managing customer interactions to build brand satisfying customers, CEM tries to integrate and address all customer contacts that will lead to long lasting positive perceptions towards the brand and the company. Understanding the various experience points, especially under the complex environment of many out-sourced functions, and managing them with the use of relevant IT tools, can ensure less customer attraction and long term profitability of the firm. The focus should shift from CRM to CEM by understanding that customer satisfaction needs a holistic approach covering all possible contact points through customer experience is delivered.

Holistic Marketing Approach: During the recession period, the holistic marketing concept, as advocated by Philip Kotler, would be of great use. The holistic marketing concept is based on the development, design and implementation of marketing programs, processes and activities that recognize their breadth and inter-dependence. Holistic marketing recognizes that 'everything matters' with marketing, and that a broad, integrated perspective is often necessary. Four components of holistic marketing are relationship marketing, internal marketing, integrated marketing and social responsibility marketing. Indian marketers in the nearest future, while facing the recession, will have to face the pressures of increasing the profit for the company on the one hand, and satisfying the customers as well as achieving well being for the society as a whole. In the process, Indian marketers will have to take cognizance of the terms like green marketing, ethical marketing etc., and apply suitable strategies to service in the recession hit economy, yet retain the reputation and image in the society.

References

Cateor Philip, Graham John and Salvan Prashant (2008), International Marketing, New Delhi, Tata McGraw Hill Publishing Co. Ltd.

Chetan Bajaj, Rajnish Tulsi and Nidhi Srivastava (2005), Retail Management, New Delhi, Oxford University Press.

G.P. Mrudula, "Wal-Mart's New Tagline for Recession Times", Marketing Mastermind, September 2008.

J.S. Panwar (2008), Marketing in the New Era, New Delhi, Response Books.

Judith Bardwick, "The Psychological Recession", Indian Management, July 2008.

Kotler Philip and Armstrong Garry (2011), "Principles of Marketing", Prentice-Hall of India Pvt. Ltd., New Delhi.

Kotler Philip, Keller Kevin, Koshy Abraham and Jha Mithilishwer (2011), "Marketing Management" (12th Edition), New Delhi, Dorling Kindersley, (India) Pvt. Ltd.

M.J. Xavier (2009), Marketing in the New Millennium, New Delhi, Vikas Publishing House.

Sreekumar P., "Customer Retention" Marketing Mastermind, July 2008.

V. Ramanathan, K.P.V. Ramankumar, K. Hari and B. Balaji Srinivasan, "Effective Role of CRM in the Indian Retail Market," Marketing Mastermind, July 2008.

17

Food and Grocery Retailing in India

Ch. Jayasankara Prasad, Y. Ramakrishna Prasad and A.R Aryasri

---

The world of retailing across the globe pays great emphasis on food and grocery retailing. It is different from other forms of retailing like apparel, furniture; jewellery etc., as food (wet items) and grocery are quite similar to each other. The Indian grocery retail market is characterized by a relatively large number of neighbourhood kirana stores when compared to the organized formats providing good discount and benefits to the customer. The consumers have many reasons to select a particular store above the others, the factors that are clubbed under the heads like convenience, merchandise, travel distance, price-promotions, service offerings etc. Depending on the importance the customer assigns to any of the attributes, and the availability of that attribute with the store, would influence the consumers' choice of store. The consumer behaviour of grocery buying shows that the consumers follow a hybrid fashion for store choice and there is limited loyalty when it comes to store patronage in the event of economic uncertainty.

Pricing is a relevant issue to customers as well as for retailers (Guillermo and Schleicher, 2006). Price promotions are pervasive in grocery markets. Price promotions are a commonplace promotional activity normally aimed at enhancing consumer's perceptions of value and increasing the likelihood of purchase (Devlin et al., 2007). A household can respond to price promotions by effectively cherry-picking through (1) spatial price search across stores, and (2) temporal price search across time (Dinesh, Sudheer Talukdar, 2008).

A.T. Kearney Report (2005) estimates that retailers spend from 5 percent to 10 percent of their gross revenues in category retailers spent US$ 26.7 billion on promotions in 2005, and promotional sales accounted for roughly 41.5 percent of total supermarket sales. Given such widespread use and the magnitude of the dollars spent, retail managers and academic researchers have a great interest in understanding how consumers react to retail price promotions and how promotions affect store choice behaviour.

Literature Review

As Lichtenstein *et al.*, (1993) state, price is unquestionably one of the most important factors that affect store choice. Over the years a number of researchers have focused on examining different elements of price as a determinant of store choice (Fox *et al.*, 2004). Price-related behaviours represent an important area of focus within the stream of research on patronage behaviour (Moore and Carpenter, 2006). Research into consumer behaviour with regard to pricing is ubiquitous in the marketing literature including inquiry into consumer use of reference prices (Biswas *et al.*, 2002), response to price reductions (Grewal *et al.*, 1996), prices as a signal of quality or value (Grewal *et al.*, 1998) point out that price is central to consumer behaviour due to its presence in all purchasing situations.

The literature suggests that consumers perceive price in both positive and negative roles that ultimately influence purchasing behaviour. When price is perceived as a positive cue, it signals quality, prestige or status to the consumer. In its negative role, price is perceived purely as an economic sacrifice. In both the situations, perceptions of price operate as marketplace cues that aid the consumer in their decision making process within increasingly complex market situations (Dodds, 1995).

Over the years, a number of researchers have focused on examining different elements of price as determinant of store choice (Fox *et al.*, 2004). They examined the relationship of price to grocery shopping behaviour and found that price was less important in driving consumer spending than promotions and store assortment. Seiders and Costley (1994) found price to be a major determinant of store choice in the grocery shopping context. Yavas (2003) reported price as an important driver in store choice among a battery of patronage motivations.

Retailers are constantly engaged in promotional efforts that include "incentives" such as sales and discounts to attract shoppers to their stores. Promotions help to create public awareness of the activities of the stores (Bagozzi *et al.*, 1999) and increase the likelihood of patronage. Hence, a well-managed promotional strategy attracts consumers to the store (arousal) and builds a value for money mindset in them. According to Urbany *et al.*, (2000), in-store promotions are significant with choice of store format and patronage behaviour. Thus, studies on price as a determinant has been looked at by the researchers but most of the studies were focused the western context. Studies are thus needed in the Indian context. This paper empirically examines price promotions as a retail strategy in uncertain economic situations with special reference to food and crockery retailing in India.

The Study

The study is based on primary data as well as necessary secondary data used to reinforce the model. The present study is descriptive in nature (cross-sectional design) which is the most commonly used in marketing research to identify the consumer's buying behaviour for that particular product and study the characteristics of customers. The mall intercept survey method (Dabholkar *et al.*, 1996) is adopted for the collection of primary data using structured questionnaire from 580 respondents from twenty leading supermarket retail stores in twin cities of Hyderabad and Secunderabad during November 2008-March 2009 using both descriptive statistical tools (percentiles, mean and standard deviation) and inferential statistical tools (Chi-square, correlation and regressions).

Statistical Results and Discussion

A total of one thousand retail customers were surveyed. Out of which, six hundred twenty were returned. This is an approximately sixty two percent response rate. Out of this, five hundred and eighty questionnaires were usable and rest was rendered unusable due to incomplete data.

Demographic Data: All respondents were adults. Out of which 324 were female (55.8 percent) and 256 were male (44.2 percent) with an average age of 32 years (range 20-62), modal age group 30-40 years and median age was 35 years. The majority of the respondents (69.3 percent) were married and the rest (30.7) percent were un-married. The major chunk of the respondents (56.4 percent) had graduation as their educational qualification and least 20 percent had SSC as their minimum qualification and the rest had PG as their academic qualification. The aggregated mean monthly household income was ₹ 18,000 with 48.3 percent respondents had paid employment as their occupation. A major chunk (97 percent) of the respondents lived within 4 km. from different retail store formats and about 55 percent had travelled up to 3 km. for shopping food and grocery products.

Purchase Behaviour: The information on the respondents' behaviour towards supermarket stores revealed that 26 percent have been with the retail outlets for less than one year, 38 percent have been with the retail outlets for two years and 36 percent have been with the retail outlets for more than two years. This shows that respondents have positive attitude towards supermarket store formats. Approximately 42 percent of the respondents visited the supermarkets twice in a given month, 38 percent visited at least once in a given month, 20 percent frequently visited. These results proved that respondents have a significant level of repurchase behaviour towards supermarkets.

Perceptions: The information on the respondents' perceptions towards price promotions revealed that 64 percent had *strongly agreed* with price-promotions as having influenced their choice of store format while 26 percent had *somewhat agreed* and rest 10 percent *disagreed* with price promotions. The results show that price promotions have effect on consumer store choice behaviour especially in turbulent economic times where value for money is the concept. The study further reveals that 58 percent of the respondents are quite particular and prefer retail stores where price rebates, discounts and offers are prevailed. 31 percent of respondents revealed that they are not very particular but prefer stores offering discounts and incentives. These findings are implicit that consumers prefer store formats offering price related promotions.

Inferential Statistics

The regression model for choice of supermarket store format contributed significantly and predicted 56.5 percent variation by price promotions. The evolved regression model indicated that independent variable such as price-promotions are related to dependent variable (choice of supermarket format) with a significant statistic $F(1,578)=749.891$, $p=0.000$. The coefficient summary for the evolved regression model revealed that PROM ($\beta=0.727$, $t=27.384$, $p=0.000$ was the significant predictor for choice of supermarket store format. Hence, the following regression model is evolved for supermarket store format choice decisions:

$Y = 1.314 + 0.727X$ (where Y= Supermarket store choice, X= Price -promotion).

Managerial Implications

A very clear implication of the study is that building store traffic is a key in the retailer's efforts to increase store traffic. It is likely that price-promotions would undoubtedly decrease retailers' gross margins and net profits. It is also important that, therefore that retailers' evaluate promotions for their ability to increase traffic along with ability to produce sales increase. The results proved that when there is no such substitution effect, price-promotions definitely have influence on consumers especially in an uncertain economic times where more money chases less quantity of commodity. Moreover, knowing the implications of promotional assortment on the promotional utility, retailers can propose promotional actions that not only increase store traffic but also develop the price image of the store.

Conclusion

Although the food and grocery retail market has been growing steadily at 30-35 percent compound annual growth rate over the last five years, the number of players in the market has been decreasing. Even larger retailers have not escaped the ravages of the market downturn in the last eight months. In this competitive retail market of 2000s, marketers are under constant pressure to create and sustain existing customers. The results proved that price promotions have significant bearing on consumers store choice behaviour in uncertain situations. Though it is conventional that price affects consumers' psyche yet the results are conclusive that they certainly impact consumer preferences towards grocery store formats. It is also stated that any form of price promotions may not be the panacea for marketing problems and like any form of sales promotion are only effective if not overused or abused.

References

A.T. Kearney. (2005), "Sidebar: Best Practices in Pricing and Promotion," (accessed December 16, 2005), [available at http://www.atkearney.com/main.taf?p=5, 3, 1,113#8].

Bagozzi, R.P., Gopinath, M., Nyer, P.U. (1999), "The role of emotions in marketing", Journal of the Academy of Marketing Science, Vol. 27 (2), pp. 184-206.

Biswas, A., Pullig, C., Yagchi, M.I., Dean, D.H. (2002), "Consumer evaluation of low price guarantees: the moderating role of reference pricing and store image", *Journal of Consumer Psychology*, Vol. 12 (2), pp. 107-118.

Carpenter, J. and Moore, M. (2006), "Consumer demographics, store attributes, and retail format choice in the US grocery market", *International Journal of Retail & Distribution Management*, Vol. 34 (6), pp. 434-452.

Dabholkar, P., Thorpe, D., and Rentz, J. (1996), "A measurement of service quality for retail stores: scale development and validation", *Journal of the Academy of Marketing Science*, Vol. 24 (1), pp. 3-16.

Dinesh, K. Gauri, K. Sudheer, and Debrata Talukdar (2008), 'The Temporal and Spatial Dimensions of Price Search: Insights from Matching Household Survey and Purchase Data" *Journal of Marketing Research*, Vol. XLV (April), pp. 226-240.

Dodds, W.B. (1995), "Market cues affect on consumers' product evaluations", *Journal of Marketing Theory and Practice*, Vol. 3, pp. 50-63.

Fox, E., Montgomery, A. and Lodish. L. (2004), "Consumer Shopping and spending across retail formats", *Journal of Business*, Vol. 77 (2), S25-S60.

Grewal, D., Krishnan, R., Baker, J., Borin, N. (1998), "The Effect of Store Name, Brand Name and Price Discounts on Consumers' Evaluations and Purchase Intentions", *Journal of Retailing*, Vol. 74 (3), pp. 331-352.

Guillermo D' Andrea; Martin Schleicher; Fernando Lunardini. (2006), "The role of promotions and other factors affecting overall store price image in Latin America", *International Journal of Retail and Distribution Management*, Vol. 34 (3), pp. 688-700.

James Devlin; Christine Ennew; Sally Mc Kechnie and Andrew Smith. (2007), "A study of time limited price promotions", *Journal of Product and Brand Management*, Vol. 16/4, pp. 280-285.

Lichtenstein, D., Ridgway N. and Netemeyer, R. G. (1993), "Price perceptions and Consumer shopping Behaviour: A field Study", *Journal of Marketing Research*, Vol. 30 (2), pp. 234-245.

Seiders, K., Costley, C.L. (1994), "Price awareness of consumers exposed to intense retail rivalry: a field study", *Advances in Consumer Research*, Vol. 21, pp. 79-85.

Sue Peattie. (1998), "Promotional competitions as a marketing tool in food retailing", *British Food Journal*, Vol. 100 (6), pp. 286-294.

Urbany, J. E., Dickson, P. R., Sawyer, A. G, "Insights into cross-and-within-store price search: retailer estimates vs. Consumer self-reports", *Journal of Retailing*, Vol.76, No. 2, 2000, pp. 243-258.

18

Smarting the Store Format to Manage Economic Uncertainty

M.K. Padmalatha

"Uncertainty is the only certainty there is, and knowing how to live with insecurity is the only security".

— *John Allen Paulos*

Uncertainty and change are not new to the humanity and their business activities. Every uncertainty opened doors to new horizons with remarkable development that followed. But the fruits of new era were for those who were alert, ready and adaptive to change at the quickest. The same principle applies to the business activities in the present highly sensitive global financial market. The businesses which could customize to the change readily in all aspects only can survive the uncertainty. This readiness is more so required for retailing which is a highly sensitive business with many influential factors. A time to time Store format review helps forecast weaknesses if any and a reform is a must especially during uncertain economic conditions. Shop-in-Shop format, a classic one, yet a new discovery of the current financial slump proved to be a mantra to the India retailers to manage an uncertain economy.

Economic Uncertainty: The Global Impact

The Financial Crisis of 2007 and the sharp rise in the energy and commodity prices are the two forces which led to economic uncertainty across the globe. This financial crisis was triggered by the US *Housing bubble, Sub-prime lending* and its paraphernalia. The crisis was so deep and harsh that it was termed as one of the major economic set backs which the world has seen after its evolution as a Global village.

The sudden imbalance in the economic scenario world wide is widely accepted as a phenomenon resulted out of downfall in the US economy. The US is known to be an investor than a saver while the other nation pan world saves larger than what they actually invest. With globalization at its height, American currency was accepted as a universal indicator in order to denominate their foreign exchange. The surplus which the nations held, as a result of their saving habit, were hoarded in form of dollars which lost its value due to the Financial Crisis in the US. This led to liquidity crunch and a band wagon of economic problems to create a highly uncertain economic scenario. According to Preeti Pushkele, rapid globalization expanded the uncertainty. This uncertainty led to reversal of economic conditions of foreign trade where in emerging economies have become the suppliers of foreign capital as against their trade with US.

The financial crisis which is defined as "*a situation where in the financial institutions or the assets suddenly loose a large portion of their value*" reportedly created an estimated loss of trillions of US dollars in consumer wealth. This loss of value impacted almost all sectors and caused a slowdown in the economic and business activities. During a slowdown along with GDP, other macro economic indicators like employment, investment, spending, house hold incomes and business profits fall.

Loss of consumer's confidence, decrease in spending capacities, decreased demand for goods and services are allied features which lead to low production, lay-offs and sharp rise in unemployment. Other causes are financial crisis, currency crisis, energy crisis, under consumption, price of fuel, bankruptcies, credit crunches, deflation, and foreclosures.

Economic Uncertainty in India

A slow down is US economy is said to be a dreaded

consequence to the world. The whole of Asia is hit by the recession as it is dependent on US economy. India is not an exception as its economy is also facing a kind of slowdown. According to official data, industrial growth in August 2008 fell to a mere 1.3 percent and also fears existed about the GDP achieving even 7.5 percent growth in the fiscal year of 2008. But the experts opine that the long term prospects of India are stable because of its cautious approach. The worst hit of the sectors by this slow down are industries, real estate and financial services only to be followed by retailing (Government of India, 2008).

Retailing: The Sunrise sector of India

David Gilbert defines retailing as "Any business that directs its marketing efforts towards satisfying the final consumer based upon the organization of selling foods and services as a means of distribution".

Retailing is a highly leveraged business sensitive to the economic performance and consumer behaviour. 'Sunrise Sector' in business is a term used to refer either an existing business or an emerging one with a promising hope for bright future with lucrative growth, investments and profits. This term in Indian context though associated with many sectors suits well to retailing as performance of this sector in the last two decades was remarkable and the future as prophesied by global consultants such as A.T. Kearney and Ernst and Young appear still rosy with global retail giants racing to enter India. Improving GDP, availability of disposable income, changing life style with a preference towards branded products and experiential shopping fuelled the retail boom in India making it the most attractive business with cash flow. So, retailing in India has become a *'most acclaimed'* sector in terms of business, employment and as back bone for the economy. But the current recession affected the retailer so badly that financial statements of many retailers are seen to under go havoc with nose diving figures.

Retailing in India: An Overview

"The Indian economy is soaring. I think Indian people love brands...I am excited about it and feel very positive that we are going to build a wonderful lifestyle business here."

—*Tommy Hilfiger, International Fashion Icon*

Indian Retailing which can be vastly divided into urban and rural retailing has been the 'apple of the eye' of international retailing because of its huge 'consumer class' population, average age of half of its population being below 25 years, and the vast untapped retail market under organized pattern. India is also announced as the '*most attractive retail opportunity*' surpassing China in the list of BRIC Nations.

Retail formats in India

According to Kotler, "In today's scenario, our retailer does not exist in the brick and mortar form alone. S/he can do it by using telephone, by direct mails, by using television..., by e-mails, by using the Internet or absolutely impersonally by using vending machines" (Philip Kotler, 2004).

Organized Retailing in India which operates in at least 11 segments like food and grocery, apparels, gems and jewellery, pharma, music, books and entertainment, consumer durables, footwear, health and beauty, home furnishings, mobile handsets and accessories and petrol retailing also maintains difference in the format or the store type they operate in.

Many factors like product portfolio, target customers, demographics, real-estate cost, and brand consistency influence the design of a format for a retail outlet. The scales of operations and country-specific issues are few more to be added if the retailer is an international player. In Indian context it's more suitable as north and south differ in habits while east and west differ considerably in income levels.

Also a format popular in one zone may not succeed in other zone. So, designing a format suitable for a certain retailing is a crucial task as it's the key driver in top line performance. The following are most prevalent formats seen in

Indian retailing.

Table 18.1: Most Prevalent Formats of Retailing in India

Type of Format	Features	USP	Example
Convenience Store	Limited Shelf Space, Focus on fast moving items	Convenient Locations, work for extended hours	Traditional Mom-n-Pop stores
Super markets	Wider choice, no-frills experience, self-service	Shopping experience	Nilgiris
Department Stores	Deep collection of wide range of products, better ambience, better merchandising	One stop shop, Unhurried shopping, space can leased to 'concessionaries'	Shopper's Stop
Discount Stores	Wider range with small collection, located at low cost areas	Low prices, scaled down version of departmental stores.	Subhiksha
Hypermarkets	One-stop shop for all needs, spread across a huge area, combination of FMCGs and CDs.	Consumerism, Economies of scale	Spencer's
Shopping Malls	Located in relatively nearer places, provides an ideal shopping experience, provides entertainment along with shopping.	Variety of shops available, experiential shopping	Central
Specialty stores	Stocks a narrow band of products, range of brands	Highly progressive, focus on specific consumer needs.	Titan eye +
Branded Stores	Exclusive outlet selling company's products	Owned or franchised by manufacturer	Nike, Adidas

Global convergence, cross-border businesses and improved education standards with increased exposure led to the evolution of Indian middle class with revolutionized buying behaviour. This exposure of Indian consumers to foreign goods and services became the key driver for the movement in the Indian retail industry towards modernization and standardization. The outcome was an emerging and promising organized retail sector with a market value of US$ 7 billion to US$ 30 billion by 2010.

Ripple Effects of Uncertainty on Indian Retailing

The hopes and rosy pictures stimulated by the reports of global consultants and industry experts are dampened by the Global Recession which was initiated in US economy due to its Sub-prime Crisis. The charts which were showing its futuristic paths took nose dives. Loss of consumer's confidence, decrease in spending capacities, decreased demand for goods and services are allied features which lead to low production, lay-offs and sharp rise in unemployment. Other causes are financial crisis, currency crisis, energy crisis, under-consumption, price of fuel, bankruptcies, credit crunches, deflation, and foreclosures.

The impact of recession on the financials of the retailing business was harsh due to its high-sensitivity towards the economic health of the nation. The prime factors affecting the retailing were Inflation, fear factor in the consumers due to financial crisis, Un-balanced incomes, job lay-offs, frozen recruitments, careful spending of disposable incomes and thus reduction in the foot fall and top line performance.

As no sector is insulated to the ripple effect of the slowdown, the above factors also impacted the retail sectors in the many ways resulting in the down sizing, rightsizing, closures, tab on expansion plans, mergers and acquisitions, all involving the majors. Some of the ripple effects are seen in form of news in a chronological order.

1. Vishal Retail shuts down 3 to 4 garment units, may affect 1000 workers (23-3-09).
2. Dabur puts 'New-U' wellness chain on the block? (21-3-09).
3. Future Group prunes expansion target for next fiscal by half; ends 2 JVs (19-3-09).
4. Vishal retail freezes expansion; closes large warehouses at Mumbai and Kolkatta (18-3-09).
5. Bata India to focus on large format stores across tier II and III cities: 40 small format stores closed (16-3-09).
6. Bharti Retail decides to close 4-5 non-performing stores of

'Easyday' (12-3-09).

7. Future Group to restructure business under 4 verticals...separate business under 'Value' and 'Lifestyle' retail segments (12-3-09).
8. India's largest food service provider Radha Krishna acquired by Sodexo (12-3-09).
9. Shopper's Stop shuts down 4 non-performing stores and subsidiary brands (1-3-09).
10. Reliance Fresh to close 25 stores; restructures 'value' formats to save cost (6-2-09).
11. French fashion retailer 'Etam' pulls out JV with Future Group (28-1-09).

These mind boggling events happening in the first quarter of the calendar year 2009 shows how harsh the affect of recession is on the Retailing in India creating doubts in the industry whether the so called 'Sunrise Sector' is turning towards 'Sunset'.

Retailer's response to the Economic Uncertainty

Denis Waitley said "Failure is delay not defeat".

According to Esteban Bowles (2003), "Retailing has always been a cyclic business which is directly proportionate to economic health. Sputter in economy hits the brakes on consumer spending, whereas a regain in economic health can make retailing to lead the charge".

The down turn dynamics include reduced foot fall, lower volume of sales, Cost pressure, Cash crunch, high top line revenues creating a deterioration in bottom-line performance. A recent research of McKinsey states that in US, retailers that endured both the last recessions during 1990-91 and 2000-01 are those who recouped with the situations, got to the basics and revamped their strategies to position their companies to survive the challenges.

Different strategies to fight Slowdown Blues

Strategies always helped to trouble shoot biggest of the

Health and Family Welfare' is responsible for implementation of various programmes in the areas of health and family welfare, prevention and control of major communicable diseases as well as promotion of traditional and indigenous systems of medicines.

Accordingly, it is carrying out measures like National health policy, implementing National Rural Health Mission (NRHM) in different States, conducting surveys and studies, etc. while, education strongly influences improvement in health, hygiene and demographic profile. The 'Ministry of Human resource Development' is involved in eradicating illiteracy from the country. It is concerned with universalisation of elementary education, achieving full adult literacy, lying down of National Policy on Education, meeting needs of secondary and higher education for all, etc. India has achieved impressive demographic transition owing to the decline of crude birth rate, crude death rate, total fertility rate and infant mortality rate as well as gained high literacy rate in the country (Business Maps of India, 2011).

IT and ITeS: The era of economic liberalization has ushered in a rapid change in the service industry. As a result, over the years, India is witnessing a transition from agriculture-based economy to a knowledge-based economy. The knowledge economy creates, disseminates, and uses knowledge to enhance its growth and development. One of the major functional pillars of this economy is Information Technology (IT) and IT-enabled services (ITeS) industry. The 'Department of Information Technology' has been making continuous efforts to make India a front-runner in the age of Information revolution. IT continues to be a dominating sector in the overall growth of the Indian industry. A large number of Indian software companies have acquired international quality certification. Several policies have also been framed on the key issues of IT infrastructure, electronic governance as well as IT education (Government of India, 2011).

menaces. Reducing cost, increasing financial flexibility, increasing investment for strategic advantages (including refreshing the store format), focusing on near-term revenue growth are 4 strategies as suggested by an expert of McKinsey. The experts of A T Kearney too suggest 'Change in Strategies' as the most successful ploy to fight the recession blues. While implementing all possible expertise from the above to fight the slump, a common proposal of being realistic about the potential of their business by performing a SWOT on the store format they operate, the sub-sector they belong to, the saturation levels of the market they operate in and finally their viability to face the competition was sent to all the retailers.

Reviewing Store Format as a Solution to Survive Uncertain Situations

A common solution found in all the expert opinions to fight the uncertainty is a revamp in 'Store format'. Some times it may happen to improve the foot fall or sometime it may be a part of 'right-sizing'. Here again comes in to the picture, the importance of Store format in influencing the profits.

Shop-in-Shop Format: The Need of the Hour

By now it's an established fact that suitable and profitable retail format is part of a good retail strategy. It should not only merchandise the products and services to the customers but also clearly segment the potential customers. All this is to happen while keeping a tab on the real estate and other top line figures. Here evolves a need for tailor made formats to suit the needs.

Shop-in-Shop format is one such format where in a space of retail outlet is allotted for another business to manage in synchrony with the overall ambience of the store. This is also referred to as "concessionaries" who pay for the space occupied in the outlet in order to have a privilege to maintain subsidiary business within certain premises.

While all the growth charts are diving south due to

recession, this format suits to the need and is rescue for the retailers, as it helps managing the top line and thus influence the bottom line performance.

Examples for the Shop-in-Shop Format in Indian Scenario

Shop-in-Shop format in Indian retailing started as an internal affair of a particular group where in two verticals of the same group where set operational in single premises. The idea behind the combination was to introduce product portfolios one vertical to the customers of another vertical, to provide experiential shopping, brand management and ultimately economies of scale. The Future group previously called as Pantaloon Retail India Ltd. (PRIL) has been patronizing this format with extensive use for its various business verticals. The following are examples of the S-i-S.

1. Pantaloons accommodate Gen M, aLL and Collection I stores.
2. Big Bazar accommodates E Zone.
3. Food Bazar accommodates Fit and healthy format.
4. Big Bazar accommodates Food courts of its own group Café Bollywood and Chamosa.
5. Central Mall accommodates the corners of Future Generalia.
6. Shopper's Stop accommodates Crossword, a books and leisure store.
7. Westside stores of Trent accommodate Café Taj, a coffee shop.
8. Subhiksha, a discount store accommodates pharmacy and mobile stores.
9. Titan exclusive showrooms also sell the Fast track range of eye wear and watches.
10. Food World accommodates Music World Express outlets.
11. Bajaj Automobile showrooms roofing Bajaj Finance and Bajaj Allianz insurance desks.

With the advent of foreign players into India organized retailing more experimentation with this format took place to evolve more utility. The result was:

1. Erection of Pizza Corner in Food World,
2. World Space FM services in Food World,
3. Barista offering its Italian food in Planet M and Ebony,
4. Crossword Corners in McDonald outlets,
5. Café Coffee day in Food World outlets.

Very soon the effectiveness of Shop-in-Shop format was understood and various tie-ups were seen both in goods and service retailing. Prominent of the examples are:

1. Western Union Money Transfer being offered in almost all nationalized banks.
2. ATMs of various banks inside petrol pumps, hotels and restaurants.
3. HPCL launching its retail outlets with value added services like ATMs, internet cafes, STD booths etc. The corporate tie-ups include Café Coffee Day, Western Union, ICICI Bank, Mahindra Finance and Tata Motors inside each SBU of HPCL.
4. NBFCs maintaining their 'help desk' corners in automobile showrooms.
5. HPCL's "Hamara Pumps" was an innovative initiative where in all the farming and day to day needs of rural population were met including financial services through Mahindra and Mahindra Financial Services.
6. BPCL tied-up with ITC e-choupals to provide one-stop solutions for the farmer fraternity.
7. M&B footwear corners in Shopper's Stop.

Key Drivers for Shop-in-Shop Format

Now that the classic examples fortifying the utility and success of the S-i-S format in retailing it is also deserving to know the drivers behind the success. Apart from the key factors driving the retail boom, decrease in disposable time led to the following factors which have driven the success of S-i-S format.

1. Increase in desires and demand for novelty in shopping.

2. A zeal for newer shopping culture and retailers' race to cash upon the newer customer aspirations.
3. Increasing importance for 'shoppertainment'.
4. Increasing preference for one stop solutions.
5. Improved awareness on value retailing.
6. Retailers' trying to utilize the 'impulsive' buying behaviour.
7. Price elasticity and quality consciousness.
8. Increased concentration on the store layouts in order to make the shopper spend more time at the store.
9. Gaining importance of the store format in converting the shopper to a customer.

Shop-in-Shop Format: A Ray of Hope during Uncertainty

Shop-in-Shop format as discussed earlier is a process where an allied business activity is permitted in a business premises on lease. This format is a familiar phenomenon in Indian retailing though its importance unnoticed, in forms of a bouquet stall in a Star hotel, Gifts gallery in an airport, Pharmacy in a Hospital, Book stand in the railway station, Vending machines in Corporate offices and a *Pan* kiosk in a '*desi*' restaurant.

As discussed previously financial crisis influenced both the top and bottom lines of financial statements. The reduced footfall, cautious expending of disposable incomes is an outcome of fear factor in consumers and financial crunch. It is very difficult in this scenario to draw customers with *'offers'* and *'sale'* to the stores to improve the footfall. The so called *promos* and *ad campaigns* cannot woo the customer to continue their habit of *consumerism* which generates the free flow of cash into retailing business. Under these circumstances, retailers cannot wait for the economic situations to improve or present the same merchandise to the customers all along the slump. Here comes into action the implementation of *strategies.*

The retailers need to exert a pull on customers to buy *all* the products when they come for the necessities and retain their loyalty with innovation and novelty in store ambience, product portfolio etc. while keeping the price factor under control.

All the above mentioned essential changes in retail dynamics can be easily achieved with S-i-S format. It helps in the following:

1. Cost management of the store keeper.
2. Gives point of sales to the concessionary at lower capital investment.
3. Gives customers variety in product range.
4. Act as one stop solution which reduces time waste of a customer to shop at various stores for allied products.

Contemporary Dynamics in Indian Retailing

The strategies to 'fight the financial crisis unanimously stress on smartening the store format. Amidst many recession top stories about closures, mergers and lay offs, a quick glance at the following news arise hope in retailers. These strategies involve store renovation which paves the retailers' path towards sustenance and prosperity.

The following is the list of S-i-S evolved with the advent of recession, as the retailers quickly understood its utility as a rescue. The increased density of S-i-Ss from the end of 2007 till the latest plans to display Nano in Westside Stores is the reiteration of the fact.

1. Replacing its exclusive store format, Goodyear tyres adopted S-i-S format in tie-up with car-care products and multi-brand outlets.
2. The Future Group had a volley of events like:

- Setting-up its end-to-end home solutions Home Town in e-zone.
- Money Bazar, the retail outlet from Future Money is set up in all e bazaars and Hometowns to supply credit to all the customers.
- Future Generalia sells its financial products to the visitors

of Big Bazar.

- FotoDepot, a one stop solution for all photography needs is set in 117 Big Bazars.
- Vivah, first organized wedding shopping solution store is all set to be launched in all Big Bazars.
- Navras, a gold and diamond jewellery outlet is to retail from all Big Bazars.

3. Citizen Watches plans to launch S-i-S format in big departmental stores.
4. Crossword, the books and entertainment vertical of K. Raheja Group plans to expand through small store format "Crossword Corners" as S-i-S in its departmental store Shopper's Stop and possibility to open in McDonald and Barista outlets too.
5. Microsoft's retail brand "One MS@Retail" launched its first outlet on pilot in multi-brand consumer durables store Tata Croma.
6. Apple marked its first S-i-S tie-up with launch of i-store in Music World store of RPG group to sell i-pods and accessories.
7. Ebony retail to accommodate local brands like Lifespring, Natalia, Provouge, Gini & Johny inside their departmental stores in S-i-S formats.
8. Vishal Retail is all set to revamp its stores with a food court 3H (in all marts) and liquor (in 4 marts) in S-i-S format.
9. Vishal Retail also announced its tie up in S-i-S with laundry specialists "White Tiger".
10. Reliance Vimal to open five S-i-S stores in tie-up with Khadims.
11. Rado, the Swiss watch maker to increase its point of sales from 6 to 14 in S-i-S format.
12. Barista, Italian coffee retailer opened its coffee shop in Hotel Leela Palace, Bengaluru.
13. Reliance Mart, the largest retail format in India is downsized and plans to operate in S-i-S and small store

formats.

14. Spencers' to focus on 'retailtainment' and decided to accommodate food courts and coffee shops in its premises in S-i-S format, thus tied-up with Flury's, Monginis, Daily Breads, Pizza Corner, Nirula's, Cafe Coffee Day, Barista and Tiffany for such shops.
15. Food court Red-E will start its coffee shop in Landmark, Chennai.
16. The Spanish luxury porcelain brand Lladro has stepped into S-i-S format by collaborating with Ethos Swiss Watch Studios in Chandigarh.
17. Archies plans to reach out consumers in S-i-S format through Reliance Time out.
18. Tata Nano is likely to be displayed from select Westside stores.

When all the major retailers in India are embracing the S-i-S format, especially during recession it is worth while to study the advantages in order to establish that Shop-in-Shop format is retailer's rescue during recession.

Advantages of Shop-in-Shop format

A keen study into the recent store format dynamics of the above retailers, the following are the advantages which are obviously rescue for a retailer by taking a proper care towards the bottom line performance.

1. **Increase in Point of Sales While Putting a Tab on Costs:** The example of Rado watches and Citizen watches, who vie with each other in the cost factor due to their international origin, can be said to enjoy this benefit because of their tie-ups with other branded and departmental stores where people come for daily needs. This helps the branded products to easily penetrate into the consuming class, who are otherwise hesitant to know about them.
2. **Easy to Create Brand Awareness and Manage A Brand:** The strategic alliance of Reliance Vimal with

popular footwear brand Khadims can be quoted here. Here, Khadims is a footwear brand where customers step-in even during down turn. Hence, Vimal gets a chance to manage creation of their brand without spending much on the promotional activities.

3. **Aid Bringing in Diversity into a Single Store:** This is a universal want of many customers today due to lack of disposable time. Shopper's Stop accommodating their own books and entertainment vertical Crossword in the departmental stores is an example to cater all the needs of a customer in a single platter, thus ensuring the return and withholding the loyalty of the customer.
4. **A Holistic Shopping Experience to the Shoppers:** The 21st century customers prefer 'something more' than what they expect. They prefer to cherish experience and obtain value for every moment and money they spend, more so during recession. Spencer's attempt to plug in Food courts in an alliance with international brands of bakers and fast food kiosks is the best example. The motive—to cater to the 'diversified' needs under a single roof.
5. **Increase in Foot Fall Both for the Main Store as Well as for Concessionary:** The coalition of Ebony retail with branded garment makers both domestic and international in S-i-S format is a symbiotic deal where in the departmental store will have increased footfall due to concessionary and the concessionary will have footfall because of the loyal customers of its accommodator.
6. **Provides Sharing of Extensive Network and Brand Equity:** Tata Croma's tie-up to accommodate retail outlets of Microsoft is the best example where in the extensive network of Tata Croma becomes an advantage for Microsoft, wherein the brand equity of international software giant works as a "pull" effect for Tata Croma.
7. **Improvement in Sales When Tied Up With Complimentator:** Books and entertainment is a niche vertical for any retailer. Gifts and cards are near

complimentary to books Reliance Time-Out including the famous Archies gallery will help them to improve the sales when deals strategically with the loyal customers of its complimentators.

8. **Cash upon the 'Impulsive Buying Behaviour' and Increase the Average Bill Size:** Buying gold and diamond jewellery is an impulse, even more in financial crunch. An artistic merchandise of jewellery to the customers of a super market may woo their impulses and make them buy if not in their first visit. This is the strategy behind Future group setting up its Navras in its highly popular Bigbazar.
9. **Achievement of Break even Point Easily:** Coffee Shops in India are still a venue for elite and not all shops have even foot fall. Barista found a trouble shooter for this menace by accommodating their Cafés in star hotels which are usually places of visit by the creamy layer. This involves less capital for establishment, thus easy to reach the BEP.
10. **Easy to Position Product, Brand and Time:** Vishal Retail's launch of its own food retailing vertical 3H in their own departmental stores helps cost management, brand and product positioning while minimizing the waste of time for the customers.
11. **Localization and Customization of Market for International Brands:** Reliance Digital is a multi-brand consumer durables outlet with a through knowledge of market and customer dynamics. I-stores choosing to sell its international product through these outlets help reach local customers easily.
12. **Strong Penetration:** A simple kiosk in a highly stepped-in discount store means a lot more than a standalone store. Future groups strategy to launch its Foto Depot and Future Generalia in Big Bazars provide them a strong penetration into consuming class.
13. **Development of Symbiotic Relationship:** Goodyear tyres

to start S-i-S format of stores inside multi-branded stores and car care products stores is an example to manage cost while maintaining the market share with a symbiotic relationship.

14. **Helps in Repositions if Going for 'Right-Sizing' and 'Down-Sizing':** Crossword, the books and entertainment vertical which is downsizing its standalone store can still withhold its market share with its presence in S-i-S format inside Shoppers Stop, McDonalds and Barista.
15. **Expand the Retail Footprint While Putting a Tab on Top Line Revenues:** Tata's likely strategy to showcase its Nano through all its authorised dealers of other automotives and select Westside stores will help increase the retail footprint of Nano without having a standalone store for itself.
16. **Helps Propel Sales Revenue:** The investment which is saved because of this S-i-S format of operations can be invested in enriching the product portfolio and merchandise which in turn will fuel the sales revenue.

All the above mentioned advantages are the mere needs of any retailer in India and also across the globe to sustain the recession blues. Hence undoubtedly it can be ascertained that Shop-in-Shop format is the retailer's rescue for recession.

The Road Ahead

The future of the Shop-in-Shop format seems to be very bright when taken into consideration its track record, increasing density and more and more evolutions during recession. For a few years to come the S-i-S format may a starter to the semi-urban and rural populations towards Mall culture which is already in prominence in metropolitan cities and urban areas. Meanwhile, this format is sure to serve the recession insurgencies and needs of both the shoppers and the sellers.

Conclusion

Retailing in India is still in its nascent stage. The economic slump of 2008 and 2009 has created a challenging environment to the retailing sector in general and organized retailing in specific. As a rescue, retailers relied on many strategies to avoid bottom line disasters, including implementation of Shop-in-Shop format. This format is still understood to be an enthusiastic effort, but if executed extensively can help all the retailers, small and big to beat the recession heat. All expertise, including changing store format would give obvious results only when the economy starts to regain its financial health. Though near term and mid term stance may be gloomy, the long term outlook is still hopeful. The immense opportunity lies in low consumption levels and high aspirations.

References

A T Kearney, 2003, "Reinventing the store–Implementing Strategic Change at the Ground level", *Retailing–Concepts and Cases,* ICFAI University Press, Hyderabad, pp. 39-54.

Anitha Sukhwal, June 2008, "An Integrated and Inclusive Model for the Development of Retailing In India", *Marketing Masterminds,* Vol. VIII, Issue 6, ICFAI University Press, Hyderabad, pp. 20-24.

Chandan A. C. and Shilpa Rajesh, June 2007, "Private Brands in Retailing", *Marketing Masterminds,* Vol. VII, issue 6, ICFAI University Press, Hyderabad, pp. 13-17.

Dhananjay Keskar, 2006, "Retail Industry-Poised for a Phenomenal Growth", *Retailing Industry–Changing Trends,* ICFAI University Press, Hyderabad, pp. 3-10.

Jyoti, Rana, October 2007, "Shopping Malls-The New Growth Engines", *MBA Review,* Vol. VI, Issue 9, ICFAI University Press, Hyderabad, pp. 57-60.

Kinjal, Shah, 2002, "Discount Stores: Is it the Answer?", *Retailing-The Sunrise Sector,* ICFAI University Press, Hyderabad, pp. 54-58.

Michael, Fernandes, Palash Mitra et al. 2002, "India's Retailing: Strategic Issues and Challenges?", *Retailing-The Sunrise Sector,* ICFAI University Press, Hyderabad, pp. 29-36.

Mridul, S.M., Nov 2007, "Organized Retail Sector and the Changing face of Indian Pharmacy", *Marketing Masterminds,* Vol. VII, issue 11, ICFAI University Press, Hyderabad, pp. 50-51.

Pandey, M.K. and Anchal Singh, November 2008, "Indian Retail Industry-A Sunrise Sector", *Advertising Express,* Vol. VIII, Issue 11, ICFAI University Press, Hyderabad, pp. 35-42.

Panigrahy, B.P., Dec 2005, "HPCL-New Initiatives", *Marketing Masterminds,* Vol. V, Issue 12, ICFAI University Press, Hyderabad, pp. 55-62.

Panigrahy, B.P., December 2005, "Retail Industry", *Marketing Masterminds,* Vol. V, Issue 12, ICFAI University Press, Hyderabad, pp. 17-26.

Prabhi, January 2009, "Brand Management in Recession Economy", *Advertising Express,* Vol. IX, Issue 1, ICFAI University Press, Hyderabad, pp. 35-38.

Pradip, K.D. and Gopal Das, November 2007, "Private Branding in Organized Retailing", *Marketing Masterminds,* Vol. VII, issue 11, ICFAI University Press, Hyderabad, pp. 69-70.

Preeti Pushkele, 2008, "What are the Global Imbalances?", *Global Imbalances – Implications and Challenges,* ICFAI University Press, Hyderabad, pp. 3-9.

Priya Chandrasekhar, 2002, "Retailing in India: Trends and Opportunities", *Retailing-The Sunrise Sector,* ICFAI University Press, Hyderabad, pp. 1-7.

Radhika N, 2006, "Organised Retailing in India", *Retailing Industry –Changing Trends,* ICFAI University Press, Hyderabad, pp. 3-10.

Radhika Vishvas and V. Murugaiah., July 2006, "FDI in Retailing-Challenges and Opportunities", *Marketing Masterminds,* Vol. VI, Issue 7, ICFAI University Press, Hyderabad, pp. 45-54.

Raju, M. R., December 2007, "Nitty Gritty of Brand vs Exclusive Retailing", *Marketing Masterminds,* Vol. VII, Issue 12, ICFAI University Press, Hyderabad, pp. 26-29.

Sarat Cahndra P.S., November 2007, "Organized Retailing–David vs. Goliath", *MBA Review,* Vol. VI, Issue 11, ICFAI University Press, Hyderabad, pp. 37-39.

Shajahan S. and Shankar Bharath, 2005, "Retail Industry: Challenges and Opportunities", *Retail Management–Perspectives and Cases,* ICFAI University Press, Hyderabad, pp. 39-54.

Shajahan S, 2006, "Retailing through Shopping Malls", *Retailing Industry–Changing Trends,* ICFAI University Press, Hyderabad, pp. 20-37.

Sreenivasa Chakravarthi, 2002, "Finding the Right Retail Model",

Retailing-The Sunrise Sector, ICFAI University Press, Hyderabad, pp. 37-43.

Suresh K., 2003, "Evolving Retail Formats", *Retailing–Concepts and Cases,* ICFAI University Press, Hyderabad, pp, 97-106.

www.delloitteresearch.com, 2008, "Global Economic Outlook 2007: Is a Crisis Imminent...", *Global Imbalances–Implications and Challenges,* ICFAI University Press, Hyderabad, pp. 101-111.

19

Services Sector in Times of Uncertainty

Sunitha Ratnakaram and Venkama Raju Chakravaram

Service sector includes industries like the IT-enabled services, healthcare, tourism and hotels, communications, media and entertainment, trade and retail, banking and financial services, transportation and logistics, etc. which form the mainstay of the countries across the globe. Indian economy is no exception to this fact. Service industries have been contributing to over 50 percent of the country's GDP over the last several years. Service industries are expected to significantly power India's growth in the years to come (Zeithmal, 2011).

Services have been growing at a faster rate than Industry and Agriculture in India and in other large developed economies. The average growth rate for services in India for the last several years has been significantly higher than that of industry and agriculture sectors and the GDP as a whole. In fact over the past decade there has been no year of below 5.5 percent growth for Services. This is in keeping with the trend that the more an economy gets developed, the faster is the growth of Services in comparison with the other sectors (Morgan Stanley, 2008).

The contribution of services sector to the Indian economy is 54 percent of GDP which is more than China's service sector contribution to GDP (The Views Paper, 2011). The economy showed signs of economic health before the global melt down. But, the heavy storm of the financial world touched Indian service sector also in its own way. In light of the current scenario, this paper highlights the changes that have contributed to the growth service economy. The overview of major service sectors in general and retailing in particular are also included. Various illustrations of change in consumer behaviour in many of these sectors, especially in retailing with the increase of growing service economy are also presented in the paper.

Significant market value creation has already taken place in sectors like information technology, media etc. over the past decade which has demonstrated the extent of value creation possible in the Service industries as a whole. Reforms in almost all the sectors like banking and financial services, healthcare, communications, media and entertainment, IT-enabled services etc. have added to the attractiveness of Services industries for the future (Report of RBI, 1999).

Features

Consumer Boom: The increasing income levels of the Indian population have resulted in a higher proportion of income being spent on services. A burgeoning educated, middle class population with higher disposable income and higher spending on value added services like communications, entertainment, hospitality and healthcare is taking the Indian Service industries to high levels of sustained growth. Not only the existing market, but potential market too is very promising for Indian services sector with an estimated young population of 900 million of about 1.3 billion by 2020 (Business Maps of India, 2011).

Competitive Advantages: India, with its large pool of low cost, trained manpower and other strategic advantages, has the potential to emerge as a service hub to the world economy. Today, many segments of the Service industry are globally competitive and cater to the global market. This includes areas like IT services, business process outsourcing (BPO) and contract research services in healthcare. Thus, investment in services provides opportunities for high growth which are often in tune with that possible in more advanced global markets. Further, large parts of this segment do not depend entirely on physical infrastructure which has been the biggest problem for many other industries which want to compete globally.

Social Changes: The standard of living of Indian people increased to a greater extent. There is a paradigm shift in the role played by women in industry and service sectors. Double income families, nuclear families are increasing today. Most of the consumers are exposing themselves to global services in foreign countries due to their business trips and vacation trips. This is increasing the expectations of the consumers. Consumers are in search of easier way of getting things done, like online shopping, shopping malls, express check outs etc. The consumers are ready to pay excess amount for the value addition in service delivery. These expectations of the consumers are a challenge the service provider.

Policy and Political Initiatives: When the great Soviet Union had to emerge itself into Russia and many other smaller nations had to accept *perestroika* and *glasnost.* It brought a tremendous change in the ideology and policy issues of many countries. This being a political change, it changed the future of those countries. India having embraced the policy of liberalization, privatization and globalization evidences a policy change, which was brought about in 1991. These policy changes thus, attracted many of the established companies to enter service sector, and also encouraged a good number of entrepreneurs to start their own ventures in the changed scenario.

Major Industries in Service Sector: An Overview

Health and Education: The most important services in the Indian economy have been health and education. They are one of the largest and most challenging sectors and hold a key to the country's overall progress. A strong and well-defined health care sector helps to build a healthy and productive workforce as well as stabilize population. The 'Ministry of

Media and Entertainment: Another major and upcoming service industry has been media and entertainment. It is basically an intellectual property-driven sector with small to large players spread throughout the country. It covers film, music, radio, broadcast, television and live entertainment. It plays a significant role in creating people's awareness about national policies and programmes by providing information and education to all. The 'Ministry of Information and Broadcasting' is responsible for formulation and administration of the rules, regulations and laws relating to media industry. Besides, retailing has been one of the fastest growing service sectors both in terms of turnover and employment. Many national and global players have been investing in the retail segment and are making all efforts to further expand the sector. Out of the total retail outlets in the country, most of them are related to food items.

Travel and Tourism: However, to supplement the achievements and meet the shortfalls in all the sub-sectors of the service industry, travel and tourism sector has to be developed in a sustainable manner. Being one of the largest industries in terms of gross revenue and foreign exchange earnings, it stimulates growth and expansion in other economic sectors like agriculture, horticulture, poultry, handicrafts, transportation, construction, etc. as well as gives momentum to growth of service exports. It is a major contributor to the national integration process of the country as well as preserver of natural and cultural environments. The 'Ministry of Tourism' has been undertaking several policy measures and incentives so as to boost the sector such as the announcement of the National Tourism Policy.

Retail: In India, retailing is one of the fastest growing industries. It is estimated to be the largest single sector (after agriculture) both in terms of turnover as well as employment. After leading the IT bandwagon, India is poised to grow as a retail hub. Retailing is defined to include all the business activities relating to selling of goods and services to the final consumers. It is the final link in a product supply chain.

The Indian retail sector is highly fragmented with about 15 million retailers. Out of the large number of total retail outlets in the country, majority of them relate to the food items. Since 1990s, big industrial houses like Rahejas, Piramals, Tatas, etc. have started entering the retail industry. Besides, several Indian and foreign companies have been franchising for establishing exclusive outlets for their brands, both within the country and overseas. For instance, 'Bharati Group' had entered into a joint venture with the world's largest retail chain the 'Wal-Mart'.

As a result, the Indian retail sector has been undergoing a rapid transformation in the past few years. The traditional formats of kirana stores, hawkers, grocers, etc are being gradually taken over by the modern formats of department stores, discount stores, malls, supermarkets, convenience stores, fast food outlets, specialty stores, warehouse retailers, hypermarkets, etc. For example, Pantaloon started the 'Big Bazaar' discount stores in 2002; Reliance opened its first supermarket named 'Reliance Fresh' outlet in Hyderabad and has since fanned out to several States; Subhiksha though today is undergoing the critical care treatment the growth recorded earlier was prominent.

Thus, the current face of Indian retail comprising the unorganized small and medium retailers is slowly changing into a more organized form of retailing.

As per the available estimates, of the ₹ 1,330,000 crore retail market, food and grocery retail is the single largest block estimated to be worth ₹ 7,92,000 crore (with 59.5 percent share), but the share of organized sector in this is miniscule. Clothing, textiles and fashion accessories constitute the second largest block with a 9.9 percent share at ₹ 1, 31,300 crore. But the largest segments as far as organized retailing is concerned are the time wear (48.9 percent share) and footwear (48.4 percent share) sectors. In 2007, the share of organized retail was estimated to be 5.9 percent, which was ₹ 78,300 crore.

This retail is expected to touch ₹ 2,30,000 crore (at constant prices) by 2010, constituting roughly 13 percent of the total retail market. However, the modern retail segment grew at the rate of 42.4 percent in 2007 and is expected to maintain a faster growth rate, especially in view of the fact that major global players and Indian corporate houses are entering into the market in a big way. This growth in modern retailing is linked to several factors particularly, the increasing purchasing power; rapid global interaction and integration as well as the changing consumer needs, lifestyle and attitude. Further, shopping centre business alone is estimated to become a ₹ 40,000 crore business by 2010-11 (R. Srinivasan, 2004).

Besides, the large organized retail segment, using sophisticated technology and communication network, offers several benefits to the consumers in the form of availability of quality products at lower prices; wider choice to the customers; shopping with convenience, space and entertainment; etc. It is also beneficial for the growth of the economy as a whole because it provides forward linkages for mass-marketing of processed and packaged goods. Its expanded reach and increased volumes translates into more manufacturing, more jobs, better standard of living and hence more prosperity.

Given the present scenario, foreign direct investment into the retail sector would further improve its productivity, competitiveness and efficiency. Such investments from abroad is a means to supplement and complement domestic efforts for providing opportunities for technological up gradation and access to global managerial skills and practices; optimal utilization of human and natural resources; opening up export markets; generating backward and forward linkages; providing access to international quality goods and services; etc.

Also, India is one of the most attractive markets for retail investment. Many national and global players have been investing in the retail segment and have ambitious plans for further expansion. The vast middle class with rising purchasing power are attracting global retail giants into the almost untapped retail industry. Some of the international players already present in the Indian market include fast food chains like McDonalds and Pizza Hut; Dominos; Levis; Lee; Nike; Adidas; Benetton; Sony; Sharp; Kodak; etc.

The investment opportunities in the domestic retail industry lay in most of the product categories particularly, food and grocery (the largest category); home improvement and consumer durables; apparel and eating out; supply chain infrastructure (cold chain and logistics); etc. India also has significant potential to emerge as a sourcing base for a wide variety of goods for international retail companies.

As of now, there is no policy for foreign direct investment (FDI) in retail. The government allows 100 percent FDI in cash and carry through the automatic route and 51 percent in the retail trade of single brand products. Besides, the franchise route is available for the big operators. The government also proposes further liberalization in the retail sector allowing 51 percent FDI in consumer electronics, sports goods, stationery and building equipment. The current policy regime also bars foreign retailers from selling multiple brands directly to consumers. Also, this policy framework involves numerous licensing formalities for the retailers and hence there is a demand for a single window clearance system which makes the whole process hassle-free.

All this shows that all the services hold immense potential to accelerate the growth of an economy and promote general well-being of the people. They offer innumerable business opportunities to the investors. They have the capacity to generate substantial employment opportunities in the economy as well as increase its per capita income. Without them, Indian economy would not have acquired a strong and dominating place on the world platform. Thus, service sector is considered to be an integral part of the economy and includes various sub-sectors spread all across the country.

Illustrations

A variety of illustrations that depict the change in consumer behaviour with the growth of services economy are presented below:

"We want to be respected. We want to feel acknowledged as a person and for what we are. Being ignored or being seen as an intrusion is something none of us like." This sentence is leading the growth of organized retailing in India today. We shall see few instances that prove the change in base of economy.

1. To start with food retailing, consumer of yesterday was trying to shop for his/her monthly provisions or groceries, in odd timings after office hours, roadside shops on small dingy roads, wait for the shop keeper to attend him or her. Whereas today most of such shopping is done in the centrally located shopping malls in the entire aesthetic environment and more over many of them offer valet parking too. Today, retail space has become more of an entertaining place for the consumer rather a runaway location. If a consumer would not like to take this pain also, online ordering, telephonic ordering, free home delivery anyway are available to him at his or her door step. With all these services provided by the organized retailer, customer is ready to go with him, fortunately for the consumer; unorganized sector retailer also is forced to foray into offering better services for a consumer.
2. Pharmacy retailing also is entering into organized retailing in a big way with Med plus, Apollo Pharmacy, Life Spring, Planet Health, Fortis to name a few. These days the pharmacists are calling you in first week of every month to know your monthly medicine requirements and are offering a free home delivery.
3. The changes occurred in banking and financial sector are beyond visualization of many a customers. Technology support they are providing, fast passed transactions, various other value added services provided by the banks

have remarkably changed the impression on bank, just an institution which accepts deposits and offers loans. Today's bank is much larger than this frame.

4. Chaiwalas and tea bunks are barely seen these days metros and cities where organized tea and coffee revolution has come with CCD, Starbucks, Tata Café and all others who offer more than a coffee to a customer which they call as experience. They no more sell a physical product but, an experience.
5. Apparels and accessories is one of the area where most of the organized retailing is concentrated with the brands like Raymond's, Grasim, Shopper's Stop, Pantaloons, Hyderabad central etc. working in a very big way. Sea change of difference can be found in the length and width of product line, quality of product, services delivered in these organized retail stores compared to the earlier ones.
6. Health and Personal Care is one more area to be supported with an illustration with Health and Glow, Global, La belle, Apollo to name a few. These institutions are offering world class services at lower costs, with sophisticated equipment, especially in health care. With the international standards maintained in many of these corporate chains, medical tourism is going to see a formidable growth in near future.
7. Books, music and hobby stores is the other interesting area which also has undergone dramatic changes from a small store to a bigger scale, from a retailer serviced outlet to a self service out let, from look and buy product, to listen, read, enjoy and buy product.

Conclusion

Service industries have witnessed a significant change thus, providing value creation opportunities in the economy. The IT, BT, media, commutations, retail, banking and financial services have grown immensely thus contributing to a dynamic service sector in India. There is plenty of opportunity and challenges as well for exciting changes in this sector. The organizations and the customers must leverage this situation.

20

Impact of Recession on Organized Retailing in India

I. Anand Pawar and K. Chandra Sekhar

The Indian retail market is the fifth largest retail destination globally and has been ranked the second most attractive emerging market for investment (E & Y, 2006). To maintain the growth story of Indian retail sector consistency in the future, retailers should be able to strike a balance between managing internal costs, inspire leadership and external market penetration through innovation and meeting customer expectations without affecting the quality of products and services. Retailing, in a layman's language involves the procurement of varied products in large quantities from various sources/producers and their sales in small lot for direct consumption to the purchaser. In commerce a retailer buys goods or products in large quantities from manufacturer or importers, either directly or through a wholesaler and then sells individual items or small quantities to the general public or end-user customers, usually in a shop, also called a store. Retailers are at the end of the supply chain. Marketers see retailing as part of their overall distribution strategy.

Organized Retailing vs. Unorganized Retailing

Retailing can broadly be classified into: organized and unorganized retail. Unorganized retailing refers to the traditional form of retailing with the retail outlets situated near the residential areas while organized retailing refers to the modern form of retailing with trading activities undertaken by licensed retailers generally located in commercial establishments/high-street areas.

Following is the classification and examples of organized retailers (modern format retailers).

1. Supermarkets (Subhiksha).
2. Hypermarkets (Big Bazar).
3. Department Store (Shopper Stop).
4. Unorganized Retailers (Traditional format retailers).
5. Traditional mom and pop stores (KIRANA).
6. Kiosks.
7. Street Markets.
8. Exclusive or Multiple Brand Outlets.

Global Retail Scenario

The global retail industry has been growing at a brisk pace during the last few decades. However the spread of organized retailing in different countries varies depending upon the socio-economic factors related to the country. Globally, the retail industry has grown at a brisk pace with a Compounded Annual Growth Rate (CAGR) of 7.77 percent during the period 2001-2006. The growing expanse of the top global retailers has ensured globalization of the industry; however the opportunity for growth of organized retail is immense in countries such as India, S. Korea, and Vietnam etc. where organized retailing is still at a nascent stage (E & Y, 2006).

Finding new markets through globalization efforts, four years ago, more than half (53 percent) of the top 200 retailers operated in only one country. Today, only 44 percent remain single-country merchants. This globalization trend can only intensify in the years ahead. The benefits of increased sales and greater economies of scale are too large to be ignored. The global retail industry has travelled a long way from a small beginning to an industry where the world wide retail sale alone is valued at US$ 7 trillion (Global Retail Report, 2003).

The top 200 retailers alone account for 30 percent of worldwide demand. Retail sales being generally driven by people's ability (disposable income) and willingness (consumer confidence) to buy, compliments the fact that the money spent on household consumption worldwide increased

68 percent between 1980 and 2003. The leader has indisputably been the USA where some two-thirds or US$ 6.6 trillion out of the US$ 10 trillion American economy is consumer spending. About 40 percent of that (US$ 3 trillion) is spending on discretionary products and services.

Retail turnover in the EU is approximately Euros 2000 billion and the sector average growth looks to be following an upward pattern. The Asian economies (excluding Japan) are expected to grow at 6 percent consistently till 2005-06. Positive forces at work in retail consumer markets today include high rates of personal expenditures, low interest rates, low unemployment and very low inflation. Negative factors that hold retail sales back involve weakening consumer confidence. As far as the policy is concerned, 100 percent FDI is allowed in cash-and-carry wholesale formats. Franchisee arrangements are also permitted in retail trade. 51 percent FDI is allowed in single-brand retailing.

Retail Boom in Store

According to industry experts, the next phase of growth is expected to come from rural markets, with rural India accounting for almost half of the domestic retail market, valued over US$ 300 billion. Rural India is set to witness an economic boom, with per capita income having grown by 50 percent over the last 10 years, mainly on account of rising commodity prices and improved productivity. According to the Investment commission of India, the overall retail market is expected to grow from US$ 262 billion to about US$ 1065 billion by 2016, with organized retail at US$ 165 billion (approximately 15.5 percent of total retail sales). India is expected to be among the top 5 retail markets in the world in 10 years. According to recent market research report by RNCOS titled, "Booming Retail Sector in India", organized retail market in India is expected to reach US$ 50 billion by 2011.

1. Number of shopping malls is expected to increase at a

CAGR of more than 18.9 percent from 2007 to 2015.

2. Rural market is projected to dominate the retail industry landscape in India by 2012 with total market share of above 50 percent.
3. Organized retailing of mobile handset and accessories is expected to reach close to US$ 990 million by 2010.
4. Driven by the expanding retail market, third party logistic market is forecasted to reach US$ 20 billion by 2011.

Growth Factors in Indian Organized Retail Sector

The Growth of Retail Companies in India is facilitated by certain factors like:

1. Existing Indian middle classes with an increased purchasing power.
2. Rise of upcoming business sectors like the IT and engineering firms.
3. Change in the taste and attitude of the Indians.
4. Effect of globalization heavy influx of FDI in the retail sectors in India.

Many Indian companies have entered the retail industry. This is also a factor in the growth of Indian organized retail sector. Reliance Industries Limited is planning to invest US$ 6 billion in the organized retail sector in India by opening 1500 supermarkets and 1000 hypermarkets. Bharti Telecom is planning a joint venture worth £ 750 million with Tesco a global retail giant. Pantaloon is planning to invest US$ 1 billion in order to increase its retail space to 30 million square feet. Such huge investment is also a factor in the growth of the organized retail sector in India. Global retail giants are also entering the retail industry in India and this is also one of the factors in the growth of the organized retail sector in India. The global retail giants who are entering the organized retail sector in India are:

1. Wal-Mart;
2. Tesco;
3. Carrefour SA;

4. Metro AG.

Leveraging of Information Technology in Retail

The Indian organized retail industry is the fastest growing in the world. To keep pace with the rapid expansion, companies are forced to leverage technology to bring in operational efficiency. With the government of India allowing 100 percent FDI in retail, major retail companies have started entering the Indian market. The competition is getting tougher by the day and companies are using technology as a differentiator. The following lines highlight the various operational areas of retail industry and how information technology is used for competitive advantage.

IT in Supply Chain Management

Supply Chain may be referred as the series of companies that eventually make products and services available to consumers, including all of the functions enabling the production, delivery, and recycling of materials, components, end products and services. SCM gives a value-enhancing and long-term benefit for the organization. Firms with large inventories, many suppliers, complex product assemblies, and highly valued customers have a lot to gain by good practices in SCM. The cost of inventories was over US$ 2.2 trillion in U.S in 2000. Transportation and inventory carrying cost in U.S totalled US$ 434 billion in 2000 (U.S Central Bureau's Annual Survey of Manufacturers). The best way to leverage the potential of SCM is by the efficient use of IT in this area. The importance of IT in SCM has long been acknowledged but little work has been done in this area. But with growing competition and greater emphasis to keep price as low as possible the companies are looking towards strengthening their supply chain.

IT in Purchasing Management

Electronic data interchange was developed in 1970 to

improve the purchasing process. The rapid advent of internet technology in the 1990's spurred the growth of non-proprietary and more flexible internet based e-Procurement systems. Earlier critics argued that e-Commerce have been over inflated and it results in larger expenses than its savings. Today though many well managed e-commerce firms are beginning to thrive as users realize the benefits of their services. The material user initiates the e-procurement process by entering a material request and other relevant information. This is then submitted to the purchasing department. After verification of this the buyer transfers this data to the e-procurement system and assigns qualified suppliers to bid for it. Suppliers connected to this system receive the bid instantaneously.

IT in Forecasting Demand

Forecasting provides an estimate of future demand and the basis for planning and sound business decisions. The goal of a good forecasting technique is to minimize the gap between actual and forecast demand. All the factors that influence demand, the impact of these factors and there time frame must be considered in developing an accurate forecast. Also buyers and sellers should share all the relevant information about the forecasting so that a correct decision can be made.

IT in Inventory Management

In traditional supply chain inventory management, orders are the only information firms' exchange, but information technology now allows firms to share demand and inventory data quickly and inexpensively. The inventory management directly influences how effectively the organization deploys its assets and capacity in producing its goods and services. The problem of inventory is compounded in an integrated supply chain, where a missed due date or stock out cascades downstream, affecting the entire supply chain. In this area IT is used in The Chase Production System in which the capacity is adjusted in the demand pattern. It is also used in master production scheduling, listing the exact end items to be produced in a specific period. IT is also used in material requirement planning and manufacturing resource planning.

IT in Just In Time

Just-in-time (JIT) is an inventory strategy implemented to improve the return on investment of a business by reducing in-process inventory and its associated carrying costs. When implemented correctly, JIT can lead to dramatic improvements in a manufacturing organization's return on investment, quality, and efficiency.

Organized Retailing Penetration

1. Organized retail in India is largely restricted to the urban and semi-urban regions, with consumer exposure to modern retailing formats like malls and stand-alone stores etc. for specific product categories.
2. Penetration of organized retail is projected to increase to 9.52 percent in 2009-2010, which revenues from organized retail touching US$ 43,829 million in 2009-2010.
3. Clothing and textiles/apparel dominate the organized retail sector with revenues worth US$ 4.76 billion, contributing to over 36 percent of the organized retail pie.
4. Apparel is one of the fastest growing verticals, with higher number of domestic and foreign brands, and increasing consumer willingness to pay for quality.
5. Footwear has the highest organized retail penetration, primarily due to players like Bata India Pvt. Ltd. and Liberty, with wide distribution network and customer confidence.

Recession

A Recession is a contraction phase of the business cycle. The National Bureau of Economic Research (NBER) is the official agency in charge of declaring that the economy is in a state of recession. They define recession as: "Significant decline in economic activity lasting more than a few months, which is normally visible in real GDP, real income, employment, industrial production, and wholesale-retail sales". For this reason, the official designation of recession may not come until after we are in a recession for six months or longer.

There are different causes for recession. They are the following:

1. An economy typically expands for 6-10 years and tends to go into a recession for about six months to 2 years.
2. A recession normally takes place when consumers loose confidence in the growth of the economy and spend less.
3. This leads to a decreased demand for goods and services, which in turn leads to a decrease in production, lay-offs and a sharp rise in unemployment.
4. Investors spend less as they fear stocks values will fall and thus stock markets fall on negative sentiment.

The US faced major crisis due to recession. Some of the major factors include—subprime mortgage crisis (home loan defaults), rising oil prices at $100 a barrel, global inflation, high unemployment rates and a declining Dollar value. All this slowed down the growth of the economy and as the GDP growth rate fell to 2 percent and this evidences that the recession set in. A slowdown in the US economy is bad news for India because:

1. Indian companies have major outsourcing deals from the US.
2. India's exports to the US have also grown substantially over the years.
3. Indian companies with big tickets deals in the US are seeing their profit margins shrinking.

A glance at the anatomy of the economic uncertainty in India can be seen in the following:

Share Market:

1. More people have sold the shares in the Indian share market than they bought in the recent weeks. This has added to the fall of sensex to lower points.

2. Foreign investors have pulled out from stock markets leading to heavy losses in stocks and mutual funds.
3. Stock broking houses are laying-off people.
4. Because of such uncertainty many people have started saving money in banks rather than investing.

Impact on Retail Industry

The factors that force the retail sales to go down in view of the impact are the following:

1. **Weaker Sentiments**: Customers are unwilling to make those hefty purchases. The value consciousness increases and the customer starts avoiding things that he or she might not use in near future.
2. **Liquidity Crunch:** Due to the uncertain environment and bank's reluctance to lend at a favourable rate (coupled with the fact that raising equity is almost impossible due to equity meltdown), the retailers to find themselves cash-strapped. Forget about any expansion, they are having hard time even in arranging for the working capital.
3. **Profitability Squeeze:** As customers become more value conscious and sales starts falling, the immediate reaction is to drop prices, thus squeezing the profit margins.
4. **Poor Infrastructure:** Underdeveloped supply chains, lack of strong cold chains, poor warehousing facilities, bad roads, etc. have been contributing to increased logistic costs for the retailers. Globally, the logistics cost component to the total retail price is around 5 percent, while in India it is as high as 10 percent.
5. **Rentals**: As real estate prices skyrocketed, retail rentals also touched unsustainable levels eating directly into the profit margins of retailers. Until a few months back, store rentals were 300 to 400 basis points higher than even international levels. Retail rentals in Linking Road in Mumbai, South Extension in Delhi and Brigade Road in Bangalore have risen about 50 percent in the past 3 years.

But it's not that the picture is absolutely gloomy. There are areas of respite as well; people are not going to cut down on the very essential items. Now this perception of what is essential and what is not might change from one person to another, but there is nothing to deny the fact that there are a few product categories which are considered to be essential by the mass.

Strategies

There are, however, strategies to help organized retailing to cope up with recession/slowdown. Citing such uncertainties in the markets, retailers have started taking corrective measures and build some sound strategies to keep their profits ticking. Some of those measures are:

1. Build more efficiency in operations. For example, Pantaloon India Ltd. has begun integrating the management, marketing, human resources, or HR, and information technology, or IT, departments of its units into one. The company says this one step will help it save around ₹ 165 crore a year.
2. Cut down advertising budgets and unnecessary costs related to daily activities like electricity cost, travel and transport, packaging, etc. and search for some low-cost innovative solutions for marketing their products.
3. Closure of unprofitable stores and "Right Sizing" their staff, etc.
4. Optimize costs (cut costs in a way that doesn't harm the business) and optimize resources. Key amongst them are:

- Improve labour productivity.
- Manage inventory efficiently.
- Renegotiate the rentals.

5. Adopt a revenue share model against fixed share model Optimize technology usage.
6. Implement technology especially in areas of manpower training, real estate management, supply chain and logistics management and day-to-day store operations.
7. Streamline store processes, increase store visibility,

manage staff effectively and look into store layout and product range re-evaluate store viability and expansion plans.

8. Classify stores clearly into categories: profitable, high cost-high sale, low cost-high price and unviable and take action accordingly for each category.
9. Invest in consumer research, paying close attention to the diversity present in India's geography, to be sharper in delivery Enter into alliances and leverage expertise.
10. Forge alliances and partnerships to leverage on each other's financial muscle and expertise.
11. Offer competitive in-store labels to earn higher margins—a win-win situation for both customer and retailer (the key is to improve quality of in-store brand).
12. Focus on logistics in terms of minimizing the costs and knowledge aggregation.
13. Leverage on technology and expertise of foreign players Tap under penetrated markets.
14. Think beyond the metropolitan cities, target the opportunity offered by the rapidly developing and largely under-penetrated Tier II, Tier III and rural markets.
15. Stand out of the crowd and keep offering new ideas, services, and experiences to the customers.

Conclusion

With inflation at an all time high and commodities prices rising, consumers have little left after spending on their daily necessities of food and grocery. However, the festive season has come as a respite for retail chains as people are coming out to shop for Diwali and keeping the sales register ticking for them but the sales of high value items like jewellery, high end consumer durables, furniture, etc. hasn't seen much enthusiasm from shoppers. Retailers like Big Bazaar, Vishal Mega Mart, etc. may hope for a greener balance sheet in such a scenario while lifestyle formats like Shoppers Stop, Lifestyle, Marks and Spencer might have to fight it out and rationalize their costs immensely to have a healthy balance sheet.

The cheer for retailers in such times could be the falling rentals which have slashed down by 20 percent-40 percent and is expecting further corrections. This has opened up a new opportunity for the retailers to invest in property and earn the returns later when the markets would stabilize. The need of the hour is to do away with unnecessary costs and look for alternative revenue streams. Make a sound strategy which caters to the price sensitivity of the markets and bring ways where low investments could bring higher returns for the retailers in uncertain situations.

References

Durga Prasad and Vijay, V. (2007), The Spread of organized retailing in India with special reference to Vijayawada City. Indian Journal of Marketing, Vol. XXXVII, pp. 3-5.

Ernst & Young, 2006, Great Indian Retail Story, Available at http://www.ey.com/global.

Eenadu daily news paper reported "Retail Space in Indian Cities" on 14 February, 2009, p. 14.

India Retail Handbook (2005), brought out by ICICI Bank and A C Neilsen ORG Marg.

Kalhan Anuradha (2007), Impact of malls on small shops and Hawkers, Economic and Political Weekly, Vol. XLII, 2063-2066.

KSA Technopak, (2005), Consumption outlook for 2005, Available at http://www.imagesretail.com/india_report.htm.

Philip Kotler, Keller, Koshy and Jha (2007), Marketing Management, (12e) Prentice Hall India Limited, p. 422.

Sasikumar, K and Regina S. Cleetus (2008), Impact of Corporate Retailing on Small Retail Outlets. Indian Journal of Commerce, Vol. 61 (4), pp. 68-77.

Singh, B.N (2006), The Two Retailing Revolutions", Business Today, February 5, pp. 34-35.

Swapna Pradhan (2008), Retail Management, the McGraw-Hill, New Delhi, pp. 19-24.

Upadhya, Y and Shiv K. Singh (2008), Measuring Consumer Perceived Value of Different Retail Formats. Indian Journal of Commerce, Vol. 61 (4), pp. 49-67.

Venkateswarlu, H. and Rajani, C.V. (2007), Small vs Mall, Indian Journal of Marketing, Vol. XXXVII, pp. 29-33.

21

Productivity of Indian Software Development Teams

G.P. Sudhakar

Indian IT Industry has crossed US$ 60 billion mark. It has seen the double digit growth rate every year for the past one decade. It is better to reduce compensation and provide employment to large numbers than mass layoffs and headcount reductions in this tough economic situation. Companies are struggling to retain the customers and to maintain their billing rates. There is tremendous pressure to reduce billing rates from the customers to the Indian software companies. These pressures have affected the product development and services teams more in Indian software houses. There are many soft factors which have affected the productivity of software development teams in India. This paper highlights all those factors affect the productivity of software development teams in India in uncertain economic situations. An attempt has also been done to highlight organizational experience on the same and the practices and the strategies adopted by them in a case study format.

These soft factors are important because one third of the time the teams spend on non-technical work. 21.1 percent of time they spend in meetings and talks, 9.6 percent on presentations and project organization, 6 percent of time they spend on independent qualification (Stefan and Wagner, 2008). Software development productivity has experienced irregular variations of decline and rise in the last one decade and there are no signs of improvement as well (Zhizhong, Peter and Craig, 2007). Best software development teams are at least 4 times more productive than the worst teams (Boehm,

1981). Basically, *productivity* is "a measure of efficiency with which resources are employed to produce goods or services" (K.S. White, 1999).

Factors Affecting the Productivity

According to Stefan and Wagner (2008), soft factors like programmer capabilities, personnel turnover in the team have influence on productivity of software development teams. Other soft factors that influence the productivity are support of top management, business culture, team climate, promotions, team building, motivation and appreciation.

Software team's productivity is also influenced by the factor how well coordination efforts are distributed (Robert Chiang and Vijay, 2004). If broadly specking, technology, people and process influence the productivity of software development teams.

The need to create software applications rapidly and deploy them quickly is very much there in times of economic downturn (Luke, 2008). Software application developers were forced to save money and made themselves more productive during these uncertain times (Luke, 2008).

Following are the some of the other factors affecting the productivity of Indian software development teams in this uncertain economy.

1. Loss of customer contracts because of customer losses/bankruptcy.
2. Layoffs and terminations in Indian software companies.
3. No individual's development in the organization.
4. Stopping promotions and increments for the team members.
5. Pay cuts and removing stock option plans.
6. Removing incentives.
7. Postponing reimbursements.
8. Delaying payments.
9. Deferring the joining dates of fresh/new employees.
10. Loss of human life because of suicides (in some cases).

11. Degrading morale among rest of the team members once their colleague is fired.
12. Tension because of media hype about recession and job losses.
13. High Pressure to deliver to the customer.
14. Over workload.
15. Financial difficulties because of mortgage, and vehicle loans.
16. Communication gap between team members and management.
17. Reduction of training budget by the organization.
18. No scope for learning new technologies.
19. Forced relocation of the employees by the companies.
20. Can work anywhere attitude because of fear of job loss.
21. Effect on health.

Individuals who were under paid have a tendency to look for outside/other employment. Hence, the financial decisions of the organization made before, during and after software development process have impact on software development team's productivity (Roland, 1996).

Improper Project Management

Chatzoglou and Macaulay (1997) have found that experience, knowledge, persistence of team members have influence on team productivity. The motivation of the team members and their communication with the rest of the team members plays a key role and also the tools and techniques used for project management are also important factors influencing the software development team's productivity. It is important that the project manager should work well with people and value their contributions. People related issues have impact on programmer's productivity. Individual programmer productivity can vary up to a factor of ten and team's productivity can vary up to a factor of five (White, 1999). Programmer capability or some measure of talent was rarely used in research because it is difficult to measure it programmer will be fast if the system response time is fast, consistent and predictable (Walt, 1995).

Team Climate

Team climate comprises of team vision, participative safety, team orientation and support for innovation (Katzenbach and Smith, 1993). If the disturbances are there from the customer or performing organization, the team looses the vision and common purpose. The participation from team members in the team activities reduces. There is very little scope for innovation in this tough economic situation. Innovation cannot be achieved under pressured environment. News ideas can not be developed without support for innovation. Hence, team climate has influence on productivity of software development teams. Team culture or organizational culture has also got influence on productivity of teams. Openness and freedom results into team cohesiveness and improves the capabilities of the team, which results into more productivity. According to David F. Rico, team cohesiveness and culture influence team performance.

Similarly organization structure and internal politics have also impact on programming productivity (Roland, 1996). Researchers have proved that team cohesiveness has impact on team productivity (Malgorzata). According to Malgorzata, teams with high cohesion, demonstrate lower tension and anxiety, less variation in productivity, improved team member commitment, satisfaction and communication.

Other Technical Factors Affecting Team Productivity

According to Stefan and Wagner (2008), factors such as user participation, overall constraints on program design, previous experience on programming language have influence on software development team's productivity. Researchers like DeMarco and Lister highlighted about the proper workplace with windows, natural light and quietness for better productivity. According to Roland (1996), more comfortable ergonomic environment enhances productivity. Workspace allocation directly affects programmers' productivity and software deliverables (Faisal and Ayman, 2008).

Researchers like Kitcheham and Mendes, Mohagheghi and Conradi have shown the connectivity between software reuse and productivity (Stefan and Wagner, 2008). Programming methodology, and programming language have impact on software development team's productivity (Roland, 1996, and Zhizhong et al., 2007). Object oriented programming is said to increase the productivity significantly. According to Zhizhong et al. (2007), four main factors essential to productivity are average team size, development language, development platform and development techniques.

According to Robert Chiang and Vijay (2004), a critical success factor affecting the team productivity is allowable system construction time.

According to Roland (1996), individual programmer has controllable constraints such as financial constraints, time constraints, software specifications, programming methodology, and corporate environment.

Strategies to Handle Tough Economic Situation

According to Luke (2008), software application developers should never blame end users and get into mess in this tough situation and they should support end users whenever they need help. He also stressed that when people are ready to do more with less, it is important to stream line our processes as well. One should learn to offer value to the customer in such situation. The following steps can be taken to handle the tough situations:

1. Boost the morale of team members and motivate them towards organizational and team purpose.
2. Counselling the affected employees.
3. Provide training to improve their skills and improve their confidence level.
4. Provide end user communication to the programmers.

5. Have proper stakeholder management and customer management.
6. Utilize the resources to the maximum extent.
7. Have "give more for less" attitude.
8. Provide value to the customer.

Organizational Experience

The next section of the paper highlights the organizational experience in handling tough uncertain situations in a case study format. The experience of Satyam Computer Services, Tata Consulting Services and Wipro Technologies is provided to through light on the subject.

Satyam Computer Services: Satyam Computer Services went into deep trouble in January 2009 when its founder and Chairman Ramalinga Raju confessed that the financial statements of the company were cooked over the years. Immediately World Bank banned Satyam and hired Tata Consultancy Services. Similarly Satyam has lost few customers in very short span of time. After the takeover of Satyam by Mahindra group, there was hope in the employees of Satyam about their future. As on 28 March 2009, Satyam has 41,622 associates on its role. Mahindra Satyam has put more than 10,000 non-billable employees on virtual pool in June 2009 because of economic slowdown and has given them the basic salary, Provident Fund and medical insurance comprising 40 percent to 50 percent of their actual salary. Around 400 of them were called back and assigned projects. However, majority of them are at home still on virtual pool or asked to leave after the specified time was over.

A few of the Satyam employees have even made suicide after being fired by their employer. Economic slowdown has added to the fuel of Ramalinga Raju's episode. People in the virtual pool are opting to relocate anywhere in the country some are ready to relocate anywhere in the world. However, Mahindra Satyam has provided their virtual pool staff with needed counselling, online training and skills enhancement programs and these employees were free to look for jobs elsewhere by staying at home. Sending their team-mates and colleges to virtual pool has affected the morale of the existing employees. Because of the insecurity feeling and job loss, which was result of economic uncertainty, they were spending long odd hours at work. At one point of time, teams at Satyam did not know how many customers are going to stay back and continue to take their services. It was volatile, uncertain and was in deep trouble.

In 2009, Satyam differed the joining dates to the fresh engineering graduates who were offered placements in different college campuses in the country. The experienced associates promotions and salary hikes were stopped in the company. Some of the poor performers (around 3000) were put under the skills improvement program and were constantly monitored so that their skill level improves or they may have to depart from the company. Such kinds of measures were taken at Satyam during this tough economic situation.

Tata Consultancy Services: TCS was a US$ 6 billion Company in 2008-09. It had around 143,000 associates working in 42 countries in 2009. Even though TCS is doing strong financially, economic recession has hit it's global operations to some extent. In 2009, TCS announced that they would lay off 1300 i.e. one percent of their manpower globally. At the same time they told them that they would be helping them in outplacement. TCS is very popular for providing long term employment among Indian IT companies. Because of the tough economic conditions and customer spending went down drastically resulted into TCS to reduce their headcount by one percent. To compare with global players this is very less in layoffs and TCS believe in long term association with their associates.

TCS has stopped salary hikes and differed promotions in some cases for their associates during this economic downturn. At some point in time, there were some restrictions on variable pay component of the employee. However, without major loss

TCS was able to pay their staff well and able to retain their associates. The associates also were spending long hours to retain the customers. There were cost cutting measures such as electricity power saving wherever possible. Some of the employees were brought back home to offshore to reduce the dollar expenditure and also to reduce the customer spending for the benefit of the customer. TCS reduced their onsite staff between 5 percent to 10 percent. TCS has laid off more than 100 employees in UK, which includes the marketing team in UK. Highly paid consultants became victims there because they are too expensive to keep on bench.

During this tough time, World Bank has given their projects to TCS and dropped from Satyam. Now TCS is concentrating on getting more government projects across the world. In India also they are expecting more revenues in the coming years from domestic spending. They are expecting more than a US$ 1 billion from the domestic IT spending as Infosys is targeting. Employees who were on bench were encouraged to upgrade their skills and undergo certain certification programs.

Wipro Technologies: Wipro provides integrated business, technology, and process solutions and consulting to global customers. It has around 95,000 employees working in 54 global delivery centres. It is world's first PCMM level 5 companies and it is the first organization to introduce six sigma into the software services sector. It has over 55 centres of excellence in the company to serve different industry sectors.

In FY 2009, Wipro announced that they would release 5 percent to 7 percent of their manpower because of the economic downturn. Because of the tough economic conditions, performance criteria became tougher in the company. Wipro put around 3,000 of their employees, i.e., four to five percent of it's manpower under performance scanner. Satyam and Wipro were conducting tests for their employees who are in the performance scanner. Based on these tests, the employee will be asked to improve the skills or advised to leave the organization. During this year rather than regular recruitment, there was only very need based recruitment in the company.

Founder and Chairman Azim Premji used to travel in economy class for his business trips. During 2009, there was lot of pressure on employees to prove them distinct and not to be picked for the performance scanner. There were cost cutting measures and new recruitment was reduced drastically at the lateral level as well as fresher level.

Conclusion

In conclusion, it is clear that there are factors which affect the productivity of software development team in uncertain times. It also true that organization in India could tie over the situation with small practices and strategies. Further research can be done in areas of team climate, context, culture, cohesion and their relationship to productivity of software development teams. Turbulent economic situation have impacted the world economy. Hence, doing further research on Indian software development teams adds value and useful to the growing Indian IT industry.

References

Alistair Cockburn (2003), *People and Methodologies in Software Development*, PhD Thesis, Faculty of Mathematics and Natural Sciences, University of Oslo, 2003.

B. Boehm (1981), *Software Engineering Economics*, Prentice Hall, Englewood Cliffs, New Jersey, 1981.

Clave Land (2007), "Factors affecting the development of Software", Clave Land, Available online at http://cltech.co.in/Factors-affecting-the-development-software-and-its-quality.asps.

Current IT Market (2009), "TCS lays off U.K. Staff; Infy, Wipro to cut onsite staff", Available onsite at http://www.currentitmarket.net/2009/02/tcs-lays-off-uk-staff-infy-wipro-to-cut.html#

Current IT Market (2009), "Wipro Laid off 300 more 'non-performers'", 28 April 2009, Available online at http://www.currentitmarket.net/2009/04/wipro-laidoff-300-more-non-performers.html.

Dave Willmer (2009), "Get Most out of Your remaining Staff (without killing them)", Available online at http://www.itcareerplanet.com/article.php/3812786.

David F. Rico, "Virtual Teams and the Factors of Performance", Available online at http://davidfrico.com/rico05j.pdf.

Debasmita Ghosh (2008), "Satyam Computers to axe 4,500 employees", TNN, 15 September 2008, Available online at http://economictimes.indiatimes.com/Infotech/ITeS/Satyam-Computers-to-axe-4500-employees/articleshow/3483960.cms.

Faisal A. Abu Rub and Ayman A. Issa (2008), "Effects of Workspace on Engineering Software Projects", Proceedings of the World Congress on engineering 2008, Vol. I, WCE 2008, July 2- 4, 2008, London, UK.

International Business Times (2009), "10,000 employees see their salaries slashed under Satyam's Virtual Pool Program, future uncertain", 15 June 2009, Available online at http://www.ibtimes.co.in/articles/20090615/10000-employees-see-salaries-slashed-under-satyam-virtual-pool-program-future-uncertain_2.htm.

Jon R. Katzenbach and Douglas K. Smith (1993), *The Wisdom of Teams*, Harvard Business School Press, Boston, MA, 1993.

K.S. White (1999), "Software Engineering Management for Productivity and Quality", International Conference on Accelerator and Large Experimental Physics Control Systems, Trieste, Italy, 1999

Katherine Spencer Lee (2008), "How to motivate employees in Today's Economy", cioupdate.com, December 1, 2008, Available online at http://www.cioupdate.com/career/article.php/3788066/How-to-Motivate-Employees-in-Todays-Economy.htm.

Luke Chung (2009), "Application Development During Uncertain Times", Available online at http://www.fmsinc.com/tpapers/budgets/ApplicationDevelopment.html.

Malgorzata Pinkowska, "IT Software Project Management: Impact of Team Cohesiveness on Productivity and Performance", Available online at http://www.lent.ch/pdf_diverse/Pinkowska-cohesiveness.pdf.

P.D. Chatzoglou and L.A. Macaulay (1997), "The Importance of human factors in planning the requirements capture stage of a project", International Journal of Project Management, Vol. 15, No. 1, pp. 39-53.

Rajiv D. Banker, Srikanth M. Datar and Chris F. Kemerer (), "Factors Affecting Software Maintenance Productivity: An Exploratory Study".

Richard Turner and Barry Boehm (2003), "People Factors in Software Management: Lessons from Comparing Agile and Plan-Driven Methods", The Journal of Defence Software Engineering, December 2003.

Robert Chiang and Vijay S. Mookerjee (2004), "Improving Software Team Productivity", Communications of The ACM, May 2004, Vol. 47, No. 5, 2004

SiliconIndia (2008), "Wipro to cut 1000 heads of non-performance", 09 Sep 2008, Available online at http://www.siliconindia.com/shownews/Wipro_to_cut_1000_heads_for_nonperformance-nid-46257.html.

SiliconIndia (2009), "TCS to aid in outplacement of laid-off employees", 11 March 2009, Available online at http://www.siliconindia.com/shownews/TCS_to_aid_in_outplacement_of_laidoff_employees-nid-53421.html.

Stefan Wagner and Melanie Ruhe (2008), "A Structured Review of Productivity Factors in software Development", Technical Report, Technische Universität München, 2008.

Stefan Wagner and Melanie Ruhe (2008), "A Systematic Review of Productivity Factors in software Development", Technical Report, State Key Laboratory of Computer Science, Institute of Software, 2008.

Walt Scacchi (1995), "Understanding Software Productivity", *Advances in Software Engineering and Knowledge Engineering,* Volume 4, pp. 37-70, 1995.

Zhizhong Jiang, Peter Naude and Craig Comstock (2007), "The Variation of Software Development Productivity 1995-2005", World Academy of Science, Engineering and Technology 27, 2007.

Index

Index